WHAT TEST-TAKERS ARE SAYING ABOUT LEARNINGEXPRESS PREPARATION GUIDES

"The information from the last two study guides I ordered from your company was invaluable. . . . Better than the $200 6-week study courses being offered. . . . After studying from dozens of books I would choose yours over any of the other companies.'"

S. Frosch

"Excellent . . . It was like having the test in advance!"

J. Kennedy

"Without this book, I wouldn't have understood the test."

R. Diaz

"Told me everything that was going to be on the test [and] gave me a good understanding of the whole process, too."

J. Molinari

"The best test-prep book I've used!"

H. Hernandez

"I felt 100% prepared when I took the Suffolk County exam this past June. I scored a 96 on it. I had taken it previously and only scored an 82. Your guide helped me add 14 points to my score!"

R. Morrell

CIVIL SERVICE CAREER STARTER

Second Edition

LEARNINGEXPRESS

NEW YORK

Copyright © 2000 Learning Express, LLC.

All rights reserved under International and Pan-American Copyright Conventions. Published in the United States by LearningExpress, LLC, New York.

Library of Congress Cataloging-in-Publication Data

Civil service career starter. — 2nd ed.
     p.   cm.
   Includes index.
   ISBN 1-57685-302-0
   1. Civil service positions—United States.   2. Civil service—
United States—Examinations.   I. LearningExpress (Organization)
JK716.C465
650.14—dc21   97-8771
                                                 CIP

Printed in the United States of America
9 8 7 6 5 4 3 2 1
Second Edition

Regarding the Information in this Book
We attempt to verify the information presented in our books prior to publication. It is always a good idea, however, to double-check such important information as hiring procedures and minimum requirements with your local, state, or federal agency, as such information can change from time to time.

For Further Information
For information on LearningExpress, other LearningExpress products, or bulk sales, please write to us at:
   LearningExpress®
   900 Broadway
   Suite 604
   New York, NY 10003

Visit LearningExpress on the World Wide Web at www.LearnX.com

CONTENTS

LIST OF CONTRIBUTORS

The following individuals contributed to the content of this book.

Liz Chesla, M. A., is an adult educator and curriculum developer at Polytechnic University in New York who has also taught reading and writing at New York University School of Continuing Education and New York Institute of Technology in New York City.

Judith N. Meyers, M. A., is director of the Two Together Tutorial Program of the Jewish Child Care Association in New York City and a former Adult Basic Education Practitioner at the City University of New York.

Judith F. Olson, M.A., is chairperson of the language arts department at Valley High School in West Des Moines, Iowa, where she also conducts test preparation workshops.

Judith Robinovitz is an independent educational consultant and director of Score At the Top, a comprehensive test preparation program in Vero Beach, Florida.

I·N·T·R·O·D·U·C·T·I·O·N

WHY YOU NEED THIS BOOK

o you're thinking about a career in the civil service. Maybe you're just out of high school or college, or maybe you're considering a career change. Maybe you're exploring various kinds of careers you might pursue, or maybe you have a pretty good idea of the kind of job you want. In any case, you have all kinds of questions about working for the government:

- What kinds of jobs are available?
- What kind of salary and benefits can I expect?
- What's the difference between working for the federal government, a state government, and a county or municipal government?
- How do I find out what jobs are available?
- Which jobs are the best bets for someone without a lot of specialized training or experience?
- Will I have to take an exam?
- If there's an exam, what's going to be on it? How can I prepare for it?
- What kinds of other resources are out there for people who want to pursue a civil service career?

This book answers all these questions. The focus is on entry-level jobs that require little or no special education or experience; in fact, many of the jobs discussed in this book require nothing more than a high school diploma or GED. However, if you have a college degree or specialized training, you'll still find plenty of opportunities here for you.

JOBS, JOBS, AND MORE JOBS

You might be surprised at the variety of jobs that are available with the various levels of government. It may not have occurred to you, for instance, that the federal government (as well as some state and local governments) hires plumbers, carpenters, electricians, and other skilled laborers, at levels from apprentice through master. If you're thinking of a secretarial job, there's an enormous variety of jobs available at all levels of government—and you don't want to limit your chances by looking only for the job title "secretary." You know that your city or town hires police officers, but did you know that law enforcement opportunities are also available with the state and federal government, or that there are a lot of other kinds of law enforcement jobs besides police officer? Did you know that the U.S. Postal Service is one of the largest employers in the country, and that it hires not only mail carriers and clerks but also clerical support people, auto mechanics, nurses, computer technicians, and hundreds of other kinds of workers?

HOW TO USE THIS BOOK

This book is your starting point in sorting through what can be a bewildering array of job opportunities. Begin with Section One, "The Basics." Here you'll learn what kinds of jobs are available, what kind of salary you can expect, how to find out about job openings, how to apply, and what kind of exams or other selection procedures you'll face for various kinds of jobs with both the federal government and state and local government.

Section Two focuses in on four "best bets"—entry-level jobs with lots of employees and steady or growing hiring patterns. The four jobs covered here—postal worker, law enforcement officer, administrative assistant (and other clerical jobs), and firefighter—generally don't require much education or training beyond high school. In these chapters, you'll learn in detail about hiring patterns and salaries, the many kinds of opportunities available, the qualifications you need, application procedures, and what you're likely to encounter on the written exam for each position.

Ah yes, the exam. The first thing you need to know is that there's no such thing as *a* civil service exam. Different jobs in different jurisdictions—whether local, state, or federal—have different exams. But there are certain kinds of questions that turn up more often than not on the various civil service exams for different positions: questions that test your reading ability; your writing skill, including grammar, vocabulary, and spelling; and your ability to reason using numbers—that is, your math. Section Three, "Passing a Civil Service Exam," provides two sample tests focusing on these crucial areas, as well as chapters that give you the tips and hints you need to score well. Once you've mastered the basics, you'll be ready to move on to other more specific kinds of questions that may appear on particular civil service exams.

This book, in short, will enable you to explore your options in federal, state, and local employment. It's your starting point toward a rewarding career in civil service.

S·E·C·T·I·O·N

THE BASICS

1

If you're thinking about pursuing a civil service career, your first questions are about what kinds of jobs are available and what the salaries and benefits are likely to be, how you can find out about openings, what kinds of qualifications you need, and how you go about applying. That's what this section is all about. Chapter 1 gives you a complete rundown of jobs with the federal government, including a list of the Top 40 Federal Entry-Level Job Titles—the jobs with the largest number of employees and greatest potential for growth. Chapter 2 outlines the general process of finding out about and applying for jobs with state and local government. Chapter 3 introduces you to the Internet and shows you how to do a job search online.

C·H·A·P·T·E·R 1

GETTING A JOB WITH THE FEDERAL GOVERNMENT

CHAPTER SUMMARY

This chapter introduces you to the numerous careers available with the federal government and the benefits of working for Uncle Sam. You'll also learn about the most common entry-level positions and how to find and apply for the government jobs that are right for you.

 firefighter in Florida. A mail carrier in Montana. A secretary in South America. What do these diverse people have in common? They all work for the federal government in some of the thousands of different positions available to civilian employees. There's a whole army of people working for Uncle Sam, keeping the federal government running smoothly, in positions from accountant to zoologist and everything in between.

Every year hundreds of thousands of people apply to join the ranks of federal employees. That's not surprising—after all, a job with the federal government has a lot to offer, including a competitive salary, job security, government pension, and upward mobility. But competition is often intense, and the job search and application process can be daunting. Let's take a closer look at just what it means to work for the government, how the government hires its employees, and how you can get an edge in the job selection process.

WHY WORK FOR UNCLE SAM?

There are lots of good reasons to work for the U.S. government: plenty of opportunities, good salary and benefits, job security, and more.

Number One Employer

The federal government is the largest single employer in the United States—and one of the largest in the world. Its nearly 3 million employees (2,819,100 in 1998) work in over 2,000 different occupations that are comparable to just about every job you can find in the private sector. In 2000, due to a budget surplus, the federal government's goal was to expand its workforce with 10,000 new hires a month. Hundreds of thousands of positions open up each year from employee promotions and retirements alone, ensuring that even in times of budget cuts and downsizing, positions—and lots of them—will always be available with the federal government. And no matter how good or bad the economy, we'll always need the postal workers who deliver our nation's mail, the police officers and firefighters who

Why Work for the Federal Government

The nation's number one employer is our own U.S. government. These benefits show why.

- **Job challenge.** Government jobs are important, varied, and necessary for our country to exist.
- **Pay comparability.** Salaries are based on private sector comparisons.
- **Extra pay.** Salaries may be augmented by locality pay and special pay provisions (law enforcement pay, for instance).
- **Job security.** Federal workers are always in demand; layoffs are very rare.
- **Step increases within grade.** Time on the job can mean step increases to higher salaries.
- **Merit promotions.** It is possible to compete for merit increases in salary.
- **Health and life insurance.** Cost is shared with the government, which offers over 300 HMOs and 15 fee-for-service plans.
- **Retirement.** Workers receive benefits from the Federal Employees Retirement System and Social Security.
- **Holiday and vacation/sick days.** There are ten paid holidays every year. Employees accrue 13, 20, or 26 paid vacation days and 13 paid sick leave days per year; family and medical leaves may also be available.
- **Alternative work schedules.** Flexible hours, compressed workweek, telecommuting, part-time work and job transfers are all options.
- **Appeals and grievances.** There are outlets for complaint—among them are unions, the Merit Systems Protection Board, the Federal Labor Relations Authority, and the Office of Personnel Management.
- **Training.** Government-paid training and tuition reimbursement are available.

protect us, and all the clerks, secretaries, and maintenance personnel who support the people working for the government.

Hiring in the Executive Branch

Of the federal government's three branches—executive, legislative, and judicial—the executive branch employs by far the largest number of civilian employees. In 1998, the number of full-time permanent executive branch employees newly hired was 58,474 (non-postal workers).

Minimum Qualifications

All you need for a career with the government is a high school diploma (or GED) and, for most positions, U.S. citizenship. (There are also some part-time positions for high school students, see "Types of Employees" on page 8.) If you are a male over 18 born after December 31, 1959, you must also be registered with (or exempt from) the Selective Service. Many kinds of positions are available for people with no education beyond high school and little or no job experience. Beyond the minimum requirements, your education, skills, experience, and location will determine what specific jobs you are eligible for with the federal government.

Did You Know . . . ?

The federal government employs more blue-collar workers (including mechanics and manual laborers) than any private-sector firm in the country.

Opportunities At Home and Abroad

With its diversity of jobs and geographic locations, the federal government offers flexibility in job opportunities that's unmatched in the private sector. While the bulk of federal civilian employees work in and around Washington, D.C., there are civilian government employees in every state and in just about every country on the globe.

After the capital, California, New York, Texas, and Florida come in with the highest numbers of government employees. California has 105,371 employees working for the U.S. Postal Service (USPS) alone and about 210,000 employees in other agencies. Atlanta, Baltimore, Chicago, Denver, Los Angeles/Long Beach, New York City, Philadelphia, San Antonio, and San Diego are among the cities with the largest government civilian employee populations.

But you don't have to live in a big city to find work with the federal government. In many small towns, a large percentage of civilians are federal employees. A look in the blue pages of your local phone book will show you just how many federal agencies there are in your area. Meanwhile, over 83,000 federal employees—approximately 1.8 percent of the civilian work force—work outside of the United States in foreign countries.

Salaries

As a government employee, you'll earn a respectable income, even at the entry level. Positions that require little or no education or work experience often offer higher pay than comparable jobs in the private sector. While the same may not be true for all entry-level jobs, employees with relevant education or experience are far more likely than their private-sector counterparts to be promoted into higher-paying positions.

The table on this page offers some examples of entry-level salaries for various positions with the federal government.

Benefits

It's hard to beat the benefits and security of working for the government. Although the benefits from department to department may vary slightly, most career employees are entitled to:

- 10 paid holidays per year
- 13-26 days of paid vacation per year
- 13 days of sick leave per year
- Regular cost of living adjustments
- Death and disability insurance
- Group life insurance
- Health care (medical and dental benefits)
- Government pension

Incentive Awards Program

If you're a federal employee and find an innovative way to reduce government costs or improve government operations, you can be rewarded with a big bonus—up to half a million dollars!—through the federal government's Incentive Awards Program.

Special Employee Programs

Federal employees also enjoy the added benefit of special employee programs. Most agencies have their own programs. The USPS, for example, has the Postal Employee's Relief Fund, which provides monetary relief to employees who have been victims of natural disasters. But there are also programs available to most or all federal employees, such as the Federal Employee Education and Assistance Fund (FEEAF). The FEEAF provides grants and scholarships to federal employees and their dependents without adding to the taxpayers' burden: all of the money comes from employee contributions.

Steady Hiring

Despite recent government cutbacks, experts foresee steady hiring in the government's future. The U.S. Department of Labor's *Occupational Outlook Handbook* predicts an increase in all government employment, from 9.5 million jobs in 1995 to 10.5 million in 2005.

Job Security

One of the greatest benefits of being a federal employee is job security. Once you've completed the three-year

SAMPLE SALARIES: U.S. GOVERNMENT EMPLOYEES

Job Title	Grade	Salary
Federal Police Officer	GS-3	$18,354–$23,859
Federal Police Officer	GS-4	$20,603–$26,787
USPS Mail Handler	MH-04	$22,311–$34,894
USPS Window Clerk	PS-05	$28,539–$39,515
USPS City Carrier	CC-06	$29,206–$39,105
Data Transcriber	GS-2	$15,594–$19,622
Computer Operator	GS-5	$21,370–$27,778
Air Conditioner and Refrigeration Technician	WG-01	$18,957–$23,169
Civil Engineer	GS-7	$29,470–$37,412

For an explanation of grade, or pay level; see "Series and Grade System of Classification" on page 8.

Federal Pay Schedules

Grade	Annual Rates for Steps (in dollars)									
	1	2	3	4	5	6	7	8	9	10
1	13,870	14,332	14,794	15,252	15,715	15,986	16,440	16,900	16,918	17,351
2	15,594	15,964	16,481	16,918	17,107	17,610	18,113	18,616	19,119	19,662
3	17,015	17,582	18,149	18,716	19,283	19,850	20,417	20,984	21,551	22,118
4	19,100	19,737	20,374	21,011	21,648	22,285	22,922	23,559	24,196	24,833
5	21,370	22,082	22,794	23,506	24,218	24,930	25,642	26,354	27,066	27,778
6	23,820	24,614	25,408	26,202	26,996	27,790	28,584	29,378	30,172	30,966
7	26,470	27,352	28,234	29,166	29,998	30,880	31,762	32,644	33,526	34,408
8	29,315	30,292	31,296	32,246	33,223	34,200	35,177	36,154	37,131	38,108
9	32,380	33,459	34,538	35,617	36,696	37,775	38,854	39,933	41,012	42,091
10	35,658	36,947	38,036	39,225	40,414	41,603	42,792	43,981	45,170	46,359
11	39,178	40,484	41,790	42,096	44,402	45,708	47,014	48,320	49,626	50,932
12	46,955	48,520	50,085	51,650	53,215	54,780	56,345	57,910	59,475	61,040
13	55,837	57,698	59,559	61,420	63,281	65,142	67,003	68,864	70,725	72,586
14	65,983	68,182	70,381	72,580	74,779	76,978	79,177	81,376	83,575	85,774
15	77,614	80,201	82,788	85,375	87,962	90,549	93,136	95,723	98,310	100,987

Percentage Pay Adjustments by Geographic Locality

Salaries are calculated for each location based on the percentage amounts below. The base pay in the Base GS Pay Scale above is multiplied by the percentage adjustment and the result is then added to the base pay.

Atlanta	6.67%	Houston	12.92%	Pittsburgh	6.68%
Boston	9.32%	Huntsville	6.31%	Portland	7.80%
Chicago	9.98%	Indianapolis	6.08%	Richmond	6.61%
Cincinnati	8.31%	Kansas City	6.51%	Sacramento	8.27%
Cleveland	6.92%	Los Angeles	11.14%	St. Louis	6.17%
Columbus	7.46%	Miami	8.51%	San Diego	8.62%
Dallas	7.47%	Milwaukee	6.74%	San Francisco	13.06%
Dayton	6.67%	Minneapolis	7.92%	Seattle	7.96%
Denver	9.16%	New York	10.55%	Washington, DC	7.87%
Detroit	10.13%	Orlando	5.87%	Rest of U.S.	5.87%
Hartford	9.85%	Philadephia	8.30%		

Source: U.S. Office of Personnel Management, January 2000

probationary period, you become a career employee who is eligible for full benefits and who is protected from layoffs by several layers of employees.

Earning Christmas Cash with the Government

Every year the USPS hires thousands of temporary employees to handle the Christmas rush. In 1999, the USPS hired 40,000 temporary workers to meet the mailing demands of the Christmas season.

TYPES OF EMPLOYEES

Full-Time Positions

While the specific employee categories in the different agencies may vary, in general there are four types of full-time employees working for the federal government:

- **Temporary.** These are positions that last for less than one year. There are no special privileges or benefits, but as a temporary employee, your foot is in the government door, and that's a great advantage: not only will you have insider knowledge of job openings, but if you do your job well, you'll have a terrific advantage over other candidates.
- **Term.** These positions are created and filled for a specific period of time for the completion of a specific project or study. They may last from one to three years, sometimes more, and term employees often receive health benefits but are usually not eligible for pension. Again, term employees can find out about job openings early and those who do their jobs well have an edge in competing for more permanent positions.
- **Career-conditional.** Most entry-level civilian employees start out in this three-year probation-

ary position, during which they are evaluated and after which they become eligible for a full-time permanent position (career status). This three-year period is critical for those who wish for career status and includes most career benefits but with various restrictions. (Disability insurance, for example, is often excluded or limited for career-conditional employees.)

- **Career.** Most employees are at this full-time, full-benefit level, which they achieve after the three-year career-conditional probation period. These are usually the last positions to be affected by downsizing and layoffs.

Part-Time, Intern, and Work-Study Positions

There are also part-time, intern, and student work-study positions available with the federal government, but the parameters of these positions vary from agency to agency. In general, if you are at least 16, you can begin working part-time for the government so long as you are in good standing at your high school and remain in good standing until you graduate. Many agencies, including the USPS, also have regular part-time positions.

SERIES AND GRADE SYSTEM OF CLASSIFICATION

In the federal government, civilian employees are organized—and paid—according to the kind of work they do (called the *series*) and the level of difficulty (called the *grade*) of their position. Salaries and wages, called *schedules*, are determined by these classifications. Each grade consists of several *steps*, or raises. For example, a Civil Engineer (Series 0810, Grade 7), earns $26,470 at Step 1, $29,998 at Step 5, and $34,408 at Step 10.

Because there are nearly a hundred government departments and independent agencies, there are many different job series and pay schedules within the federal government. Still, excluding postal workers, most entry-level employees fall into one of two main series and schedules:

■ The General Schedule (GS), which includes most professional, technical, administrative, and clerical positions

■ The Wage Grade (WG) series and schedule, which includes most federal blue-collar workers

General Schedule employees account for approximately two-thirds of government civilian employees (excluding employees of the USPS); the remaining one-third are Wage Grade employees.

GENERAL SCHEDULE JOBS

There are 22 different *occupational groups* (general job categories) in the General Schedule, and each group has dozens of *job series* (related jobs), each of which have a number of different *job titles*.

Occupational Group
↓
Job Series
↓
Job Titles

Employees in different GS series—even jobs as diverse as a computer scientist and a food inspector—will receive the same salary if they are at the same grade because their jobs are considered at the same level of difficulty by the government. This is true for other schedules as well. However, whatever the schedule, there may be slight variations in salaries as a result of the Federal Employees Pay Comparability Act of 1990, which allows

such fluctuations as small salary increases for employees in areas with high cost of living. See the chart titled "Percentage Pay Adjustments by Geographic Locality."

General Schedule Occupational Groups

There are 22 different occupational groups in the GS:

GS-000   Miscellaneous Occupations Group

GS-100   Social Science, Psychology, and Welfare Group

GS-200   Personnel Management and Industrial Relations Group

GS-300   General Administration, Clerical, and Office Services Group

GS-400   Biological Sciences Group

GS-500   Accounting and Budget Group

GS-600   Medical, Hospital, Dental, and Public Health Group

GS-700   Veterinary Medical Science Group

GS-800   Engineering and Architecture Group

GS-900   Legal and Kindred Group

GS-1000   Information and Arts Group

GS-1100   Business and Industry Group

GS-1200   Copyright, Patent, and Trade-Mark Group

GS-1300   Physical Sciences Group

GS-1400   Library and Archives Group

GS-1500   Mathematics and Statistics Group

GS-1600   Equipment, Facilities and Services Group

GS-1700   Education Group

GS-1800   Investigation Group

GS-1900   Quality Assurance, Inspection, and Grading Group

GS-2000   Supply Group

GS-2100   Transportation Group

By far the largest of the groups listed above is the GS-300 group, which includes clerical and administrative workers. For more information on administrative positions, see Chapter 6 of this book. You'll also find information on federal jobs in law enforcement in Chapter 5 and in fire services in Chapter 7.

General Schedule Grade Levels

The General Schedule includes 15 grades for its positions, GS-1 through GS-15. GS 1–7 positions are generally entry-level positions; GS 8–12, mid-level; and GS 13–15, top-level. The grades also break down into professional and non-professional categories, with the professional grades requiring a bachelor's degree or higher. Nonprofessional grades are GS-1–4, GS-6, GS-8, and GS-10, while professional grades are GS-5, GS-7, GS-9, and GS-11–12.

Sources on General Schedule Jobs

Specific job descriptions and series for each occupational group are available in the government's *Handbook of Occupational Groups and Series of Classes*, as well as in the *Position Classification Standards* volumes. The Office of Personnel Management's *Qualification Standards Handbook for General Schedule Positions* provides the minimum experience and education requirements for most federal GS jobs. These books, as well as Career Brochures describing different career paths within the federal government, should be on hand certain federal offices, job kiosks, and for print out on the Internet. See chapters 1, 2, and 3 for resources.

WAGE GRADE

Wage Grade (WG) positions are blue-collar jobs that are paid by the hour rather than by annual salary. Hourly rates are determined locally, so pay scales may vary widely. There are more than 400 WG job titles, which generally fall into one of two categories:

- Positions leading to *journeyman* or *career status*— skilled trades including Machinist, Painter, and Carpenter
- Positions that don't require special training and therefore don't lead to journeyman or career status, such as Warehouse Worker and Motor Vehicle Operator

By far the largest number of WG employees—approximately 75 percent—work for the Department of Defense.

Wage Grade Job Families

Job Families in the WG system are equivalent to GS Occupational Groups. The families are:

Aircraft Overhaul Family

Ammunition, Explosives, and Toxic Materials Work Family

Electrical Installation and Maintenance Family

Electronic Equipment Installation and Maintenance Family

Engine Overhaul Family

Fabric and Leather Work Family

Film Processing Family

Fluid Systems Maintenance Family

Food Preparation and Serving Family

General Equipment Maintenance and Operations Work Family

General Services and Support Work Family

Industrial Equipment Maintenance Family

Industrial Equipment Operation Family

Instrument Work Family

Laundry, Dry Cleaning, and Pressing Family

Lens and Crystal Work Family

Machine Tool Work Family

Metal Processing Family

Metal Work Family

WAGE GRADE CAREER LEVELS		
Grade	**Level**	**Description**
WG 1–5	Helper	Receives on-the-job training
WG 6–8	Apprentice	Receives training and instruction
WG 9–11	Journeyman	Works at full performance level
WL (1–15)	Wage Leader	Equivalent to a foreman
WS (1–19)	Wage Supervisor	Hires, promotes and fires WG employees

Miscellaneous Occupations Family

Motion Picture, Radio, Television, and Sound Equipment Operation Family

Packing and Processing Family

Painting and Paper-Hanging Family

Personal Services Family

Plant and Animal Work Family

Pliable Materials Work Family

Plumbing and Pipe-Fitting Family

Printing Family

Structural and Finishing Work Family

Transportation/Mobile Equipment Operation Family

Transportation/Mobile Equipment Maintenance Family

Warehousing and Stock Handling Family

Wire Communications Equipment Installation and Maintenance Family

Wood Work Family

See the table at the top of this page for career levels for WG employees.

More Information on Wage Grade Jobs

If you are interested in a WG job, the *Guide to Federal Technical, Trades and Labor Jobs*, which focuses on federal jobs that do not require a professional or college degree, is a good resource. You may find this guide in the reference section of your local library. You may also want to contact the Department of Defense directly, by phone or on the Internet (www.odedodea.edu/pers/).

UNITED STATES POSTAL SERVICE

The USPS is such a large and specialized agency that it is in a class by itself. It has 2,000 job titles, its own job series and pay schedules, and its own unique qualification requirements. See Chapter 4 of this book for information on entry-level postal job opportunities.

HOW THE FEDERAL GOVERNMENT HIRES CIVILIAN EMPLOYEES

JOB VACANCY ANNOUNCEMENTS

When a civil service job opens within a government agency, that agency will usually issue a *Competition Notice*, *Exam Announcement*, *Vacancy Announcement*, *Civil Service Announcement* or *Announcement* (five names for essentially the same thing). These announcements should list the following information:

- Open and close dates *(filing period* or *application window)*
- Job title
- Job number
- Geographic location

- Number of vacancies
- Hiring office/agency
- Salary
- Terms (part/full time)
- Benefits
- Job duties
- Job qualifications
- Criteria for evaluation or rating (education, experience, etc.)
- Any supplemental information required by candidate
- Who may apply (*area of consideration* or *limits of consideration*)
- How to apply
- Who to call for forms or with questions
- Where to mail completed forms
- Application deadline

Area of Consideration

If an agency wants to offer the position to a limited group of current or former employees, the job announcement will list the specific type of applicants to which the job is open (*area of consideration*). When the job is offered to external candidates, the position may still be restricted to persons within a certain geographical area, so read job announcements carefully to make sure you're eligible for consideration.

TWO HIRING SYSTEMS

Civilian employees are hired in one of two ways: through the Competitive Civil Service (CCS) or through the Excepted Service (ES). The CCS was once entirely under the jurisdiction of the Office of Personnel Management (OPM). Today, most agencies do their own recruitment, review, and hiring, but they still follow most of the procedures established for the CCS. Some agencies are not affiliated with the CCS and have independent hiring procedures; these are called *excepted*

agencies, and their hiring system is called the Excepted Service.

Competitive Civil Service

The Competitive Civil Service system is designed to give applicants fair and equal treatment and to ensure that federal applicants are hired based on objective criteria. Hiring has to be based solely on candidates' knowledge, skills, and abilities (which you'll sometimes see abbreviated as *ksa*) and not on any external factors such as race, religion, sex, and so on. Whereas employers in the private sector can hire employees for subjective reasons, federal employers must be able to justify their decisions with objective "evidence" that the candidate is qualified. Thus, applicants in the competitive service are scored through a special rating system that is made up of objective criteria such as level of education, number of years of experience, and test and interview scores.

Excepted Service

Agencies that hire through the Excepted Service are exceptions: they don't follow the CCS hiring process. The largest ES agency is the USPS, which by itself is one of the largest employers in the nation. Other ES agencies include the Foreign Service, the Federal Reserve System, the Tennessee Valley Authority, the Federal Bureau of Investigation, the Central Intelligence Agency, and the General Accounting Office.

Also in the ES category are work-study students, attorneys, chaplains, foreign language specialists, noncitizen positions, student trainers, confidential secretaries, and special assistants. While these jobs may be easier to apply for than CCS jobs because they often have a simpler hiring process, ES applicants are not subject to the benefit of ensured objectivity afforded those who go through the CCS, though hiring is still far more objective than in the private sector.

If you wish to apply for positions with an ES agency, you must contact that agency directly rather than sending your application to the OPM.

HOW APPLICANTS ARE RATED

In the CCS and in many ES agencies, applicants are usually rated on a scale of 1 to 100 according to the criteria outlined on the job vacancy announcement. Veterans receive preference of an additional 5 or 10 points, making 110 the highest possible score. (See "Veterans' Preference" under "How to Apply" later in this chapter.) This rating is often based on what the job application says about education and experience. Candidates are usually grouped into a "best qualified" or "qualified" list, which is reviewed by a personnel specialist who adds veterans' points as appropriate. Applicants who score under 70 are usually considered ineligible. Then, depending upon the position, candidates may be required to take an exam or series of exams.

Whereas in the private sector a favorable response to an initial interview can make or break your application process, in the government, the interview doesn't come until much farther into the process, after you've already received a ranking based on the information you provide in your application/resume and your performance on exams. Thus, it is critical that you treat the application process and initial tests very seriously. Don't just plan on winning the employer over in an interview.

Employee Registers/Eligibility Lists

If the position is one in which there are often regular openings or in which several vacancies are expected before the next job announcement, the agency will keep a list of eligible candidates called a *register* or *eligibility list*. With such a register, the agency doesn't have to keep opening for applications and can call on a list of candidates it already knows is qualified. This makes it all the more important that you be aware of application windows, because if an agency keeps a register, it may be some time before there's another filing period. Generally, however, registers are considered old after three years, and most registers have an average life span of one year.

Unassembled Exams

If there is no exam, then the application itself is considered the "test" (also called *unassembled exam*), and the rating is based solely on the application and accompanying materials. Then, the top-ranking candidates on the "best qualified" lists are usually contacted for an interview.

Assembled Exams

If the position requires an exam, or a series of exams, agencies take one of two options:

- Hold an *assembled exam* (that is, candidates assemble at the same time and place) for all eligible candidates; or
- Call only the top ranking candidates (often called *band testing*) for the exam.

If the agency takes the first option, your initial qualification criteria are important, but your rank can be significantly raised by your performance on later tests. In the second case, however, you need to be at the top of the chart, beginning with the initial qualification criteria, in order to make it to the next stage in the hiring process.

FINDING JOB OPENINGS

Because of the diversity of jobs and sheer number of occupational titles in the federal government, you may find that there are many job titles for which you qualify. This is particularly true of clerical positions, where there are thousands of positions with similar requirements but different job titles. In some cases, you must apply to each job title and vacancy individually; in some cases, you can apply online on the Internet for more than one position at a time. In any case, you may have many opportunities to become employed by the government.

As you scan job announcements, keep your eyes open and keep in mind that your experience and skills may qualify you for several job titles and several series. Be flexible—but also be realistic. Don't waste time applying to jobs that you are not qualified for. Unlike in the private sector, you can't convince an employer to hire you because you're a quick learner. You *must* meet the minimum qualification standards to be considered.

Unlike jobs in the private sector, government job openings aren't listed in the classified section of your city or local paper. But there are several excellent, easily accessible sources of government job information.

Job Listings Through the OPM

The Office of Personnel Managment updates a list of federal job vacancies daily. If you have a touch-tone phone, you can access this information 24 hours a day, 7 days a week by calling the OPM's automated telephone system, Jobs by Phone, at 912-757-3000. While this service offers around-the-clock convenience, beware: It may take more than one phone call to find exactly the information you need.

If you have a computer modem, you can access the same information through OPM's electronic bulletin board at 912-757-3100. This board can also be reached through the Internet (through Telnet only) at *fjob.mail.opm.gov*. You'll be able to scroll through information and won't risk running up a costly phone bill. If you don't have Internet access and cost is a concern, plan to call the bulletin board at night when long distance rates are lower.

The most user-friendly of the OPM resources, however, is its World Wide Web site at *www.usajobs.com.gov*. From this page you can search for jobs by region, state, zip code, country, and department. You can also print a copy of the application forms and access information about pay scales and a list of Federal Job Information kiosks around the country. You can even create a resume online or electronically file your qualifications statement.

The OPM also issues a publication called *Federal Exam Announcement* each quarter.

Due to budget cuts and reorganization, there are no longer any Federal Job Information Centers as in the past. However, in addition to their excellent website, OPM now maintains a touch-screen system of USAJOBS kiosks nationwide and automated 24-hour telephone hotlines. See the end of this chapter for those lists.

Contacting the Hiring Agency Directly

Because the OPM is no longer responsible for overseeing hiring in most agencies, you can also get detailed job information directly from each agency; they have their

24-Hour Access to Job Information through the OPM

By telephone: 912-757-3000
By modem (BBS): 912-757-3100
Through the Internet: www.usajobs.opm.gov
By Telnet: fjob.mail.opm.gov

own personnel offices which publish their own job lists. Some agencies also have job hotlines. You can also look in your local blue pages for names and addresses to contact.

Outstanding Scholar Program

College students with excellent academic records have an inside track in the hiring process for certain kinds of jobs. The Outstanding Scholar Program (OSP) exempts students with a cumulative grade-point average (GPA) of 3.5 or above from most of the competitive requirements expected of other candidates. These scholars can then be hired at the GS-5 or GS-7 level.

Commercial Resources

The services provided by the OPM are free, except for any long-distance charges for OPM calls. There are also a host of resources available from commercial sources.

The *Federal Jobs Digest* is a bi-weekly newspaper ($34), published every other Monday, listing thousands of new government jobs both in the U.S. and overseas. The *Digest* includes job descriptions, salaries, and instructions regarding where and how to apply. A subscription to the *Digest* is available (call 1-800-824-5000), and the *Digest* can also be found online at *www.jobsfed.com* as well as at newstands and libraries. The e-mail address is *webmaster@jobsfed.com*.

Federal Jobs Digest also publishes two guides, *Working for Your Uncle*, and *U.S. Postal Exam Test 470*, which are available online or at 800-824-5000.

You can, of course, employ a private job counselor or agency to help you find the right position with the federal government.

HOW TO APPLY

Applying for a job with the federal government can be a daunting task. The job lists are huge and, as hiring continues to move out of the jurisdiction of the OPM and into the hands of the individual agencies, agencies can increasingly individualize the application process. Fortunately, the government has recently simplified the general application process a good deal.

Filing Period

All openings have a *filing period* or *application window:* a specific time period during which applications will be accepted. Be sure you are aware of the filing period so that you do not miss the deadline. It could be weeks or even years before there's another filing period for that specific job title and location.

Application Forms

The SF-71, once required for all federal job applicants, is no longer the only way to apply for a job with the government. Rather than filling out the lengthy SF-71, applicants can now use the Optional Application for Federal Employment (OF-612), a short and easy-to-use form which is reproduced at the end of this chapter. You can still use the SF-71 if you want or, for an increasing number of jobs, you can use OPM Form 1203—an optical scan form that will quickly screen and rate your application.

Resume

You may also submit a hard-copy or online resume instead of an OF-612 or SF-71. However, if your resume does not include the information that is requested on the OF-612 and in the job vacancy announcement, you *will not be considered* for the job. One vital piece of information people often neglect to include on resumes is their Social Security number. The OPM also requests that your resume or application be brief; include *only* the relevant information.

Listed below are the items that your resume must include in order for you to be considered:

- **Job information**
  Job announcement number
  Job title
  Grade(s) for which you are applying
- **Personal information**
  Full name and mailing address (including ZIP code)
  Daytime and evening phone numbers (including area code)
  Social Security number
  Country of citizenship
  Veteran's preference, if applicable
- **Education**
  The name, city, state and ZIP code, if possible, of your high school, along with the date you earned your diploma or GED
  The name, city, state, and ZIP, if possible, of any colleges or universities you attended, as well as your major(s) and type and year of degree(s) received. If you did not receive a degree, show the total number of credits you earned and indicate whether those were earned in semester or quarter hours. (You do not need to send a copy of your college transcript unless the job vacancy announcement requests it.)
- **Work experience** Include the following information for all paid and unpaid work experience relating to the job vacancy you would like to fill:
  Job title
  Duties and accomplishments
  Name and address of employer
  Name and phone number of supervisor

Dates employment began and ended (month and year)
Number of hours worked per week
Salary/wages
Indicate whether your current supervisor may be contacted.

- **Other qualifications.** The OPM requests that you provide dates for these accomplishments, but do not send documentation unless it is specifically requested.
  List any job-related training courses you've taken (include course title and year)
  List job-related skills, such as foreign languages, computer software/hardware proficiency, machinery operability, and typing speed
  List current job-related certificates and licenses
  List job-related honors, awards, and special accomplishments, such as membership in a professional or honor society, leadership activities, publications, and performance awards.

Test Scheduling Card

When you write or visit a Federal Job Information Center (FJIC) or government agency and express your desire to apply for a position, if the job requires an assembled exam, you will receive a Test Scheduling Card. This is particularly important for positions with the USPS as well as for law enforcement, firefighter, and clerical and secretarial positions. These entry-level jobs require a written test, and because there is often an oversupply of applicants, you'll need to make a reservation to take the exam. Fill out and return the Test Scheduling Card, and you'll be notified of exactly when and where you need to be to take the exam. Be aware that sometimes certain areas have such a high demand for certain jobs, including clerical workers, that these exams can be taken on a walk-in basis without a reservation; your FJIC can tell you if this is the case in your area.

How to Pitch Your Skills to the Job Announcement

Since your application often determines whether you get called for the next part of the selection process, it's important that your SF-71, OF-612, or resume highlight how your accomplishments fit into the job requirements. To help you match your application to the job announcement, request a Qualifications Information Statement. This statement specifies the exact job qualifications for the different grade levels, discusses hiring prospects, explains how education and experience will be rated, and tells you where and how to apply and what forms to use to apply. These forms are usually available for entry-level GS positions.

Some experts recommend that you also indicate the minimum grade level you will accept, keeping in mind that a step down in salary can get your foot in the door and be a stepping stone to regular promotions once you're in the system.

Remember that you will be rated primarily on related education and experience. Even voluntary experience counts, so list all that is relevant (but omit what is not). Look for key words in the job announcement (words like "teamwork," for example) and highlight duties and accomplishments that demonstrate to the agency that you have those qualities. The more concrete evidence you provide regarding your qualification, the higher you are likely to be ranked.

Veterans' Preference

If you've served on active duty in the military, you may be eligible for veterans' preference: an addition of 5 points—or 10 points, if you are a disabled veteran—to your rating in the job selection process. To be eligible, you must have been separated under honorable conditions or, if you began serving after October 15, 1976, you must have a Campaign Badge, an Expeditionary Medal, or a service-connected disability.

To claim the 5-point preference, you need to attach proof of your eligibility: a copy of your DD-214, Certificate of Release or Discharge from Active Duty, or other eligible form. For the 10-point preference, you must attach Standard Form 15, the Application for 10-Point Veterans' Preference, and the eligibility proofs it requires. For more information regarding Veterans' Preference, call the OPM at 912-757-3000. Select "Federal Employment Topics" and then "Veterans." Or go to the OPM web site at *www.usajobs.opm.gov/b.htm.*

WHAT HAPPENS NEXT?

If you are selected, usually on the basis of your application, for further consideration, you may face additional steps in the selection process, including, depending on the position, a written exam, a physical test, one or more interviews, and other requirements you might not expect of a private employer. For some positions, the written exam is the first step.

Written Exams

For most entry-level positions that require exams, the tests start out by measuring your basic reading, writing, and sometimes math skills. The agency is more interested in your ability to be trained than in knowledge you already have about the job. Sample exams on these basic skills, as well as chapters that teach you how to improve your performance in reading, grammar, vocabulary and spelling, and math, are included in this book.

Depending on the position, the exams may also assess your common sense and logic or your memory. And then there may be different kinds of questions that test specific work-related skills. For instance, postal workers are required to memorize and check addresses; clerical workers are tested on aspects of filing such as alphabetization. The exams usually present scenarios that would arise in a typical job situation and are almost always multiple choice.

In general, you can re-take tests if you fail, and because registers are often discarded after one year, you can re-take the test during the next testing period in order to improve your score—and therefore your rank on the register.

Physical Performance Tests

The majority of civilian government jobs don't require any special physical ability, but there are several important exceptions. At the USPS, for example, many jobs require physical strength and stamina, so the USPS requires all applicants to be able to lift 70 pounds in order to be considered. But there's no further testing for physical ability.

However, firefighters and law enforcement employees, among others, *do* need special physical capabilities and skills, and they must pass a series of physical tests before they can be hired. These physical ability tests may include timed runs, obstacle courses, ladder climbs, weight lifting, weight pulling, sit-ups, and push-ups.

Interviews

Interviews for government positions almost always come *after* your agency has already determined that you are otherwise qualified for the job. These interviews often serve more as a final checkpoint in the hiring process than a first step as in the private sector. Most interviewers will go into detail about the type of work the job entails, the benefits of the position, and the procedures of the agency. They will also probably ask questions that will help them ascertain how motivated, cooperative, intelligent, and logical you are, as well as what kind of work habits, goals, and personal values you have.

Give yourself an edge in the interview by showing some knowledge of the agency and its business. During your application process, seek out others in the position you desire. Find out what their work is like and what qualities are valued. If you know something about the position and the agency, you'll demonstrate your interest and your motivation, two characteristics employers value highly.

You'll also be more likely to succeed if you're able to explain, comfortably, any gaps in your education or experience. Tell the truth; you'll be respected if you can admit to past failures or faults, especially if you can explain how you overcame, or plan to overcome, them.

Finally, you should be able to discuss your short- and long-term career goals. Clearly, if your goals are in line with the goals of the department, you're in a better position to be hired. Here again your research—talking to people already working with the department—and your overall awareness of the business of the agency will help.

Other Requirements

Before you're hired, Uncle Sam wants to make sure you're government material. That's why you will be asked to fill out a Declaration for Federal Employment (OF-306). This form is used to determine your "suitability" for working for the federal government and to authorize a background investigation. You must answer personal questions on subjects like loan defaults, felonies, and misdemeanors. Please note: Answering yes to questions does not automatically disqualify you, but your answers will be taken into consideration during the selection process.

You must also certify that all of the information you've provided is accurate and correct to the best of your knowledge, and your application will be checked. If investigators find you have falsified information in your application or resume, you may suffer one of three possible consequences: you won't be hired; you'll be fired; or you may be jailed or fined.

Many positions—especially those that deal directly with public safety, like the police and firefighter series and jobs that require security clearance—require an employee who not only meets all qualifications criteria and excels in all stages of the hiring process but who also meets certain citizenship standards. That's why before employees are hired for these jobs, they may be subject to one or more of the following:

- a background investigation
- a drug screening test
- a medical examination
- a psychological evaluation or personality test

These "checks" may significantly lengthen the hiring process, but they're important to ensure the well-being of all the citizens who interact with these employees.

FEDERAL EMPLOYMENT INFORMATION SERVICES

USAJOBS TOUCH SCREEN COMPUTER KIOSKS

These kiosks, located throughout the nation, provide current worldwide Federal job opportunities, online information, and the ability to request application packages. The touch-screen technology is easy to use. Touch Screen Computer kiosk locations are generally available Monday through Friday during normal business hours.

Alabama
Huntsville
520 Wynn Drive, NW

Alaska
Anchorage
Federal Building
222 W. Seventh Avenue
Room 156

Arizona
Phoenix
VA Medical Center
650 E. Indian School Road
Building 21, Room 141

Arkansas
Little Rock
1223 W. Seventh Street

California
Sacramento
801 I ("i") Street

Colorado
Denver
Department of Social Services
Employment Center
2200 W. Alameda Avenue, #5B

Connecticut
Hartford
Federal Building
450 Main Street
Lobby

District of Columbia
Washington, DC
Theodore Roosevelt Federal Building
1900 E Street, NW
Room 1416

Florida

Miami
Downtown Jobs and Benefits Center
Florida Job Service Center
401 NW Second Avenue
Suite N-214

Orlando
Florida Job Service Center
1001 Executive Center Drive
1st Floor

Georgia

Atlanta
Richard B. Russell Federal Building
Main Lobby
Plaza Level
75 Spring Street, SW

Hawaii

Honolulu
Federal Building
Room 5316
300 Ala Moana Boulevard

Fort Shafter
Department of Army
Army Civilian Personnel Office
Army Garrison
Building T-1500

Illinois

Chicago
77 W. Jackson Boulevard
1st Floor Lobby

Indiana

Indianapolis
Minton-Capehart Federal Building
575 N. Pennsylvania Street
Room 339

Louisiana

New Orleans
Louisiana Employment Service
1530 Thalia Street

Maine

Augusta
Federal Office Building
40 Western Avenue

Maryland

Baltimore
George H. Fallon Building
Lombard Street & Hopkins Plaza
Lobby

Massachusetts

Boston
Thomas P. O'Neill, Jr. Federal Building
10 Causeway Street
1st Floor

Michigan

Detroit
477 Michigan Avenue
Room 1196

Minnesota
Twin Cities
Bishop Henry Whipple Federal Building
1 Federal Drive
Room 501
Fort Snelling

Missouri
Kansas City
Federal Building
601 E. 12th Street
Room 134

New Hampshire
Portsmouth
Thomas McIntyre Federal Building
80 Daniel Street
1st Floor Lobby

New Jersey
Newark
Peter J. Rodino Federal Building
970 Broad Street
2nd Floor

New Mexico
Albuquerque
New Mexico State Job Service
501 Mountain Road, NE
Lobby

New York
Albany
Leo W. O'Brian Federal Building
Clinton Avenue & North Pearl
Basement Level

Buffalo
Thaddeus T. Dulski Federal Building
111 W. Huron Street
9th Floor

New York City
Jacob K. Javits Federal Building
26 Federal Plaza
Lobby

New York City
World Trade Center
Cafeteria

Syracuse
James M. Hanley Federal Building
100 S. Clinton Street

Ohio
Dayton
Federal Building
200 W. Second St.
Room 509

Oklahoma
Oklahoma City
Career Connection Center
7401 NE 23rd Street

Oregon
Portland
Federal Building
Room 376
1220 SW Third Avenue

Bonneville Power Administration
905 NE 11th Avenue

Department of Army & Corps of Engineers
Duncan Plaza

Pennsylvania
Harrisburg
Federal Building
228 Walnut Street
Room 168

Philadelphia
William J. Green, Jr. Federal Building
600 Arch Street
2nd Floor

Pittsburgh
Federal Building
1000 Liberty Avenue
1st Floor Lobby

Reading
Reading Postal Service
2100 N. 13th Street

Puerto Rico
San Juan
Torre de Plaza
Suite 1114
525 F.D. Roosevelt Avenue

Rhode Island
Providence
380 Westminster
Mall Lobby

Tennessee
Memphis
Naval Air Station Memphis
Transition Assistance Center
7800 Third Avenue
Building South 239
Millington

Texas
Dallas
Federal Building
1100 Commerce Street
1st Floor Lobby

El Paso
Federal Building
700 E. San Antonio Street
Lobby

Houston
Mickey Leland Federal Building
1919 Smith Street
1st Floor Lobby

San Antonio
Federal Building
727 E. Durango
1st Floor Lobby

Utah
Salt Lake City
Utah State Job Service
720 S. Second East
Reception Area

Vermont
Burlington
Federal Building
11 Elmwood Avenue
1st Floor Lobby

Virgin Isands
(See listing for Puerto Rico.)

Virginia
Norfolk
Federal Building
200 Granby Street

Washington
Seattle
Federal Building
915 Second Avenue
Room 110

Washington, DC
(See listing for District of Columbia.)

West Virginia
(See listing for Ohio)

Wisconsin
(For Dane, Grant, Green, Iowa, Lafayette, Rock, Jefferson, Walworth, Milwaukee, Waukesha, Racine, and Kenosha Counties, see listing for Illinois. For all other counties, see listing for Minnesota.)

Wyoming
(See listing for Colorado.)

USAJOBS BY PHONE AUTOMATED TELEPHONE SYSTEM

This automated phone system provides 24-hour-a-day, 7-day-a-week information about current employment opportunities (nationwide and worldwide); special programs for students, veterans, and people with disabilities; the Presidential Management Intern Program; salaries and benefits; and application request services.

Alabama
Huntsville
(256) 837-0894

California
San Francisco
(415) 744-5627

Colorado
Denver
(303) 236-8570

District of Columbia
Washington, DC
(202) 606-2700

Georgia
Atlanta
(404) 331-4315

Hawaii
Honolulu
(808) 541-2791

Illinois
Chicago
(312) 353-6192

Michigan
Detroit
(313) 226-6950

Minnesota
Twin Cities
(612) 725-3430

Missouri
Kansas City
(816) 426-5702

North Carolina
Raleigh
(919) 790-2822

Ohio
Dayton
(937) 225-2720

Pennsylvania
Philadelphia
(215) 861-3070

Puerto Rico
San Juan
(787) 766-5242

Texas
San Antonio
(210) 805-2402

Virginia
Norfolk
(757) 441-3355

Washington
Seattle
(206) 552-0888

From Anywhere in the Nation or the World
(912) 757-3000

Nationwide TDD Service
(912) 744-2299

USAJOBS INTERNET WEB SITE

The World Wide Web site at *www.usajobs.opm.gov* provides access to the Federal Jobs Data Base; full text job announcements; answers to frequently asked federal employment questions via Employment Info Line fact sheets; access to electronic and hard copy application forms, and online resume submission.

OTHER

You may also visit your local state employment service office. There you will find information on current federal job opportunity listings. The list may be on a printed report, on microfiche, or on computer. The method varies from state to state.

Form Approved
OMB No. 3206-0219

OPTIONAL APPLICATION FOR FEDERAL EMPLOYMENT - OF 612

You may apply for most jobs with a resume, this form, or other written format. If your resume or application does not provide all the information requested on this form and in the job vacancy announcement, you may lose consideration for a job.

1 Job title in announcement

2 Grade(s) applying for

Announcement number

4 Last name

First and middle names

Social Security Number

- -

6 Mailing address

Phone numbers (include area code)

Daytime ( )

City

State

ZIP Code

-

Evening ( )

WORK EXPERIENCE

8 Describe your paid and nonpaid work experience related to the job for which you are applying. Do **not** attach job descriptions.

1) Job title (if Federal, include series and grade)

| From (MM/YY) | To (MM/YY) | Salary $ | per | Hours per week |

Employer's name and address

Supervisor's name and phone number

( )

Describe your duties and accomplishments

2) Job title (if Federal, include series and grade)

| From (MM/YY) | To (MM/YY) | Salary $ | per | Hours per week |

Employer's name and address

Supervisor's name and phone number

( )

Describe your duties and accomplishments

NSN 7540-01-351-9178

Optional Form 612 (September 1994)
U.S. Office of Personnel Management

9 May we contact your current supervisor?

YES ☐ NO ☐ If we need to contact your current supervisor before making an offer, we will contact you first.

EDUCATION

10 Mark highest level completed. Some HS ☐ HS/GED ☐ Associate ☐ Bachelor ☐ Master ☐ Doctoral ☐

11 Last high school (HS) or GED school. Give the school's name, city, State, ZIP Code (if known), and year diploma or GED received.

12 Colleges and universities attended. Do **not** attach a copy of your transcript unless requested.

	Name	Total Credits Earned		Major(s)	Degree - Year
1)		Semester	Quarter		(if any) Received
	City State ZIP Code				
		-			
2)					
		-			
3)					
		-			

OTHER QUALIFICATIONS

13 **Job-related** training courses (give title and year). **Job-related** skills (other languages, computer software/hardware, tools, machinery, typing speed, etc. **Job-related** certificates and licenses (current only). **Job-related** honors, awards, and special accomplishments(publications, memberships in professional/honor societies, leadership activities, public speaking, and performance awards.) Give dates, but do **not** send documents unless requested.

GENERAL

14 Are you a U.S. citizen? YES ☐ NO ☐ Give the country of your citizenship.

15 Do you claim veterans' preference? NO ☐ YES ☐ Mark your claim of 5 or 10 points below.

    5 points ☐ Attach your DD 214 or other proof. **10 points** ☐ Attach an *Application for 10-Point Veterans' Preference* (SF 15) and proof required.

16 Were you ever a Federal civilian employee?

                                                                           Series Grade From (MM/YY) To (MM/YY)

    NO ☐ YES ☐ For highest civilian grade give:

17 Are you eligible for reinstatement based on career or career-conditional Federal status?

    NO ☐ YES ☐ If requested, attach SF 50 proof.

APPLICANT CERTIFICATION

18 **I certify** that, to the best of my knowledge and belief, all of the information on and attached to this application is true, correct, complete and made in good faith. I **understand** that false or fraudulent information on or attached to this application may be grounds for not hiring me or firing me after I begin work, and may be punishable by fine or imprisonment. **I understand** that any information I give may be investigated.

SIGNATURE   DATE SIGNED

GENERAL INFORMATION

You may apply for most Federal jobs with a resume, the attached *Optional Application for Federal Employment* or other written format. If your resume or application does not provide all the information requested on this form and in the job vacancy announcement, you may lose consideration for a job. Type or print clearly in dark ink. Help speed the selection process by keeping your application brief and sending only the requested information. If essential to attach additional pages, include your name and Social Security Number on each page.

- For information on Federal employment, including job lists, alternative formats for persons with disabilities, and veterans' preference, call the U.S. Office of Personnel Management at **912-757-3000, TDD 912-744-2299**, by computer modem **912-757-3100**, or via the Internet (Telnet only) at FJOB.MAIL.OPM.GOV.

- If you served on active duty in the United States Military and were separated under honorable conditions, you may be eligible for veterans' preference. To receive preference if your service began after October 15, 1976, you must have a Campaign Badge, Expeditionary Medal, or a service-connected disability. Veterans' preference is not a factor for Senior Executive Service jobs or when competition is limited to status candidates (current or former career or career-conditional Federal employees.)

- Most Federal jobs require United States citizenship and also that males over age 18 born after December 31, 1959, have registered with the Selective Service System or have an exemption.

- The law prohibits public officials from appointing, promoting, or recommending their relatives.

- Federal annuitants (military and civilian) may have their salaries or annuities reduced. All employees must pay any valid delinquent debts or the agency may garnish their salary.

- Send you application to the office announcing the vacancy. If you have questions, contact that office.

THE FEDERAL GOVERNMENT IS AN EQUAL OPPORTUNITY EMPLOYER

PRIVACY ACT AND PUBLIC BURDEN STATEMENTS

- The Office of Personnel Management and other Federal agencies rate applicants for Federal jobs under the authority of sections 1104, 1302, 3301, 3304, 3320, 3361, 3393, and 3394 of title 5 of the United States Code. We need the information requested in this form and in the associated vacancy announcements to evaluate your qualifications. Other laws require us to ask about citizenship, military service, etc.

- We request your Social Security Number (SSN) under the authority of Executive Order 9397 in order to keep your records straight; other people may have the same name. As allowed by law or Presidential directive, we use your SSN to seek information about you from employers, schools, banks, and others who know you. Your SSN may also be used in studies and computer matching with other Government files, for example, files on unpaid student loans.

- If you do not give us your SSN or any other information requested, we cannot process your application, which is the first step in getting a job. Also, incomplete addresses and ZIP Codes will slow processing.

- We may give information from your records to: training facilities; organizations deciding claims for retirement, insurance, unemployment or health benefits; officials in litigation or administrative proceedings where the Government is a party; law enforcement agencies concerning violations of law or regulation; Federal agencies for statistical reports and studies; officials of labor organizations recognized by law in connection with representing employees; Federal agencies or other sources requesting information for Federal agencies in connection with hiring or retaining, security clearances, security or suitability investigations, classifying jobs, contracting, or issuing licenses, grants, or other benefits; public and private organizations including news media that grant or publicize employee recognition and awards; and the Merit Systems Protection Board, the Office of Special Counsel, the Equal Employment Opportunity Commission, the Federal Labor Relations Authority, the National Archives, the Federal Acquisition Institute, and congressional offices in connection with their official functions.

- We may also give information from your records to: prospective nonfederal employers concerning tenure of employment, civil service status, length of service, and date and nature of action for separation as shown on personnel action forms of specifically identified individuals; requesting organizations or individuals concerning the home address and other relevant information on those who might have contracted an illness or been exposed to a health hazard; authorized Federal and nonfederal agencies for use in computer matching; spouses or dependent children asking whether the employee has changed from self-and-family to self-only health benefits enrollment; individuals working on a contract, service, grant, cooperative agreement or job for the Federal Government; non-agency members of an agency's performance or other panel; and agency- appointed representatives of employees concerning information issued to the employee about fitness-for-duty or agency-filed disability retirement procedures.

- We estimate the public reporting burden for this collection will vary from 20 to 240 minutes with an average of 40 minutes per response, including time for reviewing instructions, searching existing data sources, gathering data, and completing and reviewing the information. You may send comments regarding the burden estimate or any other aspect of the collection of information, including suggestions for reducing this burden, to U.S. Office of Personnel Management, Reports and Forms Management Officer, Washington, DC 20415-0001.

- Send your application to the agency announcing the vacancy.

C·H·A·P·T·E·R

GETTING A JOB WITH STATE AND LOCAL GOVERNMENT

2

CHAPTER SUMMARY

This chapter will show you how to tap into the rich resource of job opportunities with state, county, and municipal government. In this chapter you'll learn what types of state and local government jobs are available, how to find those jobs, and what to expect in the job application and selection process.

You don't have to work for Uncle Sam to work for the government. Hundreds of thousands of people work for state and local government in jobs that parallel just about every occupation in the private sector, from the receptionist at the public library to the maintenance crews who fill in potholes to the police officers who direct traffic and catch bad guys. There's a lot of work that needs to be done to maintain a state, county, city, or town, and many of these opportunities are available to people with little special training or experience.

WHY WORK FOR A STATE OR LOCAL GOVERNMENT?

Excellent Prospects

Now's a good time to think about working for a state or local government. The U.S. Department of Labor's *Occupational Outlook Handbook* predicts that a large percentage of job growth in the next five to ten years will be in government—particularly in state and local government. Four big growth areas in employment are health services, education, information systems, and social services—all of which are concerns of state and local government. In addition, the Bureau of Labor Statistics predicts a 10 to 20 percent increase in the number of firefighters—almost 90 percent of whom work at the municipal or county level—over the next ten years. The number of police officers, currently 600,000 nationwide, is also expected to rise as the nation's population increases.

One way to learn about a specific state is to visit the state's website. For all state home pages, use the URL *www.state._ _.us*, substituting the state's two-letter postal abbreviation for the blanks. For example, Utah is *www.state.ut.us*.

Types of State and Local Government Jobs

While specific job titles may vary considerably, state and local government jobs generally fall into one of the following categories:

- Accounting/financial management
- Agriculture/conservation
- Clerical/administrative
- Education/information services
- Engineering/architecture
- Legal/licensing
- Medical/health services
- Public safety/law enforcement
- Skilled trades/maintenance
- Social services

Diverse Opportunities and Job Security

Many of the services we take for granted in our communities are run by state and local governments. Public education (elementary and secondary schools and universities), parks, hospitals, libraries, prisons, transportation, sanitation, public utilities, fire and police departments, and courts all fall under the jurisdiction of state and local government. These government agencies and departments provide us with essential services, ensuring that even during tough economic times, state and local government jobs will still be available. And in most cases, state and local government career employees, like federal career employees, are well protected from layoffs.

And remember, you don't have to be a teacher to work in a school, or a doctor to work in a hospital, or a lawyer to work in a courthouse. All these agencies need a wide variety of personnel to fulfill their mission: clerical support staff, maintenance workers, skilled workers such as carpenters and plumbers, security guards, and on and on.

To give you a better idea of exactly what kind of jobs are out there, here's a sampling of specific entry-level job titles from around the country:

- administrative assistant
- bus operator
- clerk-typist
- corrections officer
- data entry operator
- firefighter
- highway maintenance worker
- mailroom courier
- office assistant
- park ranger
- parking meter collector
- patient relations representative
- police officer
- recycling worker
- sanitation collector
- staff assistant

- utilities billing specialist
- word processor
- youth development aide

Sizable Starting Salaries

Starting salaries range greatly from job to job, state to state, and municipality to municipality. The table on this page offers a brief sampling of salaries listed on recent job announcements.

Generous Benefits

Exact benefits, of course, will vary among government organizations, but most state and local government employees can expect a substantial benefits package, including:

- health insurance
- life insurance
- disability insurance

- paid vacation and holidays
- sick leave
- educational incentives
- pension plan

FINDING JOB OPENINGS

Like jobs with the federal government, state and local government jobs aren't usually listed in the "Help Wanted" ads; instead the agencies usually put out position announcements.

Position Announcements

Vacancy announcements—variously called *position announcements, job bulletins, notification of examination,* or some similar title—generally provide the following information:

SAMPLE ENTRY-LEVEL SALARIES: STATE AND LOCAL GOVERNMENT		
Administrative Assistant	State of Wyoming	$18,350
Bus Operator	New York City, NY	$29,120
Clerk Typist	Stamford, CT	$21,000
Corrections Officer	State of Texas	$23,610
Custodial Worker	Clearwater, FL	$18,228
Data Entry Specialist	Wake, NC	$20,970
Firefighter	Los Angeles, CA	$34,900
General Clerk	Osage, MO	$15,925
Parks Maintenance Worker	Mesa, AZ	$26,805
Police Officer Recruit	Boston, MA	$34,500
Recreation Assistant	Clearwater, FL	$17,181
Sanitation Worker	New York City, NY	$26,872
Secretary I	Huntsville, AL	$19,158
State Traffic Officer	State of California	$38,533

- Filing period (the "window" during which applications are accepted)
- Job title
- Hiring office or agency
- Salary
- Terms (whether part time or full time)
- Benefits
- Job duties
- Job qualifications
- How to apply
- Who to call for forms or with questions
- Where to mail completed forms

Public libraries and colleges usually have a list of current job and exam announcements.

The World Wide Web

Nowadays, most everyone can get on the Internet (at home, school, the library, a cybercafe, or work). Finding online state and local government job openings in many areas is a snap. As long as your state or municipality lists job openings on the Internet—and more and more of them do every day—you can access them easily. Check the end of this chapter for a list of government websites.

Many states and cities now allow you to print applications from the Internet or fill out and submit forms directly from their pages. And some states and municipalities, including California, are even beginning to administer selected civil service exams over the Internet. (Chapter 3 provides detailed information on how to use the Internet to find civil service jobs.)

USAJOBS Kiosks

Your state probably has a state job information center, which may also include municipal job information. Or your municipality may have its own local job information center. In New York, for example, there are

Department of Labor Community Service Centers around the state that provide municipal job information. See Chapter 1 for a complete list of USAJOBS touch screen kiosks.

Check Your Phone Book

Another easy way to get state and local government job information is to contact departments and agencies directly. You can call individual departments and agencies, which are listed in the blue pages of your local phone book, and request an application and information regarding job vacancies. Some agencies keep waiting lists of people who want to get a position announcement or exam bulletin if they're not hiring at the time you call.

To get a broader range of job opportunities, call the state or local personnel department (look under *Department of Personnel, Department of Employment, Human Resources, Department of Labor, Office of Personnel,* or *Office of Employment*). In the New York City phone book, for example, under "Personnel, Dept. of," there is a phone number for Applications and Filing, for Eligibility Lists Information, and for Examinations.

Fee Services

Of course, you can use a professional job service to help you find a state or local government job, and several search services are available on the Internet. Just be sure, before you commit your hard-earned money, that the search service you select is going to give you your money's worth.

How to Apply

In general, the application and selection process at the state and local level is much like the process with the federal government. Many agencies now allow you to

Job Qualifications

Qualifications for state and local jobs vary widely depending on the kind of job. Some jobs require nothing more than a high school diploma or GED, a few don't even require that much. Whatever type of job you're looking for, be sure to check the specific job qualifications on a job announcement before you apply.

State and local governments, like the federal government, rank applicants according to specific, clear criteria. If you don't meet the minimum qualifications, you won't be considered. Your interview for a state or local job often won't come until several steps into the selection process, so you can't get around not having minimum qualifications by winning an employer over in an interview.

apply online. Most agencies maintain an eligibility list on which candidates are ranked according to a clear and objective set of criteria, beginning with minimum qualifications and including exam scores if the job requires an exam. Jobs have a specific filing period, which, as with federal jobs, can be critical. If you miss the application window, you may have to wait years before another announcement.

A sample application from the State of Texas is included at the end of this chapter to illustrate the type of information you'll be asked to provide when applying for a job with a state or local government.

Follow Procedures in the Position Announcement

Application procedures vary nationwide, with each city or state setting up its own process. Vacancy announcements should tell you exactly whom to contact regarding the position. Others may include an application form or exam notification card. Many states allow you to apply instantly by filling out information on the Internet.

You can also write to the department of personnel and request application information. Many agencies or departments will also accept resumes, but as with the federal government, you need to be sure that key job vacancy information (such as the job vacancy number, if there is one) and your social security number are included. Your best bet is to read the job announcement very carefully and follow its directions exactly.

Veteran's Preference

Veterans usually get special treatment for jobs on the state and local level, especially where the selection process entails a ranking system. Veterans applying for firefighter or police officer positions, for example, often have five or ten points added to their scores. For more details, you should contact your state or local personnel department.

NEXT STEPS

What happens next, after you fill out an application? For many jobs, the first step is a written exam. After that, depending on the job, there may be more steps—many more, if you're applying for a public safety job in law enforcement or fire safety.

WRITTEN EXAMS

Many state and local government jobs have a written exam as part of the selection process. The type of test—if there is one—will vary greatly from job to job and location to location, but most exams will include at least some basic reading, writing, and sometimes math skills. You can hone your skills in these areas by taking the practice exams in this book and studying the chapters about reading, grammar, vocabulary and spelling, and math.

Beyond the basic skills, here are some of the areas most often tested for specific occupations:

- **Clerical/office support:** sorting items alphabetically and numerically, proofreading to catch discrepancies in series of numbers and letters, typing or word processing speed and accuracy, and/or stenography.
- **Corrections officer:** memory and observation, logic (placing events in a logical order), using judgment and common sense in a given situation, understanding and applying written rules and procedures.
- **Firefighter:** following directions, judgment and reasoning (for example, what you think is the most important thing to do in a certain situation), reading and understanding maps and floor plans, memory and observation. Some municipalities and counties will provide you with a study guide that they'll expect you to study before the exam, so both your understanding and your ability to remember the materials will be tested.
- **Police officer:** memory and observation, map reading, using common sense and good judgment in a given situation.

Many other jobs may not include a written test but will require various levels of certification, degrees, or job experience.

OTHER STEPS

Whether you have to go through other steps in the selection process depends on what kind of job you're applying for. Entry-level applicants for almost any public safety job—law enforcement, including corrections, and firefighting, for example—will have to pass through most if not all of these steps: one or more interviews, a physical ability test, a background investigation, a psychological evaluation, and a medical evaluation. Clerical workers, on the other hand, may have only an interview—or perhaps not even that much, in which case your written exam score and your application pretty much determine whether or not you get the job.

Physical Ability Test

People who are applying for almost any physically demanding job, including police officer, firefighter, or sanitation worker, can count on having to pass a physical ability test. These tests vary widely from municipality to municipality. In some cases, you'll be tested on the number of push-ups and sit-ups that you can do in a certain amount of time, how quickly you can run a mile, how much weight you can bench press, and similar general tests of physical fitness.

Other tests may be more closely job-related, usually resembling a sort of obstacle course. Sanitation workers, for instance, might have to drag a heavy object and then lift and toss it as if they were throwing it into a collection truck, and then carry several other objects a certain distance. Firefighters might have to crawl through a tunnel, climb stairs, drag a hose, drag a dummy, raise and climb a ladder, and jump over a wall—all with full protective gear on and under a certain amount of time.

Whatever the type, physical tests are usually timed; you have to complete a given exercise, or the whole obstacle course, in a given length of time. In some cases, the test is basically pass-fail: if you come in under the time, you pass; if you don't, you fail. In other cases, your time becomes part of your ranking on the eligibility list; the better your time, the more likely you are to be hired.

If your job requires a physical ability test, you'll need to be in tip-top shape before you go into it. It's important that you do very well on your first try, especially if your score weighs heavily in your ranking. A few cities will allow you to retake the physical test if you fail, but most will not allow you to retake the exam until the next application period.

Interviews

In the private sector, an initial interview is often one of the very first parts of the process of getting hired. You submit your application or resume, and the company calls you in for an interview to see if you're the kind of person they want. In the public sector, an interview—if there is one—is likely to come later in the process. On the basis of your application and any supporting materials, as well as your exam scores, the agency has already decided you're the kind of person they want, and they just want to make sure. You'll probably face most of the standard kinds of interview questions: who you are, what your experience is and how it suits you for this job, where you want to be in six months or five years. While the interview doesn't give you a chance to make up for a spotty application or bad test scores—you won't be called if you have them—it does give you the chance to convince the interviewer you have good oral communication skills and poise.

People applying to public safety jobs, including police officer, corrections officer, or firefighter, are likely to face a different kind of interview, and there may be more than one. You may have an individual interview with the chief or deputy chief, or you may face a board of several people which may include civilians or officials from outside the department. In most cases, the primary concern in this type of interview is your communication skills, interpersonal skills, and judgment. You'll probably be asked why you want to be a firefighter, police officer, or correctional officer; what qualities you have that will make you good at the job; and questions about your background. You may also be presented with hypothetical situations that are job related but measure your ethics rather than your knowledge of the job. For example, you may be asked what you'd do if you caught a fellow officer stealing during an investigation.

Background Investigation

Some municipalities do at least a cursory background check of almost all potential employees. For most jobs, that means nothing more than a careful private employer might do—checking that you did in fact get your diploma from Anywhere High or that you did really work for XYZ Corporation.

Law enforcement officers and firefighters go through a much more detailed background investigation. You may not even be aware that you're being investigated, but if the background investigator—often a detective in the police department—uncovers any discrepancies in your application or other information you've submitted, you can be sure you'll be questioned about it. Thus, it's critical that you be open and honest throughout all stages of the application and selection process.

Psychological Evaluation

People applying for public safety jobs are also subject to a psychological evaluation. These are stressful jobs, so hiring departments want to make sure you're emotionally stable. After all, your life and the lives of others are often at stake. The psychological examination for police officers is generally more extensive than for firefighters and correctional officers; you'll be tested to determine that you won't be hampered by serious emotional disturbances, nervous disorders, or drug and/or alcohol dependence. Sometimes the psychological evaluation consists of one or more written tests; sometimes an interview with a psychiatrist is also included.

Medical Evaluation

To work for the state, county, or city, you may be asked to submit a letter from your doctor certifying that you are in generally good physical health, particularly if your job involves physical stress. You may also have to submit to a drug test.

Candidates for public safety positions usually have to be examined by a doctor of the department's choosing. The medical exam is like a regular physical; your blood pressure, height, weight, and so on will be recorded, your eyes and ears will probably be checked, and you may have a blood and/or urine test, including a drug test. But that's about all. If you've made it this far, you'll probably have a job offer waiting for you once you get the doctor's okay.

HOW TO PREPARE

The best way to prepare for any hiring process is to talk to people already in the position you desire. They can best tell you what the job demands are and what you can expect both in the hiring process and on the job.

Just the Facts

State departments of labor perform many services to those looking for employment. For example, in 1999 the Georgia Department of Labor provided the following, without charge, to its job seekers:

320,434 Referrals to job openings
136,812 Placements on jobs
286,777 Workshop activities
117,940 Counseling interviews

You can learn what qualities are most valued by those departments and what techniques successful candidates have used to get in shape (both physically and mentally) for exams and interviews.

You can use the practice exams in this book to help you get ready for the parts of your test that include reading, writing, and math skills. LearningExpress also publishes more specific guides on the tests and selection process for many civil service jobs. If you're interested, see the back of this book for a complete list of titles, or stop by your local bookstore.

CONTACTS FOR GOVERNMENT JOBS, LISTED BY STATE

Alabama

Alabama Employment Service Division:
www.dir.state.al.us/es
334-242-8003
Alabama State Jobs: *www.personnel.state.al.us*

Alaska

Division of Personnel: *http://notes.state.ak.us/wa*
Department of Labor: *www.labor.state.ak.us*
907-465-4430; 800-587-0430

Arizona

Arizona JobBank: *www.ajb.org/az*
Arizona Department of Economic Security:
www.de.state.az.us
Arizona Labor Market Information:
www.de.state.az.us/link/economic/webpage
602-542-4966; 800-488-9191

Arkansas

Whatajob!: *www.whatajob.com*
Arkansas Government Jobs:
www.ar.statejobs.com
Arkansas Employment Security Dept.:
www.state.ar.us/esd
501-682-2127

California
CalJOBS/Online Job and Resume Bank:
www.caljobs.ca.gov or www.spb.ca.gov/index
Federal Jobs in California:
ftp://ftp.fedworld.gov/pub/jobsca.txt
Employment Development Dept.:
wwwedd.cahwnet.gov
Labor Market Information: www.calmis.ca.gov
916-653-1502; CalJOBS: 800-758-0398
Job Line for federal jobs in CA: 916-445-0838

Colorado
Department of Labor and Employment:
www.ajb.org/co
Colorado Workforce Center Locations:
www.employsvcs.cdle.state.co.us/WFCs
About Colorado Dept. of Labor and Employment:
www.cdle.state.co.us
303-830-3000, 303-376-6700

Connecticut
Department of Labor: www.ctdol.state.ct.us
860-263-6000, 860-566-2501, 860-344-2044

Delaware
Delaware's Virtual Career Network:
www.vcnet.net
State Jobs: www.state.de.us/spo/weekly
Delaware Dept. of Labor: www.state.de.us/labor
Other: www.delawareworks.com
302-739-5458, 302-856-5966, 302-577-8277

Florida
JobsDirect: http://jobsdirect.state.fl.us
Dept. of Labor and Employment Security:
www.fdles.state.fl.us
Workforce Florida Job Search:
www.floridajobs.org/pdi-jobsearch
305-377-5180, 305-377-5747

Georgia
Georgia Career Information System:
www.gclc.peachnet.edu
State Government Jobs: www.gms.state.ga.us
Georgia Dept. of Labor: www.dol.state.ga.us
404-656-2725

Hawaii
Job Service of Hawaii: http://hi.jobsearch.org
800-586-8700 (Honolulu)
Other: www.aloha.net/~edpso

Idaho
Idaho Dept. of Labor: www.labor.state.id.us
Idaho's Workforce Development:
www.idahoworks.state.id.us
208-334-6252, 208-334-2568

Illinois
Illinois Job Search: www.il.jobsearch.org
Dept. of Employment Security:
www.ides.state.il.us/html/jobs
888-367-4382; 317-232-3101

Indiana
Jobs with State of Indiana:
www.state.in.us/jobs/jobbank
Access Indiana: www.ai.org/jobs
317-232-2655

Iowa

Iowa Workforce Development:
www.state.ia.us/gov/wd
Iowa Jobs: *www.state.ia.us/jobs*
800-JOB-IOWA
515-281-5387

Kansas

Kansas Dept. of Human Resources:
www.kansasjobs.org
913-296-5390

Kentucky

Kentucky Job Bank: *www.ajb.org/ky/seeker*
502-955-8272

Louisiana

Louisiana Dept. of Labor:
www.1dol.state.la.us/state/jobs
Workforce Development Office: 225-925-4311,
504-568-5812

Maine

Maine Dept. of Labor:
www.janus.state.me.us/labor
Maine Career Centers:
www.mainecareercenter.com
888-457-8883; 800-760-1573; 207-287-3788

Maryland

Maryland's Job Bank: *www.md.jobsearch.org*
410-767-2173
State Job Opportunities:
www.dop.state.md.us/howopen.html
410-767-4715

Massachusetts

Mass. Division of Employment and Training:
www.ma.jobsearch.org
MDET: *www.detma.org*
617-338-0909; 800-5JOBNET; 888-454-9675

Michigan

Michigan works!: *www.michworks.org*
Michigan Career Center: *www.state.mi.us/career*
517-241-4000
State Jobs: *www.state.mi.us/mdcs/Index*

Minnesota

Minnesota's Job Bank: *www.mn.onestopjobs.org*
MN WorkForce Center:
www.MNworkforcecenter.org
888-GET-JOBS

Mississippi

MS Job Search: *www.ms.jobsearch.org*
Mississippi Job Fairs:
www.mesc.state.ms.us/jobfair
601-359-2348

Missouri

Missouri WORKS!: *www.works.state.mo.us*
573-882-8821

Montana

Montana Job Service: *www.jsd.dli.state.mt.us*
406-447-3222 (Helena)
State Jobs: *www.jsd.dli.state.mt.us/state*
Montana Dept. of Labor: *www.dli.state.mt.us*

Nebraska

Nebraska Job Service: www.ne.jobsearch.org
402-471-2200
State Personnel:
www.das.state.ne.us/das_dop/nejobs/per.htm

Nevada

Job Bank: www.abj.org/nv/seeker
Dept. of Personnel: www.state.nv.us/personnel
NV Employment Security Division Offices:
www.state.nv.us/detr/es
702-486-0100, 702-486-0173

New Hampshire

Dept. of Employment Security:
www.nhworks.state.nh.us
603-228-4100

New Jersey

NJ's One-Stop Jobs: www.wnipin.state.nj.us
609-777-0916
Dept. of Labor: www.state.nj.us/labor

New Mexico

Dept. of Labor: www.dol.state.nm.us/nmworks
505-841-9300 (Albuquerque); 505-827-8110

New York

CareerZone: www.nycareerzone.org
New York's Career Resource Library:
www.labor.state.ny.us/html/library
Dept. of Labor: www.labor.state.ny.us
518-457-6216

North Carolina

Employment Security Division:
www.esc.state.nc.us
919-733-7522
Office of State Personnel: 919-733-2243

North Dakota

Job Service North Dakota: www.state.nd.us/jsnd
701-328-5040 (Bismarck); 800-247-0981
State Government Jobs:
www.state.nd.us/cpers/cpdjobs/jobvacindex.htm

Ohio

Bureau of Employment Services:
www.state.oh.us/obes
513-852-3163 (Cincinnati); 614-644-4780
(Columbus)

Oklahoma

Oklahoma JOBNET: www.oesc.state.ok.us/jobnet
888-840-WORK
405-297-3050 (Oklahoma City)

Oregon

Oregon Employment Dept.: www.emp.state.or.us
503-378-8344; 503-225-2222, ext. 7777

Pennsylvania

PA CareerLink: www.pacareerlink.state.pa.us
Civil Service Jobs: www.scsc.state.pa.us
215-952-1143 (Philadelphia)

Rhode Island

netWORKri (Career Centers): www.networkri.org
401-222-3606 (Providence)
Hot Jobs:
www.dlt.state.ri.us/webdev/ets/etbull.html

South Carolina
SC Job Openings:
www.sces.org/1stop/jobbank/jobopen.htm
803-737-9935; 843-792-7025 (Charleston);
803-734-9333
State Jobs: *www.state.sc.us/jobs*

South Dakota
Dept. of Labor Job Service:
www.state.sd.us/dol/dol.htm
605-773-3148; Hotline: 605-773-3326

Tennessee
Division of Employment Security Job Search:
www.state.tn.us/labor-wfd/esdiv
State Of Tennessee Jobs:
www.state.tn.us/personnel/employ
615-741-4841

Texas
Texas Workforce Commission Job Listings:
www.twc.state.tx.us/jobs/jobs
800-735-2988; 512-463-2222
One-Stop Career Centers: *www.ttrc.dolete.gov*
Governor's Job Bank:
www.state.tx.us/jobs/gvjb/gvjb

Utah
Dept. of Workforce Services: *www.dws.state.ut.us*
State Jobs:
www.dhrm.state.ut.us/employment/bulletin
801-526-WORK

Vermont
Dept. of Employment and Training:
www.det.state.vt.us
802-658-1120 (Burlington); 802-388-4921

(Middlebury)
State Jobs: *www.state.vt.us/pers/index*
802- 828-3483

Virginia
Employment Commission's Job Seeker:
www.vec.state.va.us/seeker/seeker
757-455-3960 (Norfolk);
804-674-2368 (Richmond)

Washington
WorkSource: *http://worksource.wa.gov*
360-753-5368 (Olympia)
State Jobs: *www.wa.gov/dop*
360-586-0545 (Olympia); 206-720-3523
(Seattle)

West Virginia
WV Bureau of Employment Programs:
www.state.wv.us/bep/JOBS
State Jobs: *www.state.wv.us/admin/personel* [sic]
304-558-0342; 304-558-3950

Wisconsin
Employment Connection:
www.dwd.state.wi.us/dwe-wec
State Jobs:
www.der.state.wi.us/static/cob/cobtoc
888-258-9966; 608-242-7400 (Madison)

Wyoming
Wyoming Job Bank: *www.wyjobs.state.wy.us*
307-777-3700 (Cheyenne)

THE STATE OF TEXAS
APPLICATION FOR EMPLOYMENT

For State Agency Use Only

Job Applicant No. _____

PRINT IN BLACK INK OR TYPE. These instructions must be followed exactly. Fill out application form completely. If questions are not applicable, enter "NA." **Do not leave questions blank**. Be sure to sign when completed. The State of Texas is an Equal Opportunity Employer and does not discriminate on the basis of race, color, national origin, sex, religion, age or disability in employment or the provision of services. You may make copies of this application and enter different position titles, but **each copy must be signed**. **Resumes will not be accepted in lieu of applications.** Unless specifically stated in the job vacancy notice, resumes are not accepted at most state agencies. This application becomes public record and is subject to disclosure.

NAME _____   Social Security No. _____ - _____ - _____
          (Last)   (First)   (Middle)

MAILING ADDRESS _____ AC (_____)
         (Street)   (City) (State) (ZIP) (Country)   Home Phone

E-MAIL ADDRESS _____
List any other names used if different from name on this application. _____ AC (_____)
                            (Work Phone, Optional)

List exact title of position or type of work and location for which you wish to apply:	Job Posting Number	Closing Date
List the state agency with which you wish to apply:	Do you have any relatives working for this agency? If so, list names and relationships:	

Full-Time ☐   Part-Time ☐   Summer ☐   Temp/Project ☐   Date available for work? _____

Are you willing to work hours other than 8-5?   Yes ☐ No ☐

What days are you unable to work? _____

Are you willing to Travel? Yes ☐ No ☐   If yes, what percent of time? _____

Current Driver's License # (if required for position) _____ Commercial Driver's License Yes ☐ No ☐
                           (State)   (Number)

Are you at least 17 years of age? Yes ☐ No ☐

Geographic preference. (Be specific to city/area. If no preference, write "statewide.") _____

Have you ever been convicted of a felony or subjected to a deferred adjudication on a felony charge? Yes ☐ No ☐ If your answer is "Yes," explain in concise detail on a separate sheet of paper, giving the dates and nature of the offense, the name and location of the court, and the disposition of the case(s). A conviction may not disqualify you, but a false statement will. Note: Some state agencies may require additional information related to convictions of misdemeanors.

EDUCATION (NOTE: Applicants may be required to provide proof of diploma, degree, transcripts, licenses, certifications, and registrations.)
Indicate Highest Grade Completed: 1 2 3 4 5 6 7 8 9 10 11 12   Did you graduate from high school or receive GED? Yes ☐ No ☐

Type of School	Name and Location of School	Dates Attended From Mo.	Yr.	To Mo.	Yr.	Date Graduated Mo.	Yr.	Expected Graduation Date	Sem/Clock Hours Completed	Type of Diploma or Degree	Major/Minor Fields of Study
Undergraduate Colleges or Universities											
Graduate Schools											
Technical, Vocational, or Business Schools											

Date Received _____   Time Received _____   Received by _____

If a license, certificate, or other authorization is required or related to the position for which you are applying, complete the following:

LICENSE/CERTIFICATION (P.E., R.N., Attorney, C.P.A., etc.)	Date issued	Date expires	Issued by/Location of issuing authority (State or other authority) (City & State)	License No.

Special Training/Skills/Qualifications: List all job related training or skills you possess and machines or office equipment you can use, such as calculators, printing or graphics equipment, computer equipment, types of software and hardware. (Attach additional page, if necessary.)

_____

_____

_____

_____

Approximately how many words per minute do you type? _____ (if required for this position)

Sign Language (If required for this position)   Yes ☐   No ☐   Are you a certified interpreter?   Yes ☐   No ☐

Do you speak a language other than English? (If required for this position)   Yes ☐   No ☐
If yes, what language(s) do you speak? _____   How fluently?   Fair ☐   Good ☐   Excellent ☐

Do you write in a language other than English? (If required for this position)   Yes ☐   No ☐
If yes, which language(s) _____

Have you ever been employed by the State of Texas?   Yes ☐   No ☐   Are you currently employed by the State of Texas?   Yes ☐   No ☐

If you have been previously employed by the State of Texas, list the agency/agencies: _____

_____

Have you ever retired from Texas State Government?   Yes ☐   No ☐   If yes, indicate date retired. _____ month _____ year

MILITARY SERVICE (A copy of a report of separation from the Armed Services may be required.)

Are you a veteran?   Yes ☐   No ☐   If yes, list type of discharge status _____

Dates of Service (From/To): _____

Are you a surviving spouse of a veteran?   Yes ☐   No ☐   Are you a surviving orphan of a veteran?   Yes ☐   No ☐

If yes, complete dates of service for veteran (From/To): _____

EMPLOYMENT HISTORY

This information will be the official record of your employment history and must accurately reflect all significant duties performed. Summaries of experience should clearly describe your qualifications.

1. Include ALL employment. Begin with your current or last position and work back to your first.
2. Employment history should include **each position** held, even those with the same employer.
3. **EMPLOYER ADDRESSES MUST BE COMPLETE MAILING ADDRESSES, INCLUDING ZIP CODE.**
4. Give a brief summary of the technical and, if appropriate, the managerial responsibilities of each position you have held.
5. For supervisory/managerial positions, indicate the number of employees you supervised.

If you need additional space to adequately describe your employment history, you may use this employment history sheet or attach a typed employment history providing the same information in the same format as this application form.

Name: _____ _____

Last   First   Middle   Social Security No.

Position Title:
Employer:
Mailing Address:
City & State/ZIP:
Employer's Telephone No.: AC (   )

Starting Date			Leaving Date			Current/ Final Salary	Technical ☐	Immediate Supervisor Name:	Full-Time ☐
Mo.	Day	Yr.	Mo.	Day	Yr.		Non-Managerial ☐	Title:	Part-Time ☐
						$	Supervisory/Managerial ☐		Summer ☐

Immediate Supervisor Name:
Title:
Supervisor's Telephone No.: AC (   )
If supervisory, number of employees you supervised:

Full-Time ☐
Part-Time ☐
Summer ☐
Temp/Project ☐
Give average # of hours worked per week if part-time:

Summary of experience:

Specific reason for leaving:

Position Title:
Employer:
Mailing Address:
City & State/ZIP:
Employer's Telephone No.: AC (   )

Starting Date			Leaving Date			Current/ Final Salary	Technical ☐
Mo.	Day	Yr.	Mo.	Day	Yr.		Non-Managerial ☐
						$	Supervisory/Managerial ☐

Immediate Supervisor Name:
Title:
Supervisor's Telephone No.: AC (   )
If supervisory, number of employees you supervised:

Full-Time ☐
Part-Time ☐
Summer ☐
Temp/Project ☐
Give average # of hours worked per week if part-time:

Summary of experience:

Specific reason for leaving:

C·H·A·P·T·E·R

USING THE INTERNET TO FIND AND APPLY FOR CIVIL SERVICE JOBS

3

CHAPTER SUMMARY

This chapter introduces you to the Internet and shows you how to find government employment information online. In addition to telling you how to browse the Web and find an Internet Service Provider, this chapter will suggest a number of websites that may help you in your job search.

orget what you have heard about the complexities of finding a government job! Thanks to the Internet, job hunting is simpler and more convenient than it has ever been. Instead of combing through classified ads week after week, you can browse large databases of jobs on your personal computer. Instead of spending hours on the phone trying to get information from government agencies, you can find job resources and data online, any time of the day. If you aren't comfortable using a computer or the Internet, this is a great time to brush up on your skills — the Internet is one of the best tools you can use to explore civil service jobs. It allows you quickly to access the information you need, when you need it.

Thanks to the proliferation of personal computers (PCs), anyone can go online to research employment opportunities, find the right job, submit a resume, or even apply for a position. The beauty of job hunting online is that the Internet is open 24 hours a day, 7 days a week. Even if you don't have a computer at home or work, you can still surf the Web at these places:

- public libraries
- college or university libraries, student centers, alumni offices, and career centers
- high school placement offices
- cybercafes
- some photocopy centers
- a friend's house

Many federal, state, county, and city government agencies now maintain employment information websites. All 50 states and most large cities have their own home pages as well. The information that follows will tell you briefly how to reach these Internet sites.

USING THE INTERNET

The Internet is a massive network of worldwide computers connected to each other by modems and telephone lines. It started in the 1960s as an in-house communications system for federal offices. Today, there are several components to the Internet, the most popular of which are electronic mail (e-mail) and the World Wide Web (*www*).

To get online, you first need a computer, a modem, a telephone line, and an Internet Service Provider (ISP). Most online services, such as Earthlink, America Online, and CompuServe, are ISPs as well. Then, to use the World Wide Web to find the websites that will assist you in your job search, you need to install Web browser software on your PC. There are over two dozen browsers on the market, including Microsoft's Internet Explorer and Netscape Navigator.

Your ISP may also provide e-mail accounts to its users. If you prefer, you may sign up for a free e-mail account through websites such as *www.juno.com, www.yahoo.com,* and *www.hotmail.com.* A personal e-mail account will be essential to your online job search, allowing you to ask questions, submit resumes, and receive more information about areas that interest you.

BROWSING THE WEB

Whether you're using e-mail or browsing the World Wide Web, the best way to feel secure on the Internet is to use it. Some online browsers and services offer tutorials you can read. Or, better still, have a friend, relative, or colleague work with you. But don't be afraid to jump in and move around, experimenting with instructions, links, and icons.

Each website listed in this book has a URL (Uniform Resource Locator), which is the cyberspace address or locator of that site. Typing the URL into your Web browser's long, narrow location window will connect you to the site. Some URLs can get pretty long to type in, but you can save the ones you want to refer back to as an electronic bookmark. Another thing about URLs — you can often take off the *http://* or *www.* in front of the URL, or the letters after the last slash mark, and still get through to the website.

SEARCH ENGINES

If you don't have a specific URL address to go to, you can browse the Web in virtually millions of subjects by using a search engine. A search engine is an online tool designed to help you sort through the information on the web and find the sites most useful to you. When you open a search engine, you will generally see a search keyword box: a long, white window of space into which you can type keywords and phrases that describe the site or information you're looking for. For instance, if you type "corrections officer jobs" into your search box and click the "search" button, you will be provided with a list of websites that refer to corrections officer jobs.

You can have more than one search engine on your Web browser. Try them all and see which you prefer. Some popular ones are Netscape, AltaVista, Yahoo!, HotBot, Infoseek, Webcrawler, Lycos, and Excite. To access a particular search engine simply type the appropriate web address, such as *www.yahoo.com* or *www.infoseek.com*, into your location box. As with all other Internet services, the number of search engines continues to grow. Note that the time it takes to download the website you want will vary, depending on your hardware and software capabilities, your ISP, and the amount of Internet traffic at the time of your search.

ONLINE JOB HUNTING REFERENCES

If you want to learn more about job searching on the Internet, there are a number of good books on the subject, including:

- *The Guide to Internet Job Searching* by Osserman, Riley, and Roehm (VGM Career Horizons, 1996, 213 pages, $12.95)
- *How to Get Your Dream Job Using the Web* by Karl and Karl (Coriolis Group Books, 1997, 400 pages, $34.99)
- *Hook Up, Get Hired!* by Kennedy (John Wiley & Sons, 1995, 250 pages, $12.95)
- *Net Jobs: Use the Internet to Land Your Dream Job* (Michael Wolf & Company Publishing, 1997, 284 pages, $20).

These books are about job hunting in general. To learn about finding government and civil service jobs in particular, read on.

GOVERNMENT JOB HUNTING ON THE INTERNET

Job hunting on the Internet may seem daunting at first. But once you get the hang of it, you'll be surprised at how easy and convenient it is. You can search for jobs and information at your own pace, and you'll find all the information you need in one handy location — your personal computer.

FEDERAL JOB OPENINGS

One way to find government jobs is to go directly to the home page of a specific state or federal agency. The list at the end of Chapter 5, for example, presents URLs (and regular mailing addresses) for federal agencies that hire law enforcement candidates. The list at the end of Chapter 2 provides websites — listed by state — for specific federal, state, and local government hiring agencies. Many of these websites even have applications you can fill out and submit online.

Here are the largest federal databases available:

- USAJOBS is the Office of Personnel Management's job bank (*www.usajobs.opm.gov/a.htm.*), listing 7,500 worldwide job opportunities. Online, USAJOBS provides worldwide government job vacancies, employment fact sheets, and job applications and forms. It has online resume development and electronic transmission capabilities. The information is updated every business day.
- America's Job Bank (*www.ajb.org*) is a partnership between the U.S. Department of Labor and a network of 1,800 state-operated public employment services. AJB provides lists of both private and government jobs and gives nationwide exposure of resume pools for employers. There are also links to Career InfoNet (occupational and economic information, state profiles, and so on) and Learning

Exchange (job hunting and resume skills). These services are free to job seekers and employers alike and are funded through unemployment insurance taxes paid by employers. AJB's job postings and resumes are available on CareerNet; in public libraries; at college, university, and high school placement offices; on shopping mall job kiosks; and on military bases.

■ FedWorld (*www.fedworld.gov*) is a website funded by the Department of Commerce. FedWorld is a federal job announcement database and gateway to over 100 government bulletin boards.

STATE JOB OPENINGS

Many state employment websites also have applications you can fill out and submit online. Here are a couple of quick ways to get information and forms from specific states concerning their government openings:

■ Go to the state's home page by entering *www.state.__.us*, substituting the state's two-letter postal abbreviation for the blank. Utah, for instance, is *www.state.ut.us*.
■ Go to each state's individual AJB (America's Job Bank, Department of Labor) home page by entering *www.abj.org/__*, substituting the state's two-letter postal abbreviation for the blank. For example, Maine is *www.ajb.org/me*.

CITY AND COUNTY JOB OPENINGS

To get city and county job information, look for appropriate links on your state's home page or at America's Job Bank. Many large cities also have their own home pages these days, and job opportunities will generally be listed on these home pages. If you live in a city with its own website, this will be a great place to start looking for a job.

You can also use your search engine to find jobs in a particular area. You might, for instance, type in the keywords *Phoenix Employment* to get information about job openings in Phoenix, Arizona.

OTHER SOURCES OF GOVERNMENT JOB INFORMATION

New job seeker services are popping up all over cyberspace. Some services, such as HotJobs, are commercial (*.com* in the URL address), and some are non-profit organizations (*.org* in the address), such as the University of Chicago's Placement Office. These employment service sites offer everything from job databases to tips on job hunting to job counseling. They may or may not charge money for some or all of the services offered. They may post job listings for all occupations in the private, public, and non-profit sectors, or they may offer very specific job searches (such as for rural firefighter positions). Here are a few of the many websites:

■ Govtjobs.com (*www.govtjobs.com*) claims to be the nation's leading private website devoted to helping people find the job they are seeking in the public sector and helping government agencies and non-profits find appropriate employees.
■ FedJobs (*www.fedjobs.com*) is a privately compiled and maintained database of General Schedule (white-collar) and Wage Grade (blue-collar) jobs from 1,800 federal personnel office lists.
■ Monster.com (*www.monster.com*) claims to be the Internet's most frequently accessed career center. Monster offers keyword searches for all jobs and links to agency/search firms. Monster also posts career fairs and events and offers other job hunting services.

The following sites specialize:

- JobWeb (*www.jobweb.org*) is a not-for-profit website from the National Association of Colleges and Employers. They specialize in placing college grads in a variety of positions.
- CoolWorks (*www.coolworks.com*) lists only seasonal outdoor jobs (those found at national parks, for example).
- CareerPath (*www.careerpath.com*) searches newspaper employment ads from over 20 major cities, offers tutorials in job hunting skills, and advertises career fairs.
- E jobs (*www.ejobs.org*) links to environmental career opportunities (government, private, and non-profits) in the U.S. and Canada.

Other popular Internet employment services and databases are, in alphabetical order: Adams JobBank Online, America's Employers, Career Builder, Careers and Jobs, Career Magazine, Career Mosaic, Career Web, Computerworld's Career Page, E-SPAN, HotJobs, IntelliMatch, Job Center, Job Hunt, Med-Search, NationJob Online, Newspaper Help Wanted Ads, On-Line Career Center, Recruitment Online, the Riley Guide, Virtual Job Fair, and Ziff Davis Technology Job Database. Use your search engine to find their home pages.

THE ARMED FORCES

The armed forces offer excellent career opportunities and training for new recruits and seasoned professionals alike:

- Army (*www.goarmy.com*)
- Navy and Marines (*www.navyjobs.com*)
- Air Force (*www.afreserve.com*)

TOUCH SCREEN COMPUTER KIOSKS AND AUTOMATED TELEPHONE SYSTEMS

The Office of Personnel Management (OPM)'s USAJOBS maintains a network of self-service information kiosks located in OPM offices and many federal buildings nationwide.

At the touch of a finger, job seekers can access current job vacancies around the world, employment fact sheets, and applications and other forms. Complete job announcements can be retrieved from the kiosk. See the end of Chapter 1 for USAJOBS kiosk locations by state.

The USAJOBS Automated Telephone System is an interactive voice-response resource that can be reached at 912-757-3000 or TDD 912-744-2299 or at seventeen OPM service centers located throughout the country. (See the end of Chapter 1 or your local blue pages.) By telephone, you can access the same information available on USAJOBS kiosks; in some cases, you can even apply for jobs by phone.

JOB BOARDS

Job Boards are databases of job vacancies and descriptions. When using these databases, you may be able to search under a specific job category to find the job openings that are most suited to you. For example, the NationJob Network website, *www.nationjob.com*, has an administrative and clerical jobs page.

INTERNET MAILING LISTS

If you want job information to come to *you*, some organizations will, for a fee, automatically send you job listings via e-mail. One such organization is *www.federaljobsearch.com*. For $9.95 a month, they will match your job profile with daily searches of federal jobs and send that list to your e-mailbox. The mailing list's website tells you how to subscribe to the service by e-mailing their address. Sometimes openings are posted via these lists well before they are advertised elsewhere. Users of the same listing group may also be able to contact each other, networking by e-mail.

You can start your search for Internet mailing lists to subscribe to at these URLs:

- The Liszt Directory (*www.liszt.com*) has over 67,000 lists at 2,000 sites!
- Publicly Accessible Mailing Lists (*www.neosoft.com/internet/paml*) offers publicly accessible lists by category. Try the *employment* or *careers* categories. They guarantee that their lists are as up-to-date as possible.

BULLETIN BOARD SERVICES (BBSS)

Bulletin Board Services are not as easy to use as websites; however, they are free, and you only need a modem on your computer to access a BBS. Instead of using an Internet provider, your modem dials a number, and you follow the directions at the BBS to open databases or to submit your resume. Usually, the files that the BBS sends you have to be downloaded and unzipped (they are sent in a compressed format). If you want to find a BBS with job listings, look in your local library's reference section for a copy of *Dial Up! Gale's Bulletin Board Locator*.

USER NEWSGROUPS

Newsgroups are online sites in the Usenet portion of the Internet — there are over 10,000 of them! Newsgroups provide job listings and allow visitors to network with other visitors via e-mail. You can read messages that other users have posted and reply to the site or to the other user's e-mail address. Anyone can add information to the posting at any time. Employers may post their job announcements, and job seekers may post their

resumes in a bank, such as *news:misc.jobs.resumes*. Most Internet browsers have news readers that enable you to type in a newsgroup's address in the URL box. New user newsgroups are appearing monthly — you can browse a current list of them at *www.cis.ohio-state.edu*, a website that tracks such Internet services.

NEWSLETTERS AND GUIDES

In addition to the government's guides mentioned in this book, there are privately published guides to finding government work. *Federal Jobs Digest* is both a newsletter (25 issues/year) and a database (*www.jobsfed.com*). The publishers of *Federal Jobs Digest* also put out a guide called *Working for Your Uncle*, which can be purchased through the same sources. For more information about any of these services, call *Federal Jobs Digest* at 1-800-824-5000.

Federal Applications That Get Results by Russ Smith (Impact Publications) and *Applying for Federal Jobs* by Patricia Wood (Bookhaven Press) offer comprehensive tips on filling out government forms SF 171, OF 612, and OF 305, and on resume writing.

CAREER FAIRS

Career or job fairs offer face-to-face information on government jobs. There is usually a recruiter at the agency's booth to answer your questions and provide you with written materials to peruse at home. You can find out about upcoming job fairs on the Internet. Monster.com (*www.monster.com*) posts career fairs and events. Most state/city employment websites have a career fair link (see the list at the end of Chapter 2). Other sources of job fair information are local employment centers, USAJOBS touch-screen kiosks, school placement offices, bulletin boards at schools and libraries, and radio/TV ads.

GENERAL INFORMATION

If you are looking to read up on the labor economy, wages and trends, or other general occupational information, go to the U.S. Department of Labor (*www.dol.gov*), your state's own DOL site (for example, *www.ctdol.state.ct.us* for Connecticut's site), or Career InfoNet (*www.acinet.org*). Career InfoNet offers interesting state profiles that you can use to compare employment situations and environments.

S·E·C·T·I·O·N 2

THE MOST POPULAR ENTRY-LEVEL JOBS

Now that you've read about finding and applying for civil service jobs in general, you're ready to get specific. This section highlights four "best bets" in civil service employment: postal worker, law enforcement officer, administrative assistant, and firefighter. These jobs usually require little or no specialized training or experience, and all of them provide ample opportunities for entry-level job seekers. Each chapter presents job descriptions; statistics on hiring, pay, and benefits; and an overview of the hiring process, including minimum requirements, what the civil service exam entails, and other steps you have to go through to get the job.

C·H·A·P·T·E·R
WORKING FOR THE U.S. POSTAL SERVICE 4

CHAPTER SUMMARY

This chapter discusses entry-level career opportunities at the United States Postal Service (USPS). It offers a rundown of the types of jobs available and their requirements, application and hiring procedures, and advice on how to locate openings and opportunities in your location.

erhaps you'd like to greet customers at the window. Maybe you'd rather work behind the scenes, sorting some of the millions of pieces of mail delivered each day. Or perhaps you'd like to be a carrier, delivering mail door to door, customer by customer. Whatever your interest, you should know that a job with the United States Postal Service (USPS) has a lot to offer, including competitive salaries, job security, government benefits, and upward mobility. That's why every year hundreds of thousands of people seek employment with the USPS.

The USPS has over 38,000 facilities nationwide which handle an average of 630 million pieces of mail per day. Approximately 234,000 letter carriers and a fleet of over 190,000 vehicles distribute this mail across the nation. In fact, 41% of the world's mail volume is handled by the USPS, making it the world's largest mail delivery system (Japan, the second largest, handles only 6% of the world's mail volume).

Just the Facts
Visit the USPS on the Internet at www.usps.gov and explore the history, structure, and services of the world's largest delivery service.

Through a reorganization in 1969–1970, the United States Postal Service emerged in its current form from what had been the U.S. Post Office Department. The USPS was declared an independent establishment of the executive branch of the Government and to this day remains a semi-private independent organization. The President appoints a Board of Governors to oversee postal operations, but all income is generated through postal services, and the USPS has not taken one cent of U.S. taxpayers' money since 1982.

The USPS currently employs over 800,000 workers and, since the end of its restructuring earlier in the last decade, it has hired an average of about 30,000 employees each year. It's one of the largest employers in the nation—bigger than Ford, Chrysler, and General Motors *combined*. In fact, almost 1 in every 170 people in the domestic workforce work for the USPS. About one half of postal employees are in one of the seven major entry-level positions that are be the focus of this chapter, positions that require the passing of the 470 Battery Exam, a national standardized entrance examination. The section at the end of this chapter entitled "Other Opportunities" offers information on other entry-level positions with the USPS, including administrative and part-time positions.

THE MAJOR ENTRY-LEVEL JOBS

Listed below are the seven major entry-level positions at the USPS, all of which require the passing of the 470 Battery Examination (see page 8 for more information on this national standardized exam). If you're looking at employment with the USPS, it's likely that you'll be considering one of these positions.

- **Window Clerk:** Window Clerks are the people who serve you at the post office. They have a variety of duties, including selling stamps, weighing packages, preparing money orders, and answering your questions about USPS policies and services.
- **Mail Carrier, City:** City Carriers deliver mail to city businesses and residents. They usually have a set route on which they deliver and collect mail, by foot or vehicle depending upon their area. They spend much of their time out on their own.
  Rural: Rural Carriers, like City Carriers, deliver and collect mail but to rural businesses and residents along a set route. They have a wider variety of duties than City Carriers because they often have more direct contact with customers and provide services that city residents generally get only in local post offices. (Rural Carrier applicants must take a separate but similar entrance test, the 460 Examination.)
- **Mail Handler:** Mail Handlers load and unload mail from trucks and bins and help in the initial sorting phases. They also cancel stamps.
- **Mail Processor:** Mail Processors run equipment that processes mail. They also do some loading and sorting of mail in the initial stages of distribution.
- **Distribution Clerk:** Distribution Clerks begin the process of distributing mail. They sort mail by destination location.

- **Flat-Sorting Machine Operator:** Flat Sorting Machine Operators read ZIP codes to sort mail in the next phase of distribution. They also do some loading and unloading of mail.
- **Mark-Up Clerk:** Mark-Up Clerks work with mail that's undeliverable, correcting addresses, rerouting, and/or returning mail to sender.

Just the Facts
Did you know . . . the USPS delivers more mail in one day than Federal Express does in a whole year?

WORKING FOR THE USPS

USPS employees generally fall into three categories:

- *Career Bargaining Employees*, who are entitled to all benefits and who are represented by unions. They may be full-time or part-time regular employees.
- *Career Non-Bargaining Employees*, who also receive benefits (scaled to their hours) but are not represented by unions. They are part-time flexible employees.
- *The Supplemental Work Force*, which is composed of casual or temporary employees who do not receive benefits and are not represented by unions. This category also includes transitional employees, as described below.

Let's look at each of these categories in more detail.

Career Bargaining
Full-time—There are about 765,000 full-time employees within the USPS. These employees work at least 40 hours a week (8 hours a day, Monday through Friday) and have full benefits. Their overtime rate is 1 ½ times their hourly equivalent. Employees who work the night shift receive a higher wage.

Part-time regular—There are about 8,000 part-time regular employees, half of whom are clerks. Part-time regular employees work on a fixed schedule of less than 40 hours per week. They are career employees who earn hourly wages which increase according to a set schedule.

Career Non-Bargaining
Part-time flexible—There are about 85,000 of these career employees. Though they can be called in at any time and their schedule can be changed without their consent, they are guaranteed at least 4 hours of work a day (20 hours a week) and do receive benefits scaled to their hours. And, after one to two years (the exact number varies from office to office), part-time flexibles are automatically moved into full- or part-time regular status. In the meantime, they often move around within their offices to meet particular needs and therefore can gain experience in several positions. Though these employees are called "part-time," many work more than 40 hours a week. But they are not covered by any bargaining unit agreement and are paid hourly like part-time regulars.

Supplemental
Part-time casuals/temporaries—These employees are generally hired to meet the cyclical demands of the industry. Employees are limited to two 90-day appointments in a given year but may be offered an extra 21 days of employment with the USPS to meet delivery demands in December. The two assignments must

have a minimum 6-day break in service in between. Most casual/temporary employees do manual clerk or mail handling work. These are not career employees and are not eligible for benefits. They are hired year round, but particularly around Christmas and other busy times of year. (In 1999, 40,000 casual workers were hired nationwide to meet the mailing demands of the Christmas season.)

Many part-time casuals work July through December and then January through June for a full year of employment, but then they must wait a full year until they can work for the USPS again. Part-time casual/temporary employees do not need to take an entrance test (i.e., the 470 Battery Exam) for employment. Interested candidates can simply apply at their local post office. Pay for part-time casual/temporary employees generally falls between minimum wage and $12 an hour.

Transitional employees—Because the USPS is becoming more and more mechanized, there has been a decrease in the number of some full-time positions available. The USPS has formed an agreement with its employee unions that while going through transitions resulting from automation (e.g., employees need to be retrained, new positions are established and/or old ones are eliminated or restructured), it will hire transitional employees for a limit of 359 consecutive days. These temporary employees are technically part-time flexible employees, but they usually work a full 40 hours a week. These employees are at the lowest step of the part-time flexible schedule, however, so they're really more like casual employees. This class of employee began in 1992 with 9,732 transitional employees; in 1998 there were over 17,000.

A note about Rural Carriers: Because of the unique nature of their job, Rural Carriers are a separate category of employee within the USPS. About half of the USPS Rural Carriers are Rural Carrier Substitutes, part-time, non-career employees who cover routes for regular Rural Carriers on their days off. In 1998 there were more Rural Substitutes than Rural Carriers (56,265 and 52,241, respectively). For more information on this employment option, see the section entitled "Other Opportunities" at the end of this chapter.

Just the Facts
According to the USPS Annual Report for 1998, $1.6 billion in salary and benefits are paid out every two weeks to USPS employees.

GRADES AND PAY SCALES

The bulk of USPS positions are classified into a certain *category* and *grade*. For example, most clerks (distribution, window, etc.) are in the PS (Postal Service) *category*. Within this category, each clerk position falls into a certain *grade*, usually from 1–10, based upon the level of skill and training required for each position.

The grade for each position determines the salary. For example, an entry-level Window Clerk, who has to deal with the public and have a general knowledge of USPS services and policies, will start at PS Grade 5, and earn $28,500 a year. Entry-level Mail Processors, on the other hand, do not deal with the public and start at PS Grade 4 with an annual salary of $27,000. They may, of course, move into higher grades as they gain experience.

USPS PAY SCHEDULE: AT A GLANCE			
Postal Service (PS) Salaries			
Full-Time Annual			
Step	**Grade 4**	**Grade 5**	**Grade 6**
A	27,008	28,539	30,167
B	27,836	29,323	30,907
C	28,664	30,107	31,647
D	29,492	30,891	32,387

* Provided by the USPS.

RAISES

USPS employees are awarded raises which include a COLA (cost-of-living adjustment) on a regular basis. The salary schedule for most positions is broken down into 15 steps, labeled A–O. The table above shows the salaries for Postal Service Grades 4, 5, and 6; steps A–D. The step increase waiting period for a postal clerk, Grades 1-3, is 44 weeks between steps. For grades 4-7 the waiting period is 36 weeks between steps; and for Grades 8-10, 30 weeks. So, the longer you are with the USPS, the quicker your raises come around.

And how high are those raises? If you're a Distribution Clerk, PS Grade 5, for example, your Step A salary is $28,539. Your Step B salary is $29,323, an increase of $784 or 2.75%. And your Step C salary is $30,107, an additional increase of $784. The overall increase from Step A ($28,539) to Step O ($39,515) is an impressive $10,976, or 38%, over about 12 years. If you move up in grade during those years, however, you can expect your income to increase by another 5–6%.

HIRING FROM WITHIN

Because the benefits of working for the USPS are so desirable, many people accept part-time positions and wait for a full-time opportunity. Thus, most full-time vacancies at the USPS are filled from within by part-time employees, making it difficult to get a full-time job from the start with the USPS. Logically, when full-time positions open up, preference is usually given to part-time employees who are already familiar with the work rather than to someone who has simply done well on the Battery Exam. The good news, as we've already noted, is that even "part-time" employees (part-time flexible) often work full-time hours and receive benefits. So while you're waiting to move into a full-time Career Bargaining status, you still have a highly desirable position. Your wages will be hourly rather than salaried and your duties may be diverse, but your foot will be in the door and you do get benefits. And if you do good work, you'll have an advantage when you bid for a full-time slot or another position.

Bidding for Jobs

Competition for open positions can be heavy, so the USPS has instituted a job bidding process. When a vacancy occurs, employees submit written requests—"bids"—for that position. Assuming all candidates meet the qualifications for that position, the candidate with the highest seniority (measured in years of service with the USPS) is given the position. However, if you want to move into a supervisory position, you will need to do more than just bid—you'll need to take an exam and possibly get further training and, of course, you must be able to lead and manage people and resources.

Job "Detours"

Sometimes the exams for the positions you're interested in may not be offered for some time—even two or three years. Should you wait? Well, you might be better off if you can attain a position other than the one you desire and *then* move into the position you prefer. Once you have been employed by the USPS for at least a year, you're eligible to take the entrance exam for any position. You simply need to request that exam when a position is vacant. So, if you have been hired as a Mail Handler but want to become a Carrier, you don't need to retake the 470 Battery Test; you simply have to take the secondary tests for that specific position (Carriers, for example, have to pass a driving test). If you have been a good employee—on time, reliable, a fast learner—chances are that your supervisor will be glad to give you the test for a position you are qualified to fill.

APPLYING TO BECOME A POSTAL WORKER

MINIMUM REQUIREMENTS

To be eligible for employment with the USPS, you must meet certain minimum requirements:

- You must be 18 years of age or older, or 16 if you're already a high school graduate
- If you are a male, you must be registered with the U.S. Selective Service
- You must be a U.S. citizen or a legal resident alien
- You must be able to lift 70 pounds

- You must have 20/40 vision in one eye and 20/100 in the other (glasses are permitted)
- If you are applying for a job that requires driving, you must have a valid driver's license and a safe driving record

If you meet all of the above requirements, you may apply for a position with the United States Postal Service.

THE HIRING PROCESS

The United States Postal Service divides its hiring process into four parts, and further divides the fourth part into three separate stages, as follows:

1. Recruitment
2. Examination
3. Register
4. Suitability & Selection
   a. Suitability
   b. Selection
   c. Appointment

We'll go through each one of these steps in detail to let you know what you'll face, and what will be expected of you, at each step along the way.

STEP ONE: RECRUITMENT

As you read earlier, the USPS employs well over 800,000 workers. Maintaining a workforce of that size—filling new positions and positions that are open due to promotion or retirement, and covering positions when people are sick or on vacation—requires a significant recruitment effort to make sure there are enough qualified people to keep the mail moving. Keep in mind that operating the Postal Service doesn't just happen weekdays from 9–5. The USPS moves an average of 630 million pieces of mail every day, much of the work being done overnight.

To recruit the most qualified applicants, nearly every postal district maintains a Job Information Line that lists current exams and job openings. Openings are also listed at local post offices and announced in local newspapers. These are all meant to get the word out to the public—that's you—when a post office has openings or plans to "open" a test.

While the USPS makes recruitment a high priority, you need to tune in to the right resources (the Job Information Lines, state employment offices) or you'll miss out on the opportunities recruitment brings your way. See the section entitled "Tracking Down Job Openings" for more information on how to keep abreast of current postal employment opportunities in your location.

When you find out about an upcoming examination, that's the time to move on to Step Two: Examinations, detailed below.

Note that certain positions, including Casual Employment, do not require an examination. Casual employment, an important path into the USPS, is discussed at the end of this chapter in the section entitled "Other Opportunities."

STEP TWO: EXAMINATION

To determine whether those who are interested in working for the Postal Service are in fact qualified, the USPS has put in place an extensive screening process, the first part of which is a qualifying examination. In the case of those entry-level jobs that require the 470 Battery Examination, the following procedures apply.

The Application

When a local Postal District or post office decides that there are, or soon will be, enough openings to merit offering an examination, they announce what is known as an "application period." The application period is the period of time in which applications for an exam will be accepted. It often lasts just a few days and is announced with little advance notice.

During the application period you need to go to the post office that is offering the examination and fill out an application card. If an entire city, county, or postal district is offering an examination, you may be able to get your application card at any post office within that city, county, or district; alternatively, you may be required to get an application card at one specific application center. If you're unsure about where to pick up your application, call the post office that is offering the examination and ask them directly.

Upon receipt of your application card, the post office will mail part of the card back to you along with sample exam questions, a sample answer sheet, and the time and location of the exam. Make sure you hold on to the part of the application card that is returned to you because it will serve as your "admission ticket" to the written test.

The 470 Battery Examination

The 470 Battery Examination is a national standardized test given by the USPS to evaluate the skill levels of applicants to the following entry-level positions:

- Window Clerk
- City Carrier
- Mail Handler
- Mark-Up Clerk
- Mail Processor
- Flat-Sorting Machine Operator
- Distribution Clerk

The test, implemented in 1994, was designed to replace a set of different exams for these positions and to streamline the testing process.

The 470 Battery Examination tests memory, attention to detail, reasoning, and ability to follow directions, and is broken into four sections:

- Part A: Address Checking (95 questions, six minutes)
  Task: Determine if two addresses are alike or different
- Part B: Memory for Addresses (88 questions, five minutes)
  Task: Memorize the locations of 25 addresses in five minutes
- Part C: Number Series (24 questions, 20 minutes)
  Task: Determine the series in sets of numbers
- Part D: Following Oral Directions (20–25 questions, 25 minutes)
  Task: Mark test booklet and answer sheet based on oral directions

A score of 70 percent is considered passing, though unlikely to get you hired. Due to the intense competition for postal jobs, you'll want to aim for a score in the high eighties to nineties. To score your best you'll need to practice. Chapters 8 and 13 in this book will help you sharpen your general test-taking skills and pinpoint areas needing improvement. For extensive practice based on official USPS 470 Exams, call LearningExpress at 1-888-551-JOBS and ask about our Postal Worker guides, which come complete with sample 470 Battery Exams and instructional chapters written by experts for each of the four sections of the exam.

Veteran's Preference

The Postal Reorganization Act of 1970 gives veterans of the U.S. military special privileges and preferences in scoring and selection. Veterans are granted an additional five or ten points on the postal exam, making for a best possible score of 110. In addition, veterans entitled to the ten point preference are allowed to "re-open" exams not open to the general public, and any veteran who misses an exam because of engagement in active military service is allowed to file an application for an exam within 120 days prior to or after discharge.

The scores of veterans from re-opened or delayed examinations are merged with the scores of all other test takers—except "compensable disabled veterans" (i.e., veterans who are eligible to be compensated for a disability). Their scores are ranked against each other and placed above *all* other scores. Contact your local post office's personnel department for more information.

STEP THREE: THE REGISTER

After having taken the 470 Battery Examination, you will receive notification of how you did in the mail. If you scored 70 or better on the exam, you will be told your actual score; if you scored below 70, however, you will just receive a notice stating that you did not pass (with determination and study, hopefully you won't ever see one of these). The names of all applicants who scored 70 or above are placed on what is known as a register, a list used by the USPS to rank all eligible applicants in order of score, from highest to lowest.

Registers remain valid for two years and may be extended beyond that depending on hiring needs and the availability of applicants on other registers. When local postal facilities need to fill positions, they turn to their registers, starting from the top, and continue the screening process by selecting names from the list.

STEP FOUR: SUITABILITY & SELECTION

Once the USPS has put out the word and *recruited* applicants, once it has screened the basic skills of those appli-

WORKING FOR THE U.S. POSTAL SERVICE

cants and narrowed the group through an *examination*, and once the names of those who have passed the examination have been ranked on a *register*, it's time to evaluate the *suitability* of those applicants.

As the final step of the hiring process, the postal facility considering you for employment must determine your ability to become part of a team and your fit with the tasks and duties of a postal worker. To do this, the USPS has developed a three-stage process:

- Suitability
- Selection
- Appointment

Suitability

After receiving your completed application, the personnel office of the postal facility that is considering you for employment will review your application and begin a **Background Investigation**. As part of this investigation, the personnel department will contact former places of employment and schools you have attended to determine what kind of worker you have been and what kind of employee you will be. In addition the department does a criminal records check and military records check, and verifies your citizenship/resident alien status.

In addition to the background investigation, the hiring postal facility will ask you in for a **Personal Interview**. This face-to-face meeting is an opportunity for the hiring personnel to get to know you and, of course, to further evaluate your suitability for postal employment. You and the interviewer will also go over any questions that have come up regarding your application and background investigation and any discrepancies between the two.

After the personal interview, you may be required to pass a **Physical Agility Test**. While tests for different positions vary, remember that postal work can be arduous. Standing or walking for hours, carrying heavy sacks of mail, and moving containers all require physical strength and stamina. If you can comfortably lift 70 pounds and have a full range of motion in your fingers and limbs, you should be ready for the test. It's a good idea, however, to contact your local personnel office once you have received your application package to get the specific requirements for the position you are being considered for.

Finally, you will be required to pass a **Drug Test**. Failure to pass the drug test may result in disqualification from the selection process.

Selection

In accordance with the Rehabilitation Act of 1973, the USPS cannot make any examination of your medical state until a job offer has been made. Therefore, once you have passed all stages of the hiring process and have been found to be otherwise suitable, you will be offered employment on the condition you are medically fit to accept it. The **Medical Examination**, separate from the physical agility test, is used to confirm your ability to withstand the hard work often required of postal employees. Carriers must walk several miles every day, mail sorters must be able to hear over bustling machinery—like a general physical, the medical examination gauges your overall physical health and your fitness for postal employment.

Appointment

Once you have passed the medical examination and have fulfilled the condition of your offer of employment, you will be appointed to a position with the USPS. As the first order of business, all postal employees are required to take an oath of office. Next up is Employee Orientation, a period usually lasting a few days, in which you'll learn about postal policy, including attendance, pay schedules, and other rules.

After the orientation period you will report to your work location and begin on-the-job training. You'll work under supervision, and your daily duties will be explained to you. If the position for which you've been hired requires special skills, you'll receive that training first and then move on to your work location. During your initial appointment, your performance will be evaluated as a continuation of the suitability screening process.

TRACKING DOWN JOB OPENINGS

One of the most important things when looking for a job with the USPS is how to find out where the job openings are. Most states are made up of more than one postal district, and the districts themselves consist of hundreds of individual post offices. Because the hiring process at the USPS is decentralized—in other words, individual postal districts and post offices hire based on their own needs and on their own schedule—there's no one place to locate current openings, and there's no one person to call to find out about upcoming tests. Instead, you're going to have to find out for yourself where the opportunities are. While many post offices announce open and upcoming exams in local papers and circulars, the following are three important resources you should also keep in mind.

Postal Job Information Lines
The first thing to note is that most <u>postal districts</u> maintain what is known as a Postal Job Information Line. This is a number you can call to get automated information about current openings and current or upcoming tests. It's usually a simple recording, listing the current job opportunities and open examinations and providing you with either a phone number or an

address for an application or further information. Check the governmental listing in your phone book to find the Job Information Line, Employment Line, or Personnel Department for your district. If you can't find it, call your local post office and tell them what you're looking for; they should be able to point you in the right direction.

Don't Forget Your Local Post Office
While Job Information Lines list current openings, they are often maintained at a district level. A district can have hundreds of individual post offices under its jurisdiction. Some smaller post offices, especially in rural areas, may keep their recruiting closer to home. Instead of asking the district office, which could be hundreds of miles away, to announce their openings, they may post openings at their own location or in local papers. You may want to call or visit your local post office directly to see if they have any openings, especially if you live in a rural or outlying area, or if you are interested in working for a smaller post office rather than for a high-volume urban facility.

State Employment Offices
Another place to keep in touch with is your state's Department of Labor employment offices. These offices provide placement services and, through their vast computer databases, are often aware of jobs that may not be listed in other sources, including openings at local postal facilities. Check the state governmental listings in your phone book under "Department of Labor, Job Placement Services" for the office nearest you. The Internet address is *www.dol.gov/*.

OTHER OPPORTUNITIES

Besides the seven major entry-level jobs discussed earlier in this chapter, several other employment opportunities are available to the entry-level applicant at the USPS. Some of these positions require tests other than the 470 Battery Examination but otherwise follow the same hiring process. Some positions require no testing at all and have their own hiring procedures. The following sections present three alternative paths to employment with the USPS that you should be familiar with:

- Casual Employment
- Rural Carrier and Rural Carrier Associate
- Remote Encoding Centers and other Administrative Positions

CASUAL EMPLOYMENT

One of the most overlooked opportunities with the USPS is Casual Employment. Officially categorized as part of the USPS's supplemental workforce, Casual Employees fill short-term demands in postal facilities all over the U.S.

While these positions, as discussed earlier, offer no benefits and no guarantee of hours, they are an opportunity to take seriously. Often a test may not be open in a given district, yet a significant number of casual positions are open. A casual position is an opportunity to gain valuable experience with the USPS and to get the inside word on future opportunities. While former Casual Employees gain no official preference in the hiring process, a boss usually remembers a good employee and working as a casual may be an opportunity to get yourself remembered. Further, many individuals find the flexibility of Casual Employment—a few months on, a few months off—fits their schedule perfectly.

Casual Employees are usually hired directly from the public, with openings being announced on local Job Information Lines or in State Employment Offices. Occasionally, to fill demand, a postal facility may turn to its register of applicants to recruit casuals, meaning that individuals awaiting review may find temporary employment as casuals while continuing to have their name on an active register. There are no tests or examinations for Casual Employment, unless specific skills are required. If the position requires driving, for example, you'll need a valid driver's license and a clean driving record.

To find our about Casual Employment opportunities in your area, check the listings at your local post office or call your district's Job Information Line.

RURAL CARRIER AND RURAL CARRIER ASSOCIATE

The Rural Carrier position is held by many to be one of the most desirable positions available with the USPS. Away from the hustle and bustle of the city, the Rural Carrier spends many hours alone, traversing the countryside, breathing in fresh air, delivering mail door to door.

However, the road to becoming a Rural Carrier is not an easy one. First, you must become a Rural Carrier Associate (RCA), a non-career appointment whose primary duty is to provide relief to Rural Carriers for vacations, holidays, and illnesses. Many RCAs, as they are known, work just one or two days a week, filling in for other Rural Carriers as the need arises. After one year of employment as an RCA, you become eligible to bid for the Career position of Rural Carrier. However, this bidding process is based on seniority. If a route opens up, Rural Carriers from other routes have the first opportunity to bid on the open route; then RCAs can bid, in order of seniority.

Because of the nature of the commitment and the irregular work hours, the recruiting for RCAs is often more active than for other positions at the USPS. The hiring process is the same as for the other major entry-level jobs described in this chapter. The required test is the 460 Examination, which is *identical* to the 470 Battery Examination, but because of the special nature of the RCA position it is classified separately.

To find out about RCA opportunities in your area, check the listings at your local post office or call the Job Information Line for your district.

ADMINISTRATIVE POSITIONS

The second largest group of entry-level postal employees, after the 470 Battery Examination positions, is what is known as Administrative Positions, all of which require passing a separate exam: the Clerical Abilities, or 710, Examination. These positions which are clerical in nature, include Data Conversion Operator, Clerk-Stenographer, and Clerk-Typist.

Apart from the exam, the hiring process for administrative positions is the same as for the 470 Battery Examination positions. The Clerical Abilities (710) Examination tests your skills in the following areas:

- **Clerical Aptitude**—insert names and/or numbers alphabetically or numerically into lists provided
- **Address Checking**—compare three addresses or names to see if they are alike or different
- **Spelling**—choose the correctly spelled version of a word from a list of five options
- **Math**—perform mathematical computations: addition, subtraction, multiplication, and division
- **Verbal Abilities**—follow directions (similar to the "Following Oral Directions" section of the 470 Battery Examination)

- **Vocabulary**—determine the meaning of a particular word in a sentence
- **Reading Comprehension**—read a paragraph and answer questions based on what you have read

As with the 470 Battery Examination, when you apply for an administrative position you will receive a set of sample questions to help you prepare. In addition, most of these positions have a required typing test.

Remote Encoding Centers: An Opportunity Worth Exploring

An interesting job opportunity at the USPS is the result of a technology called "remote encoding." Currently, optical recognition computers read mail as it is sorted and apply bar-codes to individual pieces of mail. However, many handwritten addresses can't be read by computers—that's where Remote Encoding Centers (RECs) come in.

Data Conversion Operators located at an REC read the handwritten addresses, which are piped in over computer lines from sorting facilities, and electronically send the appropriate bar-code back to the post office, where a sticker is then applied to the piece of mail. Data Conversion Operators must be able to quickly read an address and then type into a computer terminal the correct information.

In 1998 new software was designed to increase to 50 percent the rate at which the Remote Computer Readers (RCRs) can read and resolve handwritten addresses. This technology reduces the amount of time workers spend keying data by hand at the RECs. For this reason, hiring at these centers is part career employee and part long-term temporary or transitional employee. Nevertheless, RECs constitute an immediate employment opportunity worth exploring. Not every district has a Remote Encoding Center, and hiring at the centers can follow a different course than for other entry-level jobs; to find out if your postal district has one, call your personnel department at your local post office.

Job Tip

For more information on employment with the USPS and the 470 Battery Exam, visit the LearningExpress web site at:

www.LearnX.com

and read about our customized Postal Worker preparation guides, or call LearningExpress toll-free at 1-888-551-JOBS to order directly.

C·H·A·P·T·E·R 5

LAW ENFORCEMENT OFFICER

CHAPTER SUMMARY

This chapter describes a variety of law enforcement careers at all levels of government. It discusses the job responsibilities of police officers, state troopers, corrections officers, and federal law enforcement officers. It also offers a look at the typical hiring process, starting salaries, and tips on tracking down job openings.

I f you're interested in a career in law enforcement, you won't be lacking in possibilities. From the U.S. government on down to your local police department, an enormous assortment of job opportunity is out there. Your main tasks are deciding what kind of job you might want and determining the qualifications you'll need to get hired.

Certain basic roles are common to many of the positions described in this chapter. These include preventing crime, keeping the peace, providing protection and security, enforcing the law, and investigating crimes. However, even if a particular job carries each of these responsibilities, one role may be emphasized more than another. For example, a corrections officer may concentrate primarily on supervising prison inmates, while a special agent for the Secret Service may focus on setting up complex protection and security systems. Keep this in mind as you read these job descriptions and consider the work that interests you most.

Where you would be working is another consideration. Mostly outdoors or indoors? In a large metropolitan area? At a remote border post? Will a job require you to relocate frequently? Will you spend a lot of time on the highway? Traveling across the U.S.?

With regard to requirements and application procedures for these jobs, you'll find that some general guidelines apply to most. For instance, plan on having to be in good physical shape, a competent driver, and capable of passing a background check. Other attributes may not be specifically required—such as strong communication skills, computer training, related work experience, college education, a military background—but can improve your chances. Because there are often many more applicants than there are job openings, every extra advantage matters.

When you're exploring opportunities in this field, remember that each job could either become your lifelong profession or serve as a stepping stone to other careers. Maybe you'll decide to start out as a municipal police officer or state trooper, then move on to a federal law enforcement position. The point is, the experience you gain in one area of law enforcement usually can be put to good use in another. You don't have to limit your choices to just one job in your lifetime—though you may need to choose one job at a time. The

information provided here simply gives you a good starting point in your decision-making and job-hunting process.

The accompanying chart features sample starting salaries for municipal police officers, state police officers, corrections officers, and federal law enforcement positions.

THE ALL-IMPORTANT WRITTEN EXAM

Frequently, a written exam is a crucial step in the selection process for becoming a law enforcement officer. You have to first pass a written exam to receive further consideration by the hiring agency.

Many law enforcement agencies establish a list of eligible candidates, and the written exam score determines an applicant's rank on the list. In some cases, this score is combined with other scores, such from the physical agility test or oral interview.

Candidates are typically ranked on the eligibility list from highest to lowest score. Therefore, you need to do well on the exam to boost your chances of being chosen from the list. If you pass the exam with a score of, say, 70 (the typical cut-off score for passing), it's not likely that you'll be hired when there are plenty of appli-

ANNUAL SALARIES: AT A GLANCE

Police Officer, New York City	$34,970
Police Officer, Dallas, Texas	$29,919
State Trooper, Pennsylvania	$38,515
State Trooper, Iowa	$33,833
Corrections Officer, Florida	$19,950
Corrections Officer, California	$29,713
Federal Corrections Officer	$31,570
Federal Police Officer	$35,110

cants with scores in the 90s. An exam bulletin usually specifies what the rank will be based on.

WHAT THE WRITTEN EXAM IS LIKE

Most written exams simply test basic skills and aptitudes: how well you understand what you read, your writing ability, your ability to follow directions, your judgment and reasoning skills, and sometimes your memory or your math. In this preliminary written exam, *you will not be tested on your knowledge of law enforcement policies and procedures, the law, or any other specific body of knowledge.* This test is designed *only* to see if you can read, write, reason and do basic math.

In a few places, taking the exam involves studying written materials in advance and then answering questions about them on the exam. Some of these written materials have to do with the law and police or corrections procedures—but all you have to do is study the guide you're given. You're still being tested just on your reading skills and memory, and there are good reasons for this.

Law enforcement officers have to be able to read, understand and act on complex written materials such as laws, policy handbooks, and regulations. They have to write incident reports and other materials that have to be clear and correct enough to stand up in court or a probation hearing. They have to be able to think independently, because officers get little direct supervision and don't have time to consult with superiors when violence is brewing. They have to be able to do enough math to add up the value of confiscated goods or compute the street price of a drug sold to a dealer for *x* amount per kilo. The basic skills the written exam tests for are skills law enforcement officers use every day.

Most exams are multiple-choice tests of the sort you've often encountered in school. You get an exam book and an answer sheet where you have to fill in little circles (bubbles) or squares with a number 2 pencil. A few agencies, particularly municipal police departments, will also have you write an essay or a mock police report.

Reading Comprehension Questions

Reading comprehension is a part of almost every written law enforcement exam. These reading questions are like the ones you've probably come across in school tests: you're given a paragraph or two to read and then asked questions about it. Questions typically ask you about:

- the main idea of the passage as a whole
- specific facts or details contained in the passage
- the meaning of words or phrases as they are used in the passage
- inferences and conclusions you can draw from what is stated in the passage

Grammar Questions

When the exam announcement says the exam tests writing skills, you're probably facing multiple-choice questions on grammar, spelling and/or vocabulary. Usually a grammar question asks you to choose which of four versions of a sentence is most correct.

Sometimes grammar questions also test punctuation or capitalization, usually by giving you a sentence with punctuation marks or capital letters underlined and asking you to choose which one is wrong.

Spelling Questions

Spelling questions might give you a sentence with a word missing and then ask you which of the choices is the correct spelling of the missing word. Or you might be given several different words and asked which one is spelled wrong.

Vocabulary Questions

Vocabulary questions usually ask you to find a *synonym*—a word that means the same—or the *antonym*—a word that means the opposite—of a given word. If you're lucky, that word will come in a sentence that will help you guess its meaning. If you're less lucky, you'll just be given the word and have to choose a synonym or antonym without any help from context.

Another way vocabulary is tested is to give you a sentence with a blank in it and ask you to choose the word that fits best in the sentence.

Math Questions

Math is usually a minor part of a law enforcement exam, if it's included at all. The questions usually test basic arithmetic: just adding, subtracting, multiplying, and dividing whole numbers. Most often the math questions are word problems that present everyday situations: the total value of stolen property, the number of cupcakes you need to give three to all the officers and two to all the civilians in the department, that kind of thing.

A few tests might ask you to work with fractions, decimals, or percentages, but still in real-life situations: how much is left after one person eats half and another person eats a third; the amount of mileage on a car gauge after a certain number of trips; how much you have to pay for a uniform at a 15% discount; and so on.

Memory Questions

Officers have to be able to remember lots of details about things they see and things they read, so observation and memory questions are often a part of law enforcement exams. You may be given a study booklet in advance of the exam and have to answer questions about it during the exam without referring to the book. Or you might be given a picture to look at or a passage to read right there at the exam and then have to answer questions about it, usually without referring to the picture or passage. You may even be shown a videotape and then asked questions about it later.

Judgment Questions

Obviously law enforcement officers need to have good judgment, so some exams include multiple-choice questions designed to test your good judgment and common sense. You may be given laws or procedures and asked to apply them to a hypothetical situation, or you may be asked which hypothetical situation is most likely to indicate dangerous or criminal activity. Answering these questions requires both common sense and an ability to read carefully.

Chapters 8 and 13 of this book will help you brush up on your general test-taking skills and highlight areas needing additional practice. For an in-depth look at the exam you'll actually take, call LearningExpress at 1-888-551-JOBS and ask about our *Police Officer*, *State Police*, or *Corrections Officer* guides, which contain full practice exams and instructional chapters written by experts for each of the skill areas you're likely to find on the written exam. Or visit us on the Web at *www.LearnX.com*.

TRACKING DOWN JOB OPENINGS

One of the most important things when looking for a job in law enforcement is how to find out where the job openings are. It's up to you to keep track of upcoming exams and filing periods. To get this information, you can contact a law enforcement agency directly, or use several other avenues to get the facts you need.

In Print

Law enforcement agencies commonly advertise jobs in newspapers, as well as in specialized publications, such as "Law Enforcement Career Digest." This publication can be viewed online or subscribed to. These bulletins list nationwide job vacancies and profile various law enforcement agencies, including FBI, ATF, DEA, Customs, Secret Service, U.S. Marshals, and more. You can get more information on this publication at:

Law Enforcement Career Digest
United States Law Enforcement Services, Inc.
P.O. Box 1322(K)
Severna Park, Maryland 21146
410-315-9448 or 800-359-6260
www.policecareers.com/digest

Some law enforcement career reference materials are available in reference sections in larger libraries. Three additional resources you may want to review or purchase are *The National Directory of Law Enforcement* (715-345-2772), *The Directory of Juvenile and Adult Correctional Institutions and Agencies* (301-918-1800), and *Police Salaries* (800-745-8780).

The World Wide Web

The Internet can be an excellent research tool for digging up information on job vacancies and current exams. One excellent source for all law enforcement and firefighter agencies is *www.policecareers.com*. You'll find a complete list of internet addresses to state employment offices at the end of Chapter 2. Most law enforcement agencies also maintain their own web sites, which you can find by using a search engine, such as Yahoo!, Lycos, or Netscape. Along with general information on the agency, these sites may feature minimum requirements for applying and a description of the selection process.

Another helpful Internet resource is the U.S. Office of Personnel Management's website, USAJOBS (*www.usajobs.opm.gov/*). This site features a searchable database of current federal job vacancies, application procedures, and related employment information.

You can also subscribe to "Federal Career Opportunities" online (*www.fedjobs.com*). This service provides daily updates on job openings at all levels of federal employment, including law enforcement positions. For more detailed information on how to use the Internet, see Chapter 3.

Job Information Lines

Most city, county, and state personnel offices have an automated information line listing current job vacancies and current or upcoming tests. It's usually a simple recording, listing the current job opportunities and open examinations and providing you with either a phone number or an address for an application or further information. Check the governmental listing in your phone book to find the Job Information Line, Employment Line, or Personnel Department for your area or use the website list at the end of Chapter 2, which includes job line numbers..

Some states, such as New Jersey and Massachusetts, have a statewide personnel office that administers the tests for entry-level law enforcement officers. Prison systems often recruit through a state employment office. Check the state governmental listings in your phone book under "Department of Labor, Job Placement Services" for the office nearest you, or go on the Internet to *www.dol.gov/*.

Career Fairs

One very helpful source for government job information, if your timing is right, is the career fair, where you can pick up brochures and ask face-to-face questions of a government recruiter. Job fairs are usually advertised on the radio and in the career or job listings section of your newspaper. Some are listed on the particular agency's web site, for example, the FBI's career fairs are updated monthly on *www.fbi.gov/employment/fairs*. Another source of job fair information is a nearby college or university placement office.

POLICE OFFICER

What You'll Do on the Job

Police officers perform numerous law enforcement duties related primarily to maintaining law and order and protecting people and property. The majority of law enforcement jobs in this country are in municipal police departments.

Police officers patrol the communities they serve by car, on foot or by other means of transportation. They watch for, investigate and attempt to prevent or disrupt suspicious or illegal activity. They respond to radio calls about various crimes committed or in progress—anything from burglaries or robberies to assaults, rapes, murders, and illegal drug trafficking. At the scene of a crime, they may question crime victims, witnesses or suspects, secure criminal evidence, and arrest suspects. While on patrol, Police Officers are also on the lookout for public safety hazards and may issue citations, or even make arrests, for various motor vehicle and parking violations.

Another major area of responsibility involves traffic and/or crowd control. Police officers may carry out these tasks for planned public gatherings such as parades, political demonstrations, and sports events. They also perform these functions under emergency conditions, including auto accidents, explosions, fires and natural disasters, and may provide basic medical care to accident or crime victims.

Police officers are highly trained in the use of physical force and weapons to subdue or apprehend criminals. In addition to preparing detailed written reports that can be used as evidence in criminal cases, they frequently provide court testimony during criminal trials.

Qualifications

Though requirements for becoming a police officer vary among police departments, typically you must be a U.S. citizen and meet a minimum age requirement (usually between the ages of 18 and 21) at the time of appointment. A valid driver's license and a good driving record are required. You must pass a written test, personal interview, background investigation, psychological testing, drug screening, physical performance tests, and a physical exam (including vision and hearing tests). A high school diploma or GED may meet the educational criteria. However, some college education may be required or preferred in the selection process. You may need to be a resident of the city or county in which you apply. If you have served in the military, you may receive what is known as "veterans preference points" on the written test.

STATE AND LOCAL LAW ENFORCEMENT AGENCIES			
Type of agency	Number of agencies	Full-time employees	Part-time employees
Local police	13,578	521,985	61,453
Sheriff	3,088	257,712	22,412
State police	49	83,742	1,303
Special police	1,316	56,229	12,003
Texas constable	738	2,310	599
Total	**18,769**	**921,978**	**97,770**

Training Involved

Most police officer recruits undergo formal training in a police academy that lasts several weeks or months. This includes classroom instruction in subjects related to the law and law enforcement procedures as well as skills training, for example, in self-defense techniques and the use of firearms. New recruits also can expect a period of on-the-job or field training under the supervision of experienced officers. Employment generally is considered to be probationary based on successfully completing a department's designated course of training.

Applying for the Job

For information about application requirements and testing procedures, contact the personnel or recruiting office of the police department(s) where you want to apply. In some locations, you can apply for a job online. Call your local police department to see if they have a web site.

STATE POLICE OFFICER

What You'll Do on the Job

The primary responsibility of state police officers (sometimes known as state troopers) is to patrol and enforce laws that govern the use of state and interstate highways, turnpikes and freeways. In addition to enforcing motor vehicle laws, they also may enforce criminal laws and assist other law enforcement agencies with criminal investigations, especially in counties without a local police force or a large sheriff's department. Ensuring public safety, providing emergency assistance and offering general assistance to motorists are other typical duties.

While on patrol, state police officers are on the lookout for motor vehicle violations, such as exceeding the speed limit, and any evidence of unsafe driving.

They can stop motorists and check for valid driver's licenses, vehicle registrations and valid vehicle inspection stickers. This can include using computerized equipment to tap into state or interstate data bases and run identification and vehicle checks, for example, to determine if a vehicle is stolen or a driver is wanted for criminal violations. When justified, they can issue citations, search vehicles or make arrests.

State police officers frequently respond to the scene when emergencies occur on the highways such as car accidents or fires or when vehicles break down and block traffic. Depending on the situation, they may direct traffic, render first aid, call for emergency equipment or assist in other ways. The written reports and possibly diagrams that these officers prepare when accidents occur are used for evidence in any subsequent legal proceedings. To maintain public safety on the highways, these officers also perform actions necessary to alleviate unsafe road conditions caused by road damage, debris on the roads, bad weather or other factors. State police officers commonly provide help to motorists in non-emergency situations as well, such as giving directions or offering information about local services and facilities.

Qualifications

Requirements for this position vary among the states, generally according to their prevailing civil service regulations. In most states, you must be a U.S. citizen between 21 and 29 years of age at the time of appointment and a resident of the state in which you are applying. Other typical requirements include passing a written test, personal interview, physical examination (including vision and hearing tests), physical performance tests, some form of psychological testing, possibly a polygraph and drug screening, and a thorough background investigation. A high school diploma or GED may satisfy the minimum educational requirements. Some level of college education may be required; in most states it serves as an advantage in the hiring process.

Training Involved

Selected recruits for state police officer positions participate in a formal training program, which may range in length from 3 to 4 months. This training covers general policing methods as well as subjects specific to this position. These include instruction in state motor vehicle codes, patrol and surveillance techniques, and pursuit driving. After completing this training, additional on-the-job training takes place under the supervision of experienced state police officers.

Applying for the Job

For information about application requirements and job openings, contact the State police department's personnel or recruiting office. State civil service commissions may also be able to provide information about application and testing procedures. In many states, you can now apply for a job online.

CORRECTIONS OFFICER

What You'll Do on the Job

Corrections officers guard and supervise prisoners confined to penal institutions. While this basic role doesn't change, their specific duties will vary depending on the size and type of institution—federal or state penitentiaries, city or county jails, reformatories or detention centers—and the level of security or supervision required by an institution (minimum or maximum security).

Corrections officers monitor the behavior of inmates at all times to maintain order, enforce the rules of the institution, and prevent escape. They routinely search inmates and cells for prohibited items or materials. They also make sure that cells and outer facilities remain secure, for example, that locks, window bars or doors have not been tampered with. A constant duty is being on the lookout for any signs of tension or disruptive conduct among inmates which could lead to physical disputes or emergency situations such as riots.

The disciplinary role of corrections officers is vital and can involve the use of force or weapons. However, it is their further responsibility to *protect* inmates. They have a duty to ensure the health, safety and well-being of inmates while they are institutionalized; and, for those inmates who eventually will be released, help prepare them to lead productive lives outside the institution. You can find more information online at *www.bop.gov/recruit.html.*

Qualifications

Employment requirements for corrections officers vary depending on the institution. In general, federal prisons, large institutions and/or maximum security facilities may have more stringent requirements than small and/or minimum security facilities. Most often, you must be at least 21 years old and have a high school diploma or a GED. Good physical health and emotional stability are standard criteria so you can expect some kind of medical, fitness and psychological testing. Polygraph (lie detector) tests, drug screening and background investigations are also common. You may or may not be required to pass a written test (such as a civil service examination). Related work experience and higher education rate highly in the hiring process; one or the other is required by some institutions, especially at federal institutions.

Training Involved

Corrections Officers in federal prisons receive formal training through the Federal Bureau of Prisons. On-the-job training directed by experienced officers is customary at the state and local level, often supplemented with specialized formal training courses. Many state facilities, however, have adopted or plan to adopt formal training programs like those conducted for federal institutions.

Applying for the Job

For information about career opportunities for corrections officers, you can contact correctional institutions and facilities in your area; State departments of corrections; State civil service commissions; the Federal Bureau of Prisons; or the Federal Office of Personnel Management (OPM). You may also want to contact national organizations in this field, such as The American Correctional Association, 4380 Forbes Blvd., Lanham, MD 20706-4322 (301-918-1800) *www.corrections.com/aca/*; and Office of International Criminal Justice, 180 N. Wacker Dr., Suite 300, Chicago, IL 60606; *email: oicjinc@aol.com; www.acsp.uic.edu.* and the National Employment Listing Service, 916-392-2550.

Job Tip

For more information on employment in law enforcement, visit the LearningExpress web site at *www.LearnX.com* and read about our exclusive customized police officer, state police officer, and corrections officer exam preparation guides, or call LearningExpress toll-free at 1-888-551-JOBS to order directly.

FEDERAL AGENCIES

The U.S. Government provides numerous opportunities for those interested in a law enforcement career. Many federal agencies, for example, maintain their own police forces and investigative or security units. In 1999, there were 28 Federal officers per 100,000 U.S. residents. Typically, each agency provides general law

enforcement training, often through the Federal Law Enforcement Training Center in Glynco, Georgia, as well as specialized training relative to its particular mission (for example, to enforce federal immigration laws or drug laws, to ensure the safety of government officials, or to protect government property and lands). Whatever its mission or jurisdiction, these agencies frequently work in tandem, lending their expertise to criminal investigations or assisting each other in emergency situations.

Some federal agencies have the authority to test and hire applicants directly while many others work through the Office of Personnel Management (OPM) to fill job openings (online, go to *www.usajobs.opm.gov/*). When this is the case, the OPM typically accepts applications for employment with a specific federal agency; administers the appropriate written tests; and then submits an eligibility list of qualified candidates to the agency for consideration. (If you already work for a federal agency, you may be able to apply directly to another agency rather than go through the OPM.)

The OPM operates Federal Job Information kiosks in major metropolitan areas across the country. When written tests are required by an agency that works through the OPM, these tests generally will be given at federal facilities. This is also where you can find out about current job openings and request the application forms you'll need. At the end of Chapter 1, you'll find a list of computerized job-search kiosks operated by the OPM across the country, plus federal job hotline numbers and other on-line services you can use.

You can expect a lot of paperwork when you're applying for federal jobs—and it's crucial that you provide every piece of paper that's requested. Announcements that are made for federal job vacancies—for example, by the OPM or directly through a federal agency—indicate what information is needed to apply. For most federal jobs, you can apply using a resume, a form known as the Optional Application for Federal Employment (available through the OPM), or some similar kind of written statement. You also may be asked to send along other documents, such as a college transcript or a certificate of discharge from military service.

Keep in mind, too, that federal jobs are classified a certain way to indicate the experience, salary level and other features of the job. These classifications are known as "grades." With your application, you usually need to indicate the job title; the announcement number of the job; and the grade(s) assigned to the job. See Chapter 1 for a full explanation of job series and grades.

The following are some descriptions of federal agencies, the kind of work you'll encounter, and the training involved for becoming a law enforcement officer with the U.S. Government.

Bureau of Alcohol, Tobacco, and Firearms

The Bureau of Alcohol, Tobacco and Firearms (ATF) is responsible for the administration and criminal enforcement of federal laws involving alcohol, tobacco, firearms and explosives. With regard to criminal activity, the agency serves to prevent the illegal possession, use and trafficking of such commodities as liquor, cigarettes and guns. Read more about the agency online at *www.atf.treas.gov/*.

SPECIAL AGENT
What You'll Do on the Job

Special Agents perform investigative work related to federal laws that are regulated by the ATF Bureau. They conduct investigations aimed at uncovering the illegal manufacture, possession, trafficking or smuggling of cigarettes and liquor. They investigate similar kinds of criminal activities with regard to firearms and explosives as well.

Depending on the type of case, Special Agents may set up surveillance operations, work undercover or instigate raids. Questioning informants, witnesses and suspects are key duties to gather information and physical evidence of violations. With proper legal warrants, Special Agents are authorized to conduct searches and seize contraband or physical evidence. In addition, they help prepare cases for criminal prosecution and give court testimony when needed.

Qualifications

Among other requirements for a Special Agent position, you must be a U.S. citizen between the ages of 21 and 37. You will need to take the Treasury Enforcement Agent (TEA) written examination. After passing the TEA exam, you then must pass a personal interview, a background investigation, drug screening and physical exam (including vision and hearing tests). A four-year degree from an accredited college or university is required. In some cases, the equivalent in work experience or education plus work experience may be considered instead.

Training Involved

As a Special Agent trainee, you'll receive eight weeks of training in general law enforcement and investigative techniques at the Federal Law Enforcement Training Center in Glynco, Georgia. This training includes courses in surveillance techniques, rules of evidence, undercover assignments, arrest and raid techniques and the use of firearms. Specialized training is later provided that covers the specific duties of ATF Special Agents, such as instruction related to laws enforced by the ATF Bureau, case report writing, firearms and explosives operations, bomb scene searches and arson investigations.

Applying for the Job

You may contact your local OPM area office regarding the TEA Examination, which is administered by the OPM. More information on testing and application procedures is available through the Bureau of Alcohol, Tobacco and Firearms, Personnel Division-Employment Branch, Washington, D.C. 20226. A job information line can be reached at 202-927-8610. The ATF website is *www.atf.treas.gov/*.

DRUG ENFORCEMENT ADMINISTRATION

Enforcing U.S. laws regarding illegal drug trafficking and preventing drug abuse are the chief responsibilities of the Drug Enforcement Administration (DEA). Through its investigative activities, the DEA seeks to track down major suppliers of narcotic and dangerous drugs both in the U.S. and abroad. Read more about the DEA online at *www.usdoj.gov/dea/job/ads.htm*.

SPECIAL AGENT
What You'll Do on the Job

DEA Special Agents coordinate their investigative efforts with other federal, state and local law enforcement agencies, especially to open the channels of information about methods used and people engaged in the illegal trafficking of drugs. They are heavily involved with the international community as well. Working with foreign governments, agencies and law enforcement officials, they help to develop intelligence networks, investigate unlawful drug trade, institute drug control and anti-drug abuse programs, and other such services. They also enforce federal laws by monitoring the transactions of drug companies and other legitimate channels of narcotic and dangerous drugs.

Qualifications

Candidates for DEA Special Agent positions must be U.S. citizens between the ages of 21 and 35 at the time of appointment. Although no written test is required, you will need to pass a physical examination (including vision and hearing tests) and a thorough background investigation. Any form of drug abuse, past or present, would be grounds for immediate disqualification. To qualify, you must have a degree in any field from an accredited college or university and either (a) one year of work experience; or (b) an overall GPA of 2.5 on a 4.0 scale and a 3.5 GPA in your major field of study, with an academic standing in the upper 1/3 of a graduating class or major subdivision (for example, a college's school of business or division of arts and sciences), membership in a scholastic honor society, plus one year of graduate study.

Training Involved

Applicants for DEA Special Agent positions participate in 14 weeks of basic training at the FBI Academy in Quantico, Virginia. This training includes courses in narcotic laws, arrest techniques, surveillance techniques, search and seizure laws, firearms use, practical exercises and self-defense.

Applying for the Job

Applications should be sent directly to the nearest DEA office for hiring consideration. Certain forms and pieces of documentation must be provided with your application. This may include a resume or Optional Application for Federal Employment, a Background Survey Questionnaire (OPM Form 1386) and a completed college transcript. More information on testing and application procedures is available through the Drug Enforcement Administration, Office of Personnel, 1405 I Street N.W., Washington, D.C. 20537 or at *www.usajobs.opm.gov*.

FEDERAL BUREAU OF INVESTIGATION

As its name implies, the chief responsibility of the Federal Bureau of Investigation (FBI) is to investigate violations of federal laws. The FBI is part of the U.S. Department of Justice and has jurisdiction in over 260 types of criminal cases. Its vast files—with everything from fingerprint records and criminal aliases to shoe prints and carpet fiber samples—can also be tapped to help with criminal investigations.

SPECIAL AGENT
What You'll Do on the Job
The FBI expects to hire 500 Special Agents in fiscal year 2000. Due to the broad scope of the FBI's law enforcement mission, Special Agents can be put to work on literally hundreds of types of cases. Among these are investigations into organized crime; bank robberies; espionage; terrorism; civil rights violations; embezzlement; extortion; bribery; fraud; public corruption; finance, commerce and trade law violations; kidnapping; and attacks or assassination attempts on federal officials.

While Special Agents usually work on high-security cases and have the FBI's sophisticated resources at their disposal, their basic duties are common to most investigative work. This may involve undercover activities and surveillance operations; reviewing relevant records and documentation; questioning informants, witnesses and suspects; and arresting suspects and seizing evidence.

Qualifications
To qualify as an FBI Special Agent, you must be a U.S. citizen between the ages of 23 and 37. You will need to take a series of written tests which are computer-scored at FBI headquarters in Washington, D.C. After passing these tests, you will participate in a formal interview.

You also must pass a thorough background investigation and physical exam (including vision and hearing tests). Candidates typically need to rank well above average in each area to be considered, due both to the nature of the work and the high level of competition for these positions.

Training Involved
Newly appointed Special Agents receive training at the FBI Academy in Quantico, Virginia. Training lasts approximately 16 weeks and consists of classroom instruction in a number of subject areas, a physical fitness program and firearms training.

Applying for the Job
The FBI uses a centralized hiring system that is not subject to OPM appointment regulations. You may apply on the Internet at *www.fbi.gov/employment/agent4.htm*. Applications can also be submitted to the nearest FBI field office or to FBI headquarters in Washington, D.C. More information on testing and application procedures is available through an FBI field office or at its headquarters (Federal Bureau of Investigation, Ninth Street & Pennsylvania Avenue, Washington, D.C. 20535).

OTHER FEDERAL AGENCIES

In addition to those described above, law enforcement positions are also available through the following federal agencies. Online listings can be found at *www.usajobs.opm.gov/* and *www.fedworld.gov/jobs/jobsearch.*

SPECIAL AGENTS AND CRIMINAL INVESTIGATORS
U.S. Department of State
Recruitment Division
P.O. Box 9317
Arlington, VA 22219
www.state.gov/www/careers/index

U.S. Department of the Interior
Bureau of Land Management
Personnel Service
18th & C Streets N.W.
Washington, D.C. 20240
www.doi.gov/hrm/doijobs.html

Bureau of Indian Affairs
Personnel Service
1951 Constitution Avenue N.W.
Washington, D.C. 20245
www.doi.gov/bureau-indian-affairs.html

U.S. Fish and Wildlife Service
Personnel Division
Room 3454
18th and C Streets N.W.
Washington, D.C. 20240
peronnel.fws.gov/

Department of Defense
Office of Inspector General
Personnel Division
400 Army Navy Drive
Arlington, VA 22202-2884

www.dticaw.dtic.mil/prhome/
www.odeodea.edu/pers/

U.S. Air Force
Office of Special Investigations
Bolling Air Force Base
Washington, D.C. 20332-6001
www.af.mil/careers/

U.S. Department of Labor
Office of Inspector General
Human Resources Management Division
200 Constitution Avenue N.W., Room S-5513
Washington, D.C. 20210
www.dol.gov

U.S. Naval Investigative Service
Career Services Department
Washington, D.C. 20388-5025
www.navyjobs.com

Federal Protective Service
18th and F Streets N.W., Room 2306
Washington, D.C. 20405

Immigration and Naturalization Service
Border Patrol Examining Unit
425 I Street N.W., 2nd floor
Washington, D.C. 20536-0001
www.ins.usdoj.gov/graphics/workfor/index.htm

Internal Revenue Service
1111 Constitution Avenue N.W., Room 1034
Washington, D.C. 20224

U.S. Customs Service
Office of Human Resources
Enforcement Division
P.O. Box 7108
Washington, D.C. 20044
www.customs.treas.gov/career/career.htm

U.S. Marshals Service
Personnel Management Division
Law Enforcement Recruiting Branch
600 Army Navy Drive
Arlington, VA 22202-4210
www.usdoj.gov/marshals/careers/careers.htm

U.S. Secret Service
Personnel Division
1800 G Street N.W.
Washington, DC 20223
www.treas.gov/uss/

FEDERAL POLICE OFFICERS

U.S. Park Police
Personnel Office, 1100 Ohio Drive S.W.
Washington, D.C. 20242
www.doi.gov/u.s.park.police/

U.S. Capitol Police
Public Information Office
119 D Street N.E.
Washington, D.C. 20510
www.usajobs.opm.gov/e151.htm

U.S. Department of Justice
950 Pennsylvania Ave., N.W.

Washington, D.C. 20530-0001
gopher://justice2.usdoj.gov/

Library of Congress Employment Office
James Madison Memorial Building
101 Independence Avenue S.E.
Washington, D.C. 20540
www.loc.gov/hr/employment

U.S. Government Printing Office
Employment Branch, Room C-106, Stop: PWE
North Capitol and H Streets N.W.
Washington, D.C. 20401
www.access.gpo.gov/employment/index

U.S. Supreme Court
Personnel Office, Room 3
One First Street N.E.
Washington, D.C. 20543
www.uscourts.gov/employment/opportunity

Department of Defense
Washington Headquarters Services
Personnel and Security
Washington, D.C. 20301-1155
www.odedea.edu/pers

FEDERAL BUREAU OF INVESTIGATION

Preliminary Application for
Special Agent Position
(Please Type or Print in Black Ink)

Date: _____

I. PERSONAL HISTORY

Name in Full (Last, First, Middle)	List College Degree(s) Already Received or Pursuing, Major, School, and Month/Year:

Marital Status: ☐ Single ☐ Engaged ☐ Married ☐ Separated ☐ Legally Separated ☐ Widowed ☐ Divorced

Birth Date (Month, Day, Year) Birth Place:	Social Security Number: (Optional)	Do you understand FBI employment requires availability for assignment anywhere in the U.S.?

Current Address

_____   Home Phone _____
Street   Apt. No.   Area Code   Number

Work Phone _____
City   State   Zip Code   Area Code   Number

Are you: CPA ☐ Yes ☐ No   Licensed Driver ☐ Yes ☐ No   U. S. Citizen ☐ Yes ☐ No

Have you served on active duty in the U. S. Military? ☐ Yes ☐ No If yes, indicate branch of service and dates (month/year) of active duty. Include military school attendance (month/year):

How did you learn or become interested in FBI employment as a Special Agent?	Have you previously applied for FBI employment? ☐ Yes ☐ No If yes, location and date:

Do you have a foreign language background? ☐ Yes ☐ No List proficiency for each language on reverse side.

Have you ever been arrested for any crime (include major traffic violations such as Driving Under the Influence or While Intoxicated, etc.)? ☐ Yes ☐ No If so, list all such matters on a continuation sheet, even if not formally charged, or no court appearance or found not guilty, or matter settled by payment of fine or forfeiture of collateral. Include date, place, charge, disposition, details, and police agency on reverse side.

II. EMPLOYMENT HISTORY

Identify your most recent three years FULL-TIME work experience, after high school (excluding summer, part-time and temporary employment).

From Month/Year	To Month/Year	Title of Position and Description of Work	# of hrs. Per week	Name/Location of Employer

III. PERSONAL DECLARATIONS

Persons with a disability who require an accommodation to complete the application process are required to notify the FBI of their need for the accommodation.

Have you used marijuana during the last three years or more than 15 times? ☐ Yes ☐ No

Have you used any illegal drug(s) or combination of illegal drugs, other than marijuana, more than 5 times or during the last 10 years? ☐ Yes ☐ No

All Information provided by applicants concerning their drug history will be subject to verification by a preemployment polygraph examination.

Do you understand all prospective FBI employees will be required to submit to an urinalysis for drug abuse prior to employment? ☐ Yes ☐ No

Please do not write below this line.

C·H·A·P·T·E·R 6

ADMINISTRATIVE ASSISTANT

CHAPTER SUMMARY

This chapter discusses entry-level clerical and administrative assistant positions in federal, state, and city government. It offers a rundown of job requirements and duties, application and hiring procedures, employment resources, and a look at typical salary ranges.

Just about every government agency, be it federal, state, or city, needs people to handle the day-to-day details of office work. These individuals fall into an entry-level category known as clerical workers and administrative assistants.

In general, clerical and administrative assistant personnel provide support to higher-level employees by performing such routine office work as:

- answering telephones
- correspondence
- stenography (taking dictation in shorthand)
- handling incoming and outgoing mail and filing
- operating office machines (typewriters, copiers, fax machines, computers, mail processing equipment, etc.)
- data entry and information management

They may also complete research projects and prepare reports, or be given assignments that demand specialized skills, such as proficiency with a 10-key adding machine or experience with word processing or spreadsheet software.

"Clerical and administrative support" is a broad description of a job whose exact responsibilities can vary greatly, depending on the agency you work for. For example, take a look at the job description for a clerk (a GS-300 position) with the Internal Revenue Service:

Perform various clerical duties such as maintaining records, extracting, sorting, and filing tax returns and other related correspondence.

Note how the job responsibilities relate directly to the activities of the Internal Revenue Service.

Following are two job vacancy announcements for a clerical and administrative assistant from state-level agencies, followed by one from a city agency. Clearly, the mission or focus of each agency influences the kind of work you do.

Administrative assistant needed in the Florida Department of Military Affairs (DMA) to perform the following duties: review and process requests for state and federal medals, ribbons, and appurtenances. Write narratives for award orders and certificates. Serve as liaison between the DMA and other military related organizations. May be required to travel on military aircraft in conjunction with duties.

Administrative secretary to work for the state of North Dakota Highway Patrol. Duties include directing calls and providing information on motor vehicle registration, traffic laws, etc.; dispatches and receives messages via two-way radio; collects revenue and prepares reports.

Clerk position in the Mesa, Arizona Human Resources Department. Job involves extensive pub-lic contact, with little supervision. Performs a variety of secretarial and clerical work, provides information on personnel office procedures to visitors and over the phone.

Below is a list of typical state agencies that employ clerks and administrative assistants. Because each agency has its own focus, you can see how varied the work may be for these positions.

Department of Agriculture and Consumer Services
Department of Banking and Finance
Department of Business and Professional Regulations
Department of Corrections
Department of Highway Safety and Motor Vehicles
Department of Juvenile Justice
Department of Labor and Employment Security
Department of Law Enforcement
Department of Military Affairs
Department of Revenue
Department of Transportation
Department of Veterans Affairs

JOB PROSPECTS

There is an abundance of career opportunities for clerical and administrative support at all levels of government. For example, of the 22 General Schedule occupational groups working for the federal government (see Chapter 1), GS-300—the General Administrative, Clerical and Office Services Group—employs by far the most GS employees. In fact, nearly half a million employees—about half of all civil service positions—fall into this job category. That's because clerks are needed in every government agency and facility and because there are so many different types of clerks working for the government.

You may think that federal jobs are limited to the Washington, D.C. area, but the U.S. government employs entry-level administrative assistants and clerks in offices and facilities all over the country. The Internal Revenue Service, for example, employs thousands of clerical and administrative support personnel in 11 different states. Other agencies, some of which are military, that employ clerical-related employees include:

- The National Park Service (Glacier National Park, MT)
- Department of the Air Force (Grand Forks, ND)
- Department of Labor (Dallas, TX)
- Department of the Interior (Vernal, UT)

The locations listed here are just some of the many cities in which these agencies employ administrative assistants.

States can have up to 75 agencies located both within the capital city and throughout the state. A high concentration of clerical and administrative assistant jobs can be found in the government offices of the state capital; however, when you begin your job search, you'll find that recruitment announcements often include a specific geographic location of the agency you'll work for, and this can be anywhere that agency has an office. If you'd like to work for the state prison or state university system, for example, you'll find opportunities in the counties and cities where these institutions are located.

As for the local level, clearly, the bigger the city, the more government agencies there are. For example, there are almost 50 city government agencies in New York City; a smaller city, such as Charlottesville, VA, has 13 agencies.

JOB TITLES TO LOOK FOR

If you're interested in becoming a clerk or administrative assistant, it's important to know, at least at the federal level, that many job series that fit this description don't necessarily have the word "clerk" or "administrative assistant" in their title. Thus, it's important that you read job announcements carefully. If you're looking just for "clerk" or "administrative assistant," you may miss out on excellent job opportunities.

At the federal level, there are 38 job series in GS-300, each of which have from several to several dozen individual positions that are clerical or administrative in nature. Here are some of those job series:

GS-302—Messenger Series

GS-318—Secretary Series

GS-332—Computer Operation Series

GS-350—Equipement Operator Series

GS-382—Telephone Operator Series

GS-385—Teletypist Series

For a complete listing of GS-300 job titles, consult the *Dictionary of Occupational Titles,* published by the U.S. Department of Labor's Employment and Training Commission.

At the state and city level, you're more likely to see the following titles in the clerical and administrative category:

Accounting Clerk

Administrative Clerk

Administrative Secretary

Business Machine Operator

Clerical Assistant

Clerk Typist

Entry Level Clerk

Data Entry Clerk

General Office Clerk

Mail Clerk

Office Assistant

Personnel Clerk

10-Key (adding machine) Operator

The following are sample starting salaries for clerical and administrative assistants in various locations.

- Casper, WY = $19,200
- Indianapolis, IN = $18,346
- Hickory, NC = $18,120
- Nashville, TN = $17,193
- Houston, TX = $19,488
- Portland, OR = $18,594

MEETING THE REQUIREMENTS

Minimum requirements for clerical and administrative assistants vary from job to job and agency to agency. Overall, you must be a U.S. citizen or have applied for citizenship to qualify for any government job.

For many entry-level clerical and administrative jobs in city and federal government, the typical minimum requirements are:

- You must be at least 16 years old
- You must have a high school diploma or its equivalent
- Males over age 18 must also be registered with (or exempt from) the Selective Service.

It's not unusual for state agencies to require applicants to:

- Be at least 21 years old
- Have a bachelor's degree from an accredited college or university *and* one year of administrative assistant experience, *or* a master's degree. (Administrative or clerical experience can sometimes substitute on a year-to-year basis for the required college education.)

Although you don't need any experience to qualify for a GS-1 position with the federal government, you'll need three months of office experience for a GS-2 and six months' experience for a GS-3 position.

Experience Pays

When it comes to working for the government, the term "entry level" doesn't necessarily imply that this is your first job. It's a category of employees defined by pay scale, experience, and skills. As with most private sector jobs, it pays to have some experience, even if it isn't required. That's because the higher the position pays, the more education and/or experience is required of the candidate.

For example, at the federal level, you don't need any experience to get a GS-1 clerical position, while up to three years of experience can land you a GS-5 spot. The GS-1 annual salary ranges from $13,870 to $17,351, and a GS-5 job pays from $21,370 to $27,778 annually.

The same rule of thumb applies to state and city agencies, but in addition to office experience, your education is taken into account when it comes to title and pay level. The following chart shows the title, necessary education and experience, and pay scales for a clerk in Salt Lake City, Utah.

EDUCATION AND SALARY: AT A GLANCE

Title	Education and Experience	Annual Salary Range
Clerk 1	High school diploma, no experience	$17,448 to $24,060
Clerk 2	High school diploma and one year office experience *or* one year postsecondary (college) education	$19,236 to $26,640
Clerk 3	High school diploma and three years' office experience	$20,520 to $28,716

KSAs and E & T

Although clerical and administrative assistant jobs are termed entry level, some of these positions demand a bit of preliminary knowledge and/or experience. You can acquire such hands-on skills as typing or using such office equipment as an adding machine or word processor by working in a private sector company or by taking classes with a business skills school.

The skills and experience you'll need to have are described in the job vacancy announcement. You're likely to encounter two acronyms in a job announcement or on an application that relate to your previous experience:

- E & T = Experience and training
- KSAs = Knowledge, skills, and abilities

Both of these acronyms mean about the same thing. You may be asked to describe your E & T or KSAs in an interview, on a job application, or in a cover letter to a personnel office (if applicable). Here's where you let your prospective employer know what prior experience you have gathered, the specific training you've completed, or the skills and abilities you've honed that enable you to do the job.

Here is a sample of typical KSAs from a job vacancy announcement for an administrative assistant:

- Knowledge of administrative procedures and practices
- Effective communication
- Ability to collect, organize, and evaluate data such as accounting, personnel, or purchasing
- Report writing
- Ability to prepare correspondence and administrative reports
- Utilize problem-solving techniques

- Work independently *and* work well with others
- Plan, organize, and coordinate multiple work assignments

THE HIRING PROCESS
Federal Government

If you want a clerical or administrative assistant position in the federal government, you'll first have to pass what is known as a clerical and administrative support examination (see Chapters 8 and 13, Civil Service Practice Exams 1 & 2, for more information). This test is offered on a walk-in basis at various regional or state test sites around the country. You don't have to apply for this examination, all you need to know is the test schedule and the address of the test site in your area. The best way to find this out is to contact your local Federal employment (USAJOBS) sources. Chapter 1 prsents a complete list of USAJOBS touch screen kiosks and automated phone systems. Chapter 2 provides a list of federal, state, and city websites for job searches and labor information.

If you pass the clerical and administrative support exam with a 70 or higher, you may apply for a position by submitting a copy of the Notice of Results from this test and a completed application to the agency announcing the job vacancy. Contact numbers and addresses are included in the job announcement.

To apply, you'll use either the SF 71 application or the Optional Application for Federal Employment, OF 612. You can get these forms by calling the Office of Personnel Management at 912-757-3000, or by printing out the online application found at *www.usajobs.opm.gov*. (See Chapter 1 for a complete rundown of the federal government's hiring process and a sample OF 612 application.) You may apply for some jobs with a resume; the job announcement will include detailed instructions on the procedures to follow.

After you apply, you'll be ranked on an eligibility list according to your exam results and your application or resume. If your name is selected by the agency, you'll be contacted for an interview.

State and Municipal Government

Procedures for applying to state and local agencies can vary greatly, so it's important that you read job announcements carefully. In general, you'll have to submit an application to the agency that is hiring (keep in mind that some states and cities don't have a central personnel office and individual agencies are in charge of hiring new employees). The job announcement, again, will include instructions on how and where to get an application and where to submit it.

Many, but not all, state and local agencies require applicants to pass a written test that assesses skill areas relevant to the position, and then the agency ranks candidates according to their score on the test. Due to the number of applicants for each job, some agencies, particularly at the local level, are restructuring their selection process to eliminate the use of written tests. Agencies that don't administer a written test often rate candidates on the basis of their job application, KSAs (or E & T), and an oral interview (see below).

If you are required to take some form of written exam, the test will focus on abilities that are relevant to the job. For example, if the position you want is in an accounting office, you'll be tested in some of the following areas:

■ Bookkeeping
■ Business Problems
■ Filing
■ General Accounting Principles
■ Governmental Accounting Procedures
■ Math
■ Office Procedures

For a clerical or administrative assistant job that involves correspondence, composing memos, filing, and answering phones, you'll take a test that assesses the following areas:

■ Filing
■ Grammar
■ Office Knowledge
■ Public Relations
■ Reading
■ Reasoning
■ Spelling
■ Visual Comparison
■ Vocabulary

Skills Tests

To get a clerical or administrative assistant job, you may need some hands-on skills, whether it's in using an adding machine or a word processor, filing, taking dictation, or just typing.

Like the written test, an agency may choose to administer a skills test to an applicant, or require some other form of proof that you meet the necessary skills requirements. This sort of test involves taking a typing or dictation test, an adding machine test, a filing test, or some other test in which you show your prospective employer that you can do the job.

If the agency you apply to doesn't require you to pass a skills test, you may be asked to present documentation of your skills, for example, that you type 35 words a minute or that you are proficient with a 10-key adding machine. This kind of documentation can come from a business college or other private training company.

Agencies may rank candidates on an eligibility list according to their score on a written exam, a skills test, or a combination of the two. As with the federal government, candidates are selected from the eligibility list and scheduled for an interview. Agencies may choose candidates randomly or in rank order.

Oral Interview

If your name is chosen from the eligibility list, you'll attend an interview with personnel from the hiring agency. Most oral interviews consist of structured questions based on job tasks. You may be asked to describe your skills and experience or to comment on how well prepared you are for the job.

If the agency you apply to doesn't use a written exam or skills test, chances are you'll be ranked on an eligibility list according to your score on the oral interview. In this case, you may be required to attend another interview with the hiring agency.

HOW TO BEGIN YOUR JOB SEARCH

The traditional channels for finding out about jobs are through state/city agency personnel offices and federal, state, and city job hotlines. An agency may also advertise positions in the newspaper and post them at public libraries and job placement offices in colleges and universities.

There are several other job sources that you may not have considered but which can expand your horizons in your employment search.

Government Phone Listings

The "blue pages," which are found in your local telephone company's phone book, are an excellent source of information if you need to find out which federal, state, and local government agencies have offices in your area. The blue pages contain comprehensive listings of city government agencies, plus local listings for state and federal agencies, including the Office of Personnel Management (OPM), whose headquarters are in Washington, D.C. Access to federal government job openings is available 24 hours a day by calling the OPM Job Line at 912-757-3000.

A number of agencies at the state and city level of government have their own personnel office, so if you already know which agency you'd like to work for, you can look up the agency by name and find a sub-listing for "personnel." The number you get may be a job hotline with recorded information on current job vacancy announcements, examination dates, and application information; or someone on the other end may be able to give you information on where that agency posts job vacancies and how to apply.

Online Job Resources

America's Job Bank (AJB) is a computerized network that links the 1,800 state employment services offices in the U.S. It offers access to over 1,521,000 jobs—about five percent of which are in government agencies—including entry-level clerical and administrative support positions.

You can find AJB on the World Wide Web (*www.ajb.dni.us/*). You can find AJB links to almost every state by keying in *www.ajb.org/_ _/*, where the state's 2-letter postal abbreviation fills in the blanks. (Delaware, for example is *www.ajb.org/de/*. In addition to the Internet, AJB is accessible via computer systems in high schools, colleges and universities, public libraries, and transition offices on military bases around the world.

Another helpful Internet resource is the U.S. Office of Personnel Management's website, USAJOBS (*www.usajobs.opm.gov/*). This site features a searchable database of current federal job vacancies, application procedures, and related employment information.

Federal Research Service, Inc. is a private company that publishes current federal government job opportunities. You'll have to subscribe either to its online service (*www.fedjobs.com*) or its printed bulletin to find out about these jobs. The online service is updated daily, and the booklet is published biweekly.

State (and some larger city) employment offices are accessible via the Internet. Below is a list of Internet addresses of employment offices *each* state (we've included the phone number for state personnel agencies and, where available, job information lines in case you don't have Internet access). Some of these sites are devoted solely to government job listings; others contain a mix of government and private sector jobs. (Don't scratch private sector employment from your list, particularly if the government job you want requires some previous office experience.) These websites include useful search functions to help you find clerical and administrative support positions in your area, along with hiring procedures, detailed job announcements, salary ranges, and contact numbers. Some of these sites even feature on-line applications!

Alabama

www.dir.state.al.us/es/
www.personnel.state.al.us/
(334) 242-8003

Alaska

www.state.ak.us/local/jobs.html/
Job Information Line (800) 587-0430

Arizona

www.state.az.us/employment.html
www.de.state.az.us
(800) 488-9194
Job Information Line (602) 542-4966

Arkansas

www.state.ar.us/esd/employment.htm
www.arstatejobs.com

www.labor.state.ak.us
(501) 682- 2127

California

www.caljobs.ca.gov
www.spb.ca.gov/index
Job Information Line (916) 653-1502
(800) 758-0398

Colorado

www.ajb.org/co/
(303) 830-3000
(303) 376-6700

Connecticut

www.ctdol.state.ct.us
(860) 566-2501
(860) 344-2044

Delaware

www.vcnet.net
www.state.de.us/spo/weekly.htm
www.delawareworks.com
(302) 856- 5966
(302) 577-8277

Florida

www.floridajobs.org/wps/onestop
http:/jobsdirect.state.fl.us/
(305) 377-5180
Job Information Line (305) 377-5747

Georgia

www.gcic.peachnet.edu/
www.dol.state.ga.us/job_ops.htm
(404) 656-3017

Hawaii
http://hi.jobsearch.org/
(808) 586-8700

Idaho
www.doe.state.id.us
(208) 334-6252
Job Information Line (208) 334-2568

Illinois
www.il.jobsearch.org
www.state.in.us/acin/personnel
(317) 232-3101

Indiana
www.state.in.us
www.ai.org/jobs/jobank.htm
(317) 233-0236

Iowa
www.state.ia.us/jobs
(800) JOB- IOWA
(515) 281-5387

Kansas
www.ink.org/public/kdhr/jobbank.html
www.state.ks.us
(913) 296- 5390

Kentucky
www.state.ky.us/agencies/personnel/jobspage.htm
(502) 955-8272

Louisiana
www.ldol.state.la.us
(504) 568-5812

Maine
www.state.me.us/labor/jsd/jobserv.htm
www.state.me.us
(207) 287-3788

Maryland
www.md.jobsearch.org
www.dop.state.md.us
(410) 767-4715

Massachusetts
www.ma.jobsearch.org
www.magnet.state.ma.us/hrd
(617) 727-3777
Job Information Line
(617) 727-3777 ext. 246

Michigan
www.mdcs.state.mi.us
(313) 256-3690

Minnesota
www.jobsearch.org
www.doer.state.mn.us

Mississippi
Internet address not available
(601) 359-2348

Missouri
www.works.state.mo.us/mw2a.htm
www.state.mo.us/oa/pers/pers.htm

Montana
www.161.7.163.2/
www.isd_server.dli.mt.gov
(406) 441-3200
Job Information Line (406) 447-3222

North Carolina
www.esc.state.nc.us
www.osp.state.nc.us/OSP/jobs
(919) 733-7922

North Dakota
www.state.nd.us/jsnd/job/htm
www.state.nd.us/jsnd/lmi.htm
(701) 328-5000

Nebraska
www.state.ne.us/personnel/per.htm
(402) 471-2075
Job Information Line (402) 471-2200

Nevada
www.state.nv.us/detr/detr.html
(702) 687-4050
Job Information Line (702) 687-4160

New Hampshire
www.nhworks.state.nh.us/
(603) 271-3261

New Jersey
www.nj.job.org
(609) 292-4144

New Mexico
www.nm.jobsearch.org

New York
www.labor.state.ny.us
www.csstate.ny.us
(518) 457-2487
Job Information Line (518) 457-6216

Ohio
www.state.oh.us/obes/
www.state.oh.us/
(216) 466-4026

Oklahoma
www.oesc.state.ok.us/jobnet/default/htm

Oregon
www.emp.state.or.us
(503) 378-8344
Job Information Line (503) 225-2222 ext. 7777

Pennsylvania
www.state.pa.us/jobpost.html
(215) 560-2253

Rhode Island
www.det.ri.us/
(401) 277-3900

South Carolina
www.state.sc.us/jobs
(803) 734-9080
Job Information Line (803) 734-9333

South Dakota
www.state.sd.us/state/executive/dol/dol.htm
(605) 773-3148
Job Information Line (605) 773-3326

Tennessee
www.state.tn.us/employsecurity
www.state.tn.us
(615) 741-4841

Texas
www.twc.state.tx.us/jobs/job
(512) 463-2222

Utah
www.udesb.state.ut.us/
(801) 536-7120
Job Information Line (801) 538-3062

Vermont
www.cit.state.vt.us/det/dethp.htm
(802) 828-3606
Job Information Line (802) 828-3483

Virginia
www.va.jobsearch.org
www.state.va.us/~dtt/menu.htm
(804) 225-2131

Washington
www.wa.gov/dop
(360) 753-5368
Job Information Line (360) 753-5368

Wisconsin
www.dwd.state.wi.us/jobnet/
www.badger.state.wi.us:70/1/agencies/der
(608) 266-1731

West Virginia
www.state.wv.us/bep
(304) 558-5946

Wyoming
www.wyjobs.state.wy.us
(307) 777-7188

PERSONAL SECTION – Entries in BLUE are required fields.

Applicant Name:

Social Security Number:

Mailing Address:

City:

County/Country:

State: Zip Code:

Home Phone:

Business Phone:

SUNCOM Phone:

E-Mail Address:

Date Available (MM/DD/YYYY):

Counties of Interest:

Minimum Acceptable Salary:

SAVE   RESET

HIGH SCHOOL

Name/Location of School: [   ]

Received..............: ○ Diploma ○ None ○ Other (Specify) ...: [   ]

Your Name if different while attending school: [   ]

[SAVE HIGH SCHOOL] [RESET]

COLLEGE, UNIVERSITY OR PROFESSIONAL SCHOOL:
(Transcripts may be required.)

You may enter up to six colleges. [ADD COLLEGE]

JOB-RELATED TRAINING OR COURSE WORK:
(Vocational, Trade, Governmental, Business, Armed Forces, etc.)

You may enter up to ten courses. [ADD COURSE WORK]

LICENSURE, REGISTRATION, CERTIFICATION:
(Examples: Driver License, Teacher Certification, RN, LPN, PE, CPA, etc.)

You may enter up to four licensures. [ADD LICENSURE]

KNOWLEDGE/SKILLS/ABILITIES (KSAs)

List KSAs you possess and believe relevant to the position you seek, such as operating heavy equipment, computer skills, fluency in language(s), etc.

NOTE: Limit text to 5 lines of text

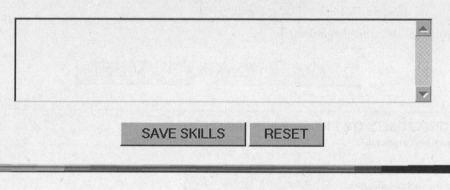

[SAVE SKILLS] [RESET]

EMPLOYMENT SECTION – You may enter up to 20 employment blocks.

Describe your work experience in detail, beginning with your current or most recent job. Include military service (indicate rank) and job-related volunteer work, if applicable. Indicate number of employees supervised. Use a separate block to describe each position or gap in employment. All information in this section must be completed.

Add periods of employment by clicking [ADD EMPLOYMENT]

NOTE: If you have no work experience, please click on "NO WORK EXPERIENCE" to complete the employment section. Your application will be considered incomplete if this section is not entered, and you will not be allowed to apply for any vacancy.

[NO WORK EXPERIENCE]

C·H·A·P·T·E·R 7

FIREFIGHTER

CHAPTER SUMMARY

This chapter describes the duties and demands of being a firefighter, one of the most highly sought after civil service jobs. You'll also learn about selection process and getting hired, from applying for the job to passing the written exam and physical ability test.

escribing firefighters without using the word "hero" would be tough. After all, their ultimate goal is to prevent or relieve human suffering and loss. They regularly put their own lives on the line to save other lives and protect property. Much of their work is physically exhausting, mentally demanding and highly dangerous. When a fire or other emergency strikes, they're on the scene battling flames, smoke, collapsing walls, chemical explosions and numerous other threats.

Behind every heroic moment, of course, are countless hours of preparation. Career firefighters are highly trained professionals. Their services are essential to every community and every stretch of land across this country. If you make this your career choice, rest assured that the need for firefighters is constant and the job prospects are promising. But this is a competitive field. Wherever you apply, you'll need to show that you've got what it takes to meet the demands of the job—and the hiring process.

WHERE THE JOBS ARE

Roughly 300,000 career firefighters are employed nationwide as paid, full-time professionals. So who hires all these career firefighters? Well, if you're in the majority—nine out of 10, according to the Bureau of Labor Statistics (BLS)—you'll be employed by a municipal or county fire department, typically serving a community with a population of 50,000 or more. Not surprisingly, large cities are the largest employers.

Full-time firefighters are also hired by federal and state government agencies to protect government-owned property and special facilities. For example, the U.S. Forest Service, Bureau of Land Management and Park Service offer both year-round and seasonal fire service jobs to protect the country's national parks, forests and other lands.

In the private sector, many large industrial companies have their own firefighting forces, especially companies in the oil, chemical, aircraft, and aerospace industries. Other employers include airports, shipyards, and military bases. Also, a growing number of companies are in the business of providing fire protection services—including on-call or on-site firefighting teams—to other businesses and institutions.

In addition to career firefighters, there are still large numbers of volunteer or "paid-call" reserve firefighters nationwide. These individuals work mostly in rural or small communities and may receive compensation only when they are called to duty.

ON THE JOB

The foremost duty of a firefighter is exactly what the job title says—to fight fires. Whether a fire breaks out at a 2-story home, a 700-room hotel or a 10,000-acre farm, the next sound you'll hear is the familiar wail of those massive red trucks barreling their way to the scene, loaded with firefighters in oversized suits, big heavy boots and odd-shaped hats.

But firefighters today do a lot more than put out fires. Natural disasters, bombing incidents, gas pipe explosions, and hazardous waste spills are just a few of the situations where firefighters often are called on to provide emergency services. Sometimes these circumstances pose the threat of fire. Other times a rescue operation may be the main order of business. Whatever the crisis at hand, something else that firefighters are trained to do is to administer and/or coordinate basic medical care to any injured persons there may be.

Fire departments also provide many non-emergency services. One highly important task is to inspect buildings and facilities for compliance with fire codes and safety regulations. Another is to educate the public about fire prevention and safety procedures. This could include giving presentations to local schools and community groups, or sponsoring campaigns aimed at making people more aware of fire hazards—sort of a local version of Smokey the Bear's "Only you can prevent forest fires" campaign. Firefighters often participate in public education efforts, but building inspection more often is handled by higher-ranked fire service personnel who have had special training.

What the average person may not be aware of is simply how much mental knowledge goes into firefighting. We see them driving the red truck, attaching a hose to a hydrant, dousing flames, busting out windows with a pickax, climbing tall ladders. These activities alone require a high level of technical skill and a great deal of physical stamina and strength. Firefighters also face serious physical risks from being exposed to flames, smoke, fumes and explosive or toxic materials, as well as from walls and buildings caving in or collapsing.

To reduce those risks, it's critical that they stay in top physical condition and master the use of various equipment and tools. But it's equally critical that they have a knowledge bank filled with scientific and technical information about combustible materials, building construction, ventilation systems, sprinkler systems, electrical circuitry, chemical reactions, and a host of other subjects. Firefighters are educated, trained and drilled again and again in each of these critical areas.

Much of this preparation and learning goes on back at the station house. At departments with full-time personnel, on-duty firefighters usually eat, sleep, and make a home away from home at the station. Between sirens, their on-duty time is devoted to practice drills, training, and education programs, equipment maintenance and other routine activities.

Although most rotate between day and night shifts, the length of their tour of duty and their shifts varies from department to department. For example, they may work four days on, then four days off, putting in anywhere from 10- to 16-hour shifts. Or they may work a 24-hour shift, followed by 48 hours off, then the cycle repeats. Whatever the work schedule, it's not the corporate nine-to-five routine.

THE PAYBACK: SALARY AND BENEFITS

As with nearly every job, firefighters earn different salaries depending on where they work and who they work for. The size and location of the department or agency makes a difference. So does a firefighter's level of experience and time on the job.

Salary data reported by the International City Management Association (ICMA) cites $24,100 as the national average salary for full-time, entry-level firefighters, and $33,000 as the average maximum salary when different levels of experience are included. These figures are an average based on all geographical locations and departments of every size.

If you work in a small city, you can expect an annual salary of roughly $19,000 to $28,000. The range can be significantly higher—from $30,000 to $55,000 and above—in large cities. Geographically speaking, salaries tend to be lowest in the southern region of the U.S. and highest out west. The table that follows will give you a sense of a firefighter's starting salary at some representative major cities.

Typical working hours for full-time firefighters range from 42 to 56 hours a week. They are entitled by law to overtime pay, which kicks in at an average of 53

ENTRY-LEVEL FIREFIGHTER SALARIES: AT A GLANCE	
Fire Department	**Salary**
Fresno, CA	$43,601
Los Angeles, CA	$34,500
Buffalo, NY	$32,117
New York, NY	$31,764
Dover, DE	$24,274
San Antonio, TX	$32,925

or more hours a week during a work period. Many departments also offer longevity pay to career firefighters, usually around $1,000 a year. This extra pay generally is separate from any salary increase that comes with a promotion.

Employee benefits packages for firefighters also vary from department to department, but they tend to be substantial. Common benefits include medical, disability, and life insurance; sick leave, vacation, and holiday pay; educational incentives; and a generous pension plan. Departments also supply uniforms and personal equipment you use on the job.

Unions play a large role in negotiating and protecting the salaries and benefits that firefighters earn. Most firefighters in medium to large departments are members of the International Association of Fire Fighters (IAFF), which maintains a national office and local chapters. The IAFF and other professional organizations also work to resolve labor disputes and sponsor governmental legislation on behalf of their members.

HIRING TRENDS

Employment of firefighters is expected to increase 14% to 26% over the next decade, according to the BLS. Some new jobs will be created in suburban communities where populations are on the rise. Other new jobs will come in small communities and rural areas where departments are in transition from a volunteer to a paid force. Employment at large, urban departments will be stable—not producing many new jobs, but holding steady on the large numbers they already employ. Overall, the majority of job openings will come about simply to replace firefighters who retire or leave the job for other reasons.

Firefighting certainly can be called "a steady job." Since fires can happen anywhere and at any time, no department that maintains a paid force is going to go out of business! On the whole, turnover is low and layoffs are rare in this profession. Even when local governments call for budget cuts, communities generally rally to keep or grow the number of firefighters their tax dollars support. For the most part, too, the job market is not subject to seasonal fluctuations. One exception is forestry firefighting, which is mostly seasonal employment and almost exclusively available through state and federal agencies.

Along with job security, you've got other pluses described earlier: relatively high wages, good benefits, a generous pension and the chance to do challenging, exciting and important work. All these pluses add up to steep competition for these jobs. Most fire departments—especially large, urban departments—have many more applicants than they do job openings.

APPLYING FOR THE JOB

Because municipal and county fire departments operate independently, no one set of qualifications and hiring procedures is used by each and every department nationwide. However, though the particulars may vary, certain standards are likely wherever you plan to apply.

In general, previous work experience looks good on the application form. Jobs in construction, mechanics, landscaping, masonry and plumbing are some that demonstrate the physical strength and dexterity needed to be a firefighter. But the basic idea is to show that you have held a responsible job, followed a boss' orders and are a team player. Also, whether it's required or not, departments tend to look favorably on applicants who have attended college. Even better is having taken courses in fire science. Keep in mind how much competition you're apt to have for a firefighting job. Any advantage you have or can give yourself—which includes preparing yourself for the written exam—really can make the difference in getting hired.

THE ELIGIBILITY LIST

Most fire departments, or the city personnel departments that handle the selection process for them, establish a list of eligible candidates; many such lists rank candidates from highest to lowest. How ranks are determined varies from place to place; sometimes the rank is based solely on the written exam score, sometimes on the physical ability test, and sometimes on a combination of factors. The point is, even if you make it through the entire selection process, the likelihood that you will be hired as a firefighter often depends on *the quality of your performance* in one or more parts of the selection process.

BASIC QUALIFICATIONS

The basic qualifications you need in order to even think about becoming a firefighter vary from city to city. You neet to find out what those qualifications are in the agency you want to serve, but some qualifications are pretty standard:

- A minimum age—sometimes 18, more often 20 or 21—and, in some departments, a maximum age, which can range from 30 to 45
- A high school diploma or its equivalent and, increasingly, some college
- A clean criminal record
- Excellent physical and mental health
- A valid driver's license and a satisfactory driving record

Some cities list their firefighter job openings on their city or county websites. See the end of Chapter 2 for state-by-state jobsite listings.

Many jurisdictions, but not all, require that you live in the jurisdiction or nearby. Many fire departments give preference to otherwise qualified veterans over civilians. This may take the form of a policy, sometimes called a "Veteran's Preference" policy, whereby points are automatically added to the written exam. Is this unfair? No. Fire companies are a lot like military units. They follow a strict chain of command, and firefighters on the line work as a team, knowing that their lives are in each other's hands. Military personnel have learned the discipline and teamwork that are vital to firefighting and emergency services. Veterans are simply better qualified than most other people.

Increasingly, fire departments are also giving preference to certified Emergency Medical Technicians (EMTs) or paramedics. As the work of fire departments becomes less involved strictly with fighting fires and more with other kinds of emergency services, many departments require qualified EMTs.

THE EXAM OR POSITION ANNOUNCEMENT

Applying to be a firefighter differs from applying for most other jobs. The differences begin with the exam or position announcement. You rarely see fire department openings advertised in the Help Wanteds. Instead, the city usually starts looking for potential firefighters by means of a special announcement. This announcement will outline the basic qualifications for the position as well as the steps you will have to go through in the selection process. It often tells you some of the duties you will be expected to perform. It may give the date and place of the written exam, or tell you where to pick up an application; or it may go as far as to outline each step of the selection process. Announcements are also found on state and city Internet sites.

THE APPLICATION

Often the first step in the process of becoming firefighter is filling out an application. Sometimes this is a real application, asking about your education, employment experience, personal data, and so on. Sometimes there's just an application to take the written or physical test, with a fuller application coming later. In any case, at some point you will probably be asked some questions you wouldn't expect to see on a regular job application. You might be asked things like whether you've ever gotten any speeding tickets or been in trouble with the law, whether you've used illegal drugs, even whether any relatives work for the city or for the fire department. Your answers to these, as well as the more conventional questions, will serve as the starting point if the department conducts an investigation of your background, so it's important to answer all questions accurately and honestly.

THE WRITTEN EXAM

In most jurisdictions, taking a written exam is the next step in the application process, though in some cases the physical ability test comes first.

The written exam is your first opportunity to show that you have what it takes to be a firefighter. As such, it's extremely important. People who don't pass the written exam don't go any farther in the selection process. Furthermore, the written exam score often figures into applicants' rank on the eligibility list; in some cases, this score by itself determines your rank, while in others it is combined with other scores, such as physical ability or oral board scores. In those places, a person who merely passes the exam with a score of, say, 70, is unlikely to be hired when there are plenty of applicants with scores in the 90s. The exam announcement may specify what your rank will be based on.

What the Written Exam Is Like

Most written exams simply test basic skills and aptitudes: how well you understand what you read, your ability to follow directions, your judgment and reasoning skills, your ability to read and understand maps and floor plans, and sometimes your memory or your math. In this preliminary written exam, *you will not be tested on your knowledge of fire behavior, firefighting procedures, or any other specific body of knowledge.* This test is designed *only* to see if you can read, reason, and do basic math.

In some places, taking the exam involves studying written materials in advance and then answering questions about them on the exam. These written materials generally have to do with fire and firefighting—but all you have to do is study the guide you're given. You're still being tested just on your reading skills and memory, and there are good reasons for this.

Firefighters have to be able to read, understand and act on complex written materials—not only fire law and fire procedures, but also scientific materials about fire, combustible materials, chemicals, and so forth. They have to be able to think clearly and independently, because lives depend on decisions they make in a split second. They have to be able to do enough math to read and understand pressure gauges or estimate the height of a building and the amount of hose needed to reach to the third floor. They have to be able to read maps so they can get to the emergency site quickly and floor plans so that they can find their way to an exit even in a smoke-filled building.

Chapters 8 and 13 of this book will help you sharpen your general test-taking skills and pinpoint areas needing improvement. For extensive practice based on the exam you'll actually take, call Learning-Express at 1-888-551-JOBS and ask about our *Firefighter Exam* guides, which come complete with full practice exams and instructional chapters written by experts for each of the areas you're likely to be tested on.

THE PHYSICAL ABILITY TEST

The physical ability test is the next step in the process for many fire departments; some put this step first. You may have to bring a note from your doctor saying that you are in good enough shape to undertake this test before you will be allowed to participate. The fire department wants to make sure that no one has a heart attack in the middle of the test. This is a clue: expect the test to be tough.

Firefighting is, after all, physically demanding work. Once again, lives depend on whether your strength, stamina, and overall fitness allow you to carry out the necessary tasks during an emergency. If you make it to the academy and later into a fire company, you can expect to continue physical training and exercises throughout your career. In fact, in some cities all firefighters are required to retake the physical ability test every year.

What the Physical Ability Test Is Like

The exact events that make up the physical ability test vary from place to place, but the tasks you have to perform are almost always job-related—they're a lot like the physical tasks you will actually have to perform as a firefighter. Many times the test is set up like an obstacle course, and usually the test is timed, with a cutoff time for passing. Often you have to wear full (heavy) protective gear, including an air pack, throughout these events. Here's an example of the events in a test that you would typically have five to seven minutes to complete:

- Dummy drag
- Hose drag
- Climb stairs
- Climb through tunnel
- Raise and climb ladder
- Jump over wall

You might be given the opportunity to do a walk-through of the course before you actually have to take the test. In the test itself, you would be timed as you went through the events, and you would have to complete the events within a set time to pass. Different departments have different policies on retesting if you fail. Some allow you to retest on the same day after a rest period. Some allow you to come back another time and try again, usually up to a set maximum number of tries. And in some departments, your first try is the only chance you get; if you fail, you're out, at least until the next testing period. Few departments will allow you to retest, if you have already passed, simply to better your time. You can usually find out just what tasks are included in the physical ability test from the exam announcement or related materials.

Many urban fire departments report that the physical ability test is the one step of the process in which the most applicants fail. People come in unprepared, they're simply not strong enough or fast enough to do all the events, while wearing heavy gear, in the time allotted. Female applicants, in particular, have high failure rates on physical ability tests because some of the events require a lot of upper-body strength.

But don't despair. The physical ability test is one area where advance preparation is almost guaranteed to pay off. Many fire departments conduct training sessions for would-be applicants, to help them get up to the required level of fitness. Some allow you to walk through and practice on the course ahead of time. If any of these opportunities are available to you, be sure to use them.

THE BACKGROUND INVESTIGATION

Most fire departments conduct background investigations of applicants who pass the written and physical tests. Firefighters have to be honest, upright citizens who can get along with both their company and the people they serve, so the fire department conducts a background investigation to make sure you're the right kind of person. You may not even know such an investigation is going on—until someone at the oral interview asks you why you wrote on your application that you never used drugs when your high school friends all say you regularly smoked marijuana on weekends.

The rigorousness with which your background will be checked depends on the policies of your department. Some conduct a fairly superficial check, calling your former employers and schools simply to verify that you were there when you say you were there and didn't cause any problems during that time.

Other departments will investigate you in a great deal more depth, asking their contacts how long and how well they knew you and what kind of person they found you to be. Did you meet your obligations? How did you deal with problems? Did they find you to be an honest person? Do they know of anything that might affect your fitness to be a firefighter? The references you provided will lead the investigator to other people who knew you, and when the investigator is finished, he or she will have a pretty complete picture of what kind of person you are.

A few fire departments include a polygraph, or "lie detector," test as part of the background investigation. As long as you've been honest in what you've said when your stress reactions weren't being monitored by a polygraph machine, a lie detector test is nothing to worry about.

ORAL INTERVIEWS AND BOARDS

The selection process in your fire department is likely to include one or more oral interviews. There may be an individual interview with the chief or deputy chief, or there may be an oral board, in which you would meet with several people. Or you may face both. Whether it's an individual interview or an oral board, the interviewers are interested in your interpersonal skills—how well you communicate *with them*—as well as in your qualifications to be a firefighter.

What the Oral Interview Is Like

In some cities, applicants who get this far in the process meet with the chief or deputy chief, who may conduct something like a typical job interview. The chief or deputy chief might describe in detail what the job is like, ask you how well you think you can do a job like that, and ask you why you want to be a firefighter in the first place. In the process, the chief will also be assessing your interpersonal skills, whether you seem honest and (relatively) comfortable in talking to him or her. You may also be asked questions about your background and experience.

This interview can be a make-or-break part of the process, with the chief turning thumbs up or down to your candidacy, or the chief may rank you against other applicants, in which case the chief's assessment of you is likely to figure into your place on the eligibility list.

What the Oral Board Is Like

The oral board typically assesses such qualities as interpersonal skills, communication skills, judgment and decision-making abilities, respect for diversity, and adaptability. The board itself consists of two to five people, who may be firefighters or civilian personnel or interview specialists. There's usually some variety in the makeup of the board: officers of various ranks and/or civilians from the personnel department or from the community.

The way the interview is conducted depends on the practices of the individual department. You may be asked a few questions similar to those you would be asked at a normal employment interview: Why do you want to be a firefighter? What qualities do you have that would make you good at this job? You may be asked questions about your background, especially if your application or background investigation raised any questions in the board members' minds.

Instead of or in addition to such questions, you may be presented with hypothetical situations that you will be asked to respond to. A board member may say something like this: "After a dwelling fire is under control, you're walking through the building checking its structural soundness. When you walk into the bedroom, you see a fellow firefighter sticking a jewelry box into the pocket of his coat. What would you do?" You would then have to come up with an appropriate response to this situation.

THE PSYCHOLOGICAL EVALUATION

Some cities, though not all, include a psychological evaluation as part of the firefighter selection process. The fire department wants to make sure that you are emotionally and mentally stable before putting you in a high-stress job in which you have to interact with peers, superiors, and the public. Don't worry, though; the psychological evaluation is not designed to uncover your deep dark secrets. Its only purpose is to make sure you have the mental and emotional health to do the job.

THE MEDICAL EXAMINATION

Before passage of the Americans With Disabilities Act (ADA), many fire departments conducted a medical examination early in the process, before the physical ability test. Now, the ADA says it's illegal to do any exam-inations or ask any questions that could reveal an applicant's disability until after a conditional offer of employment has been made. That means that in most jurisdictions you will get such a conditional offer before you are asked to submit to a medical exam.

You should know, however, that almost any disability is grounds for disqualification as a firefighter, even under the protections provided by ADA. Firefighting requires a high level of physical and mental fitness, and a host of disabilities that would not prevent a candidate from doing some other job would prevent a firefighter from fulfilling essential job functions. Even, for instance, a skin condition that requires a man to wear facial hair would disqualify that man from being a firefighter, because facial hair interferes with proper operation of the breathing apparatus.

Note, however, that a test for use of illegal drugs *can* be administered before a conditional offer of employment. Because firefighters have to be in tiptop physical shape, and because they are in a position of public trust, the fire department expects you to be drug-free. You may have to undergo drug testing periodically throughout your career as a firefighter.

STARTING OUT AND MOVING UP

Once you're hired as a firefighter, your department will make sure you get all the training you need to do the job. Many large, urban departments run their own on-site formal training programs or fire academy. Smaller departments may send new recruits to a fire academy in their region. Some stick mostly to on-the-job training supervised by experienced fire service personnel.

Academy training generally lasts several weeks, with part of the time spent on classroom instruction and part on practical training. You'll cover areas such as firefighting and prevention techniques, hazardous and combustible materials, local building codes and emergency medical procedures. You'll also learn how to use various kinds of firefighting and rescue equipment.

As you continue on the job, you'll regularly receive training to learn new skills and keep you up to date on the latest equipment and firefighting techniques. This ongoing training is aimed at improving your overall performance as a firefighter. If, down the road, you want to move up the ranks, you'll have to meet a different set of training, education and testing requirements.

For any rank promotion, factors such as your on-the-job performance, a recommendation from your supervisor, and how long you've been on the job are taken into account. But there's more. You'll also need to pass a written exam for most promotions, for example, to become a driver operator, lieutenant, captain, battalion chief, assistant chief, deputy chief or chief. You'll probably have to "show your stuff" in a physical performance test where you demonstrate techniques or use equipment relative to the position you want. You might have to become certified in specialized areas, usually through a combination of skills training and knowledge-based education programs, followed by a written certification exam.

Higher education is another requirement you may face for promotion. If you haven't done so already, you may need to take certain college classes or earn a college degree. For example, many departments require an associate's degree to become a lieutenant or captain. Generally a master's degree in public administration, business administration or a related field is required for any rank at or above battalion chief. Advanced education and training programs are available through a variety of sources, including community colleges and universities, professional organizations and state-sponsored fire academies.

Job Tip

Visit the LearningExpress web site at *www.LearnX.com* to learn more about our customized *Firefighter Exam* guides, and to find out about local firefighter exam dates for cities across the country. To order books directly, call us toll-free at 1-888-551-JOBS.

S·E·C·T·I·O·N 3

PASSING A CIVIL SERVICE EXAM

Your first step in getting most civil service jobs is passing an exam. Civil service exams vary from one position to another and from one jurisdiction (federal, state, or local) to another, but most exams include at least some questions about how well you understand what you read. Many also include some math and some way of testing how well you can write, usually with questions on grammar, vocabulary, or spelling. So this section is your first step toward doing well on your civil service exam.

Take the first practice exam in Chapter 8 to see how you would do on questions on reading comprehension, grammar, math, and vocabulary and spelling. Then study Chapters 9–12, which give you the information and practice you need to do well in these important areas. Then take the second practice exam in Chapter 13 to see how much you've improved. Once you've solidified these vital basic skills, you'll be ready to move on to preparing for the other, more specific kinds of questions that may appear on a given civil service exam.

C·H·A·P·T·E·R 8

CIVIL SERVICE EXAM 1

CHAPTER SUMMARY

This is the first of two practice exams in this book that test the basic skills required for almost any civil service exam. Use this test to evaluate your skills in reading, writing, and math, and to identify areas to focus on in the instructional chapters ahead.

ivil service exams vary widely depending both on the kind of job you're applying for and on which agency—city, state, or federal—you're applying to. But every exam tests your reading skill, at least indirectly. After all, you can't do well on the exam if you can't read and understand it. And many exams, for all different kinds of jobs, also test your writing skill—whether you recognize a correctly written sentence, use a varied vocabulary, and spell words correctly. Some exams also test your problem-solving skills using numbers; that is, they include math questions.

So the practice exam that follows tests the basic skills you're likely to encounter on almost any civil service exam: 30 questions on reading comprehension, 20 questions on grammar, 20 questions on math, and 30 questions on vocabulary and spelling, for a total of 100 questions.

Normally you would have about two hours to take an exam like this, but for now don't worry about timing; just take the test in as relaxed a manner as you can. The answer sheet you should use is on the next page. After the exam is an answer key, with an explanation of each correct answer, followed by a section on scoring your exam.

1.	ⓐ	ⓑ	ⓒ	ⓓ	35.	ⓐ	ⓑ	ⓒ	ⓓ	69.	ⓐ	ⓑ	ⓒ	ⓓ
2.	ⓐ	ⓑ	ⓒ	ⓓ	36.	ⓐ	ⓑ	ⓒ	ⓓ	70.	ⓐ	ⓑ	ⓒ	ⓓ
3.	ⓐ	ⓑ	ⓒ	ⓓ	37.	ⓐ	ⓑ	ⓒ	ⓓ	71.	ⓐ	ⓑ	ⓒ	ⓓ
4.	ⓐ	ⓑ	ⓒ	ⓓ	38.	ⓐ	ⓑ	ⓒ	ⓓ	72.	ⓐ	ⓑ	ⓒ	ⓓ
5.	ⓐ	ⓑ	ⓒ	ⓓ	39.	ⓐ	ⓑ	ⓒ	ⓓ	73.	ⓐ	ⓑ	ⓒ	ⓓ
6.	ⓐ	ⓑ	ⓒ	ⓓ	40.	ⓐ	ⓑ	ⓒ	ⓓ	74.	ⓐ	ⓑ	ⓒ	ⓓ
7.	ⓐ	ⓑ	ⓒ	ⓓ	41.	ⓐ	ⓑ	ⓒ	ⓓ	75.	ⓐ	ⓑ	ⓒ	ⓓ
8.	ⓐ	ⓑ	ⓒ	ⓓ	42.	ⓐ	ⓑ	ⓒ	ⓓ	76.	ⓐ	ⓑ	ⓒ	ⓓ
9.	ⓐ	ⓑ	ⓒ	ⓓ	43.	ⓐ	ⓑ	ⓒ	ⓓ	77.	ⓐ	ⓑ	ⓒ	ⓓ
10.	ⓐ	ⓑ	ⓒ	ⓓ	44.	ⓐ	ⓑ	ⓒ	ⓓ	78.	ⓐ	ⓑ	ⓒ	ⓓ
11.	ⓐ	ⓑ	ⓒ	ⓓ	45.	ⓐ	ⓑ	ⓒ	ⓓ	79.	ⓐ	ⓑ	ⓒ	ⓓ
12.	ⓐ	ⓑ	ⓒ	ⓓ	46.	ⓐ	ⓑ	ⓒ	ⓓ	80.	ⓐ	ⓑ	ⓒ	ⓓ
13.	ⓐ	ⓑ	ⓒ	ⓓ	47.	ⓐ	ⓑ	ⓒ	ⓓ	81.	ⓐ	ⓑ	ⓒ	ⓓ
14.	ⓐ	ⓑ	ⓒ	ⓓ	48.	ⓐ	ⓑ	ⓒ	ⓓ	82.	ⓐ	ⓑ	ⓒ	ⓓ
15.	ⓐ	ⓑ	ⓒ	ⓓ	49.	ⓐ	ⓑ	ⓒ	ⓓ	83.	ⓐ	ⓑ	ⓒ	ⓓ
16.	ⓐ	ⓑ	ⓒ	ⓓ	50.	ⓐ	ⓑ	ⓒ	ⓓ	84.	ⓐ	ⓑ	ⓒ	ⓓ
17.	ⓐ	ⓑ	ⓒ	ⓓ	51.	ⓐ	ⓑ	ⓒ	ⓓ	85.	ⓐ	ⓑ	ⓒ	ⓓ
18.	ⓐ	ⓑ	ⓒ	ⓓ	52.	ⓐ	ⓑ	ⓒ	ⓓ	86.	ⓐ	ⓑ	ⓒ	ⓓ
19.	ⓐ	ⓑ	ⓒ	ⓓ	53.	ⓐ	ⓑ	ⓒ	ⓓ	87.	ⓐ	ⓑ	ⓒ	ⓓ
20.	ⓐ	ⓑ	ⓒ	ⓓ	54.	ⓐ	ⓑ	ⓒ	ⓓ	88.	ⓐ	ⓑ	ⓒ	ⓓ
21.	ⓐ	ⓑ	ⓒ	ⓓ	55.	ⓐ	ⓑ	ⓒ	ⓓ	89.	ⓐ	ⓑ	ⓒ	ⓓ
22.	ⓐ	ⓑ	ⓒ	ⓓ	56.	ⓐ	ⓑ	ⓒ	ⓓ	90.	ⓐ	ⓑ	ⓒ	ⓓ
23.	ⓐ	ⓑ	ⓒ	ⓓ	57.	ⓐ	ⓑ	ⓒ	ⓓ	91.	ⓐ	ⓑ	ⓒ	ⓓ
24.	ⓐ	ⓑ	ⓒ	ⓓ	58.	ⓐ	ⓑ	ⓒ	ⓓ	92.	ⓐ	ⓑ	ⓒ	ⓓ
25.	ⓐ	ⓑ	ⓒ	ⓓ	59.	ⓐ	ⓑ	ⓒ	ⓓ	93.	ⓐ	ⓑ	ⓒ	ⓓ
26.	ⓐ	ⓑ	ⓒ	ⓓ	60.	ⓐ	ⓑ	ⓒ	ⓓ	94.	ⓐ	ⓑ	ⓒ	ⓓ
27.	ⓐ	ⓑ	ⓒ	ⓓ	61.	ⓐ	ⓑ	ⓒ	ⓓ	95.	ⓐ	ⓑ	ⓒ	ⓓ
28.	ⓐ	ⓑ	ⓒ	ⓓ	62.	ⓐ	ⓑ	ⓒ	ⓓ	96.	ⓐ	ⓑ	ⓒ	ⓓ
29.	ⓐ	ⓑ	ⓒ	ⓓ	63.	ⓐ	ⓑ	ⓒ	ⓓ	97.	ⓐ	ⓑ	ⓒ	ⓓ
30.	ⓐ	ⓑ	ⓒ	ⓓ	64.	ⓐ	ⓑ	ⓒ	ⓓ	98.	ⓐ	ⓑ	ⓒ	ⓓ
31.	ⓐ	ⓑ	ⓒ	ⓓ	65.	ⓐ	ⓑ	ⓒ	ⓓ	99.	ⓐ	ⓑ	ⓒ	ⓓ
32.	ⓐ	ⓑ	ⓒ	ⓓ	66.	ⓐ	ⓑ	ⓒ	ⓓ	100.	ⓐ	ⓑ	ⓒ	ⓓ
33.	ⓐ	ⓑ	ⓒ	ⓓ	67.	ⓐ	ⓑ	ⓒ	ⓓ					
34.	ⓐ	ⓑ	ⓒ	ⓓ	68.	ⓐ	ⓑ	ⓒ	ⓓ					

CIVIL SERVICE EXAM 1

PART ONE: READING COMPREHENSION

Answer questions 1–6 on the basis of the following passage.

Greyhound racing is the sixth most popular spectator sport in the United States. Over the last decade a growing number of racers have been adopted to live out their retirement as household pets, once their racing career is over.

Many people hesitate to adopt a retired racing greyhound because they think only very old dogs are available. Actually, even champion racers only work until they are about three-and-a-half years old. Since greyhounds usually live to be 12–15 years old, their retirement is much longer than their racing careers. However, because greyhounds are raised with a specific "job" in mind, they are still ready to go through their puppyhood after they retire. So when you adopt a retired racing greyhound, you need to teach it how to play, and even what treats are! But your new pet will usually be housebroken in a matter of days.

People worry that a greyhound will be more nervous and active than other breeds and will need a large space to run. These are false impressions. Greyhounds have naturally sweet, mild dispositions, and while they love to run, they are sprinters rather than distance runners and are sufficiently exercised with a few laps around a fenced-in backyard everyday.

Greyhounds do not make good watchdogs, but they are very good with children, get along well with other dogs (and usually cats as well), and are very affectionate and loyal. A retired racing greyhound is a wonderful pet for almost anyone.

1. The purpose of this passage is to
   a. advertise veterinarian services
   b. explain the popularity of greyhound racing
   c. encourage people to adopt retired racing greyhounds
   d. teach people how to housebreak a puppy

2. According to the passage, adopting a greyhound is a good idea for people who
   a. do not have children
   b. live in apartments
   c. do not usually like dogs
   d. already have another dog or a cat

3. Which of the following is implied by the passage?
   a. More and more retired racing greyhounds are being adopted every day.
   b. Greyhounds sleep much more than most dogs.
   c. People should adopt greyhounds so they can stop racing.
   d. People who own pet rabbits should not adopt greyhounds.

4. One drawback of adopting a greyhound is that
   a. greyhounds are not good watch dogs
   b. greyhounds are very old when they retire from racing
   c. greyhounds are very competitive
   d. greyhounds need lots of room to run

5. This passage is most like an advertisement because it
   a. uses statistics to prove a point
   b. is distributed in a veterinarian's office
   c. says nothing negative about greyhounds
   d. encourages people to do something

6. According to the passage, a retired racing grey-hound available for adoption will most likely be
a. happy to be retiring
b. easily housebroken
c. a champion
d. high-strung

Answer questions 7–12 on the basis of the following passage.

On February 3, 1956, Autherine Lucy became the first African-American student to attend the University of Alabama, although the dean of women refused to allow Autherine to live in a university dormitory. White students rioted in protest of her admission, and the federal government had to assume command of the Alabama National Guard in order to protect her. Nonetheless, on her first day in class, Autherine bravely took a seat in the front row. She remembers being surprised that the professor of the class appeared not to notice she was even in class. Later she would appreciate his seeming indifference, as he was one of only a few professors to speak out in favor of her right to attend the university.

For protection, Autherine was taken in and out of classroom buildings by the back door and driven from class to class by an assistant to the president of the university. The students continued to riot, and one day the windshield of the car she was in was broken. University officials suspended her, saying it was for her own safety. When her attorney issued a statement in her name protesting her suspension, the university used it as grounds for expelling her for insubordination. Although she never finished her education at the University of Alabama, Autherine Lucy's courage was an inspiration to African-American students who followed in her footsteps and desegregated universities all over the United States.

7. This passage is most likely from a book called
a. *20th Century United States History*
b. *A Collection of Favorite Children's Stories*
c. *A History of the Civil War*
d. *How to Choose the College That Is Right for You*

8. According to the passage, Autherine Lucy
a. lived in a dormitory
b. sat in the front row of her class
c. became a lawyer
d. majored in history

9. Which of the following best describes Autherine Lucy?
a. quiet and shy
b. courageous and determined
c. clever and amusing
d. overly dramatic

10. Autherine Lucy expected to
a. stand out from the other students
b. have the support of the university faculty
c. join a sorority
d. be called on in class

11. Autherine Lucy never graduated from the University of Alabama because she
a. moved to another state
b. transferred to another university
c. dropped out due to pressure from other students
d. was expelled for insubordination

12. According to the passage, which of the following is true?
a. The Alabama National Guard is normally under the command of the U.S. Army.
b. In 1956, the only segregated university in the United States was in Alabama.

c. Autherine Lucy was escorted to and from class by an assistant to the president of the University of Alabama.

d. White students at the University of Alabama were pleased that Autherine Lucy was a student there.

Answer questions 13–17 on the basis of the following passage.

Following a recent series of arson fires in public-housing buildings, the mayor of a large U.S. city has decided to expand the city's Community Patrol, made up of 18- to 21-year-olds, to about 400 people. The Community Patrol is an important part of the city's efforts to at least reduce the number of these crimes.

In addition to the expanded patrol, the city also plans to reduce the seriousness of these fires, which are most often started in stairwells, by stripping the paint from the stairwell walls. Fed by the thick layers of oil-based paint, these arson fires race up the stairwells at an alarming speed.

Although the city attempted to control the speed of these fires by covering walls with a flame retardant, it is now clear that the retardant failed to work in almost all cases. In the most recent fire, the flames raced up ten stories after the old paint under the newly applied fire retardant ignited. Because the retardant failed to stop the flames, the city decided to stop applying it and will now strip the stairwells down to the bare walls.

13. One of the main points of the passage is that flame retardants
   a. reduce the number of arson fires in large cities
   b. are being stripped from walls by the Community Patrol
   c. have not prevented stairwell fires from spreading

d. have increased the speed of flames in stairwell fires

14. The mayor expanded the size of the Community Patrol in an effort to
   a. arrest and convict the city's arsonists
   b. increase jobs for 18- to 21-year-olds
   c. apply flame retardants in public-housing buildings
   d. prevent some of the stairwell fires from occurring

15. The city's *most recent* decision in an attempt to reduce the seriousness of stairwell fires is to
   a. remove all paint and retardants from stairwell walls
   b. increase the age range of community-patrol members
   c. develop a new flame-retardant material
   d. apply a non-oil-based paint to stairwell walls

16. The passage indicates stairwell fires spread extremely rapidly because
   a. the flames are fed by the oil-based paint on the walls
   b. the stairwells have no ventilation from the outdoors
   c. arsonists set the fires in several locations at once
   d. the stairwell walls are old and often bare

17. The city has decided to stop using flame retardants because the retardants
   a. send toxic fumes and gases into the buildings
   b. have failed to control the speed of stairwell fires
   c. are thick and have a flammable oil base
   d. increase the speed at which flames travel up stairs

Answer questions 18–20 on the basis of the following passage.

Detectives who routinely investigate violent crimes can't help but become somewhat jaded. Paradoxically, the victims and witnesses with whom they work closely are often in a highly vulnerable and emotional state. The emotional fallout from a sexual assault, for example, can be complex and long lasting. Detectives must be trained to handle people in emotional distress and must be sensitive to the fact that for the victim the crime is not routine. At the same time, detectives must recognize the limits of their role and resist the temptation to act as therapists or social workers, instead referring victims to the proper agencies.

18. What is the main idea of the passage?
   a. Detectives who investigate violent crime must not become emotionally hardened by the experience.
   b. Victims of violent crime should be referred to therapists and social workers.
   c. Detectives should be sensitive to the emotional state of victims of violent crime.
   d. Detectives should be particularly careful in dealing with victims of sexual assault.

19. According to the passage, what is "paradoxical" about the detective's relationship to the victim?
   a. Detectives know less about the experience of violent crime than do victims.
   b. What for the detective is routine is a unique and profound experience for the victim.
   c. Detectives must be sensitive to victims' needs but can't be social workers or psychologists.
   d. Not only must detectives solve crimes, but they must also handle the victims with care.

20. Which of the following is NOT advocated by the passage for detectives who investigate violent crimes?
   a. They should refer victims to appropriate support services.
   b. They should be aware of the psychological consequences of being victimized.
   c. They should not become jaded.
   d. They should not become too personally involved with victims' problems.

To answer questions 21–23, read the following passage and choose the word or phrase that best fits in each numbered blank.

Hand-rearing wounded or orphaned creatures requires skill. In the case of a baby bird, 21) _____, you must imitate as closely as possible the parents' methods of feeding. 22) _____, hold the beak open using thumb and forefinger. 23) _____ introduce food (a mixture of hard-boiled egg and finely ground raw meat) into the beak with tweezers or an eyedropper.

21. a. however
   b. meanwhile
   c. for example
   d. in contrast

22. a. In addition
   b. First
   c. Likewise
   d. Nonetheless

23. a. Thus
   b. Hence
   c. Meanwhile
   d. Then

Answer questions 24–27 on the basis of the following passage.

Heat reactions usually occur when large amounts of water and/or salt are lost through excessive sweating following strenuous exercise. When the body becomes overheated and cannot eliminate this excess heat, heat exhaustion and heat stroke are possible.

Heat exhaustion is generally characterized by clammy skin, fatigue, nausea, dizziness, profuse perspiration, and sometimes fainting, resulting from an inadequate intake of water and the loss of fluids. First aid treatment for this condition includes having the victim lie down, raising the feet 8–12 inches, applying cool, wet cloths to the skin, and giving the victim sips of salt water (1 teaspoon per glass, half a glass every 15 minutes), over the period of an hour.

Heat stroke is much more serious; it is an immediate life-threatening situation. The characteristics of heat stroke are a high body temperature (which may reach 106°F or more); a rapid pulse; hot, dry skin; and a blocked sweating mechanism. Victims of this condition may be unconscious, and first aid measures should be directed at cooling the body quickly. The victim should be placed in a tub of cold water or repeatedly sponged with cool water until his or her temperature is lowered sufficiently. Fans or air conditioners will also help with the cooling process. Care should be taken, however, not to overly chill the victim once the temperature is below 102°F.

24. The most immediate concern of a person tending a victim of heat stroke should be to
    a. get salt into the victim's body
    b. raise the victim's feet
    c. lower the victim's pulse
    d. lower the victim's temperature

25. Which of the following is a symptom of heat exhaustion?
    a. unconsciousness
    b. profuse sweating
    c. hot, dry skin
    d. a weak pulse

26. Heat stroke is more serious than heat exhaustion because heat stroke victims
    a. have no salt in their bodies
    b. cannot take in water
    c. have frequent fainting spells
    d. do not sweat

27. Symptoms such as nausea and dizziness in a heat exhaustion victim indicate that the person most likely needs to
    a. be given more salt water
    b. be immediately taken to a hospital
    c. be immersed in a tub of water
    d. sweat more

Answer questions 28–30 on the basis of the following passage.

Beginning next month, the Sanitation Department will institute a program intended to remove the graffiti from sanitation trucks. Any truck that finishes its assigned route before the end of the workers' shift will return to the sanitation lot where supervisors will provide materials for workers to use in cleaning the trucks. Because the length of time it takes to complete different routes varies, trucks will no longer be assigned to a specific route but will be rotated among the routes. Therefore, workers should no longer leave personal items in the trucks, as they will not necessarily be using the same truck each day as they did in the past.

28. According to the passage, the removal of graffiti from sanitation trucks will be done by
  a. sanitation supervisors
  b. sanitation workers
  c. custodial staff
  d. workers who created the graffiti

29. According to the passage, which of the following is true of sanitation routes?
  a. They vary in the amount of time they take to complete.
  b. They are assigned according to the amount of graffiti on the truck in question.
  c. They are all of equal length, though some may take longer to drive than others.
  d. They take longer to complete at certain times of the year.

30. According to the passage, prior to instituting the graffiti clean-up program, sanitation workers
  a. were not responsible for the condition of the trucks they drove
  b. had to re-paint the trucks at regular intervals to get rid of graffiti
  c. usually drove the same truck each work day
  d. were not allowed to leave personal belongings in the trucks

PART TWO: GRAMMAR

Answer questions 31–35 by choosing the word or phrase that best completes the sentence.

31. On February 27, the City Fire Department responded to a blaze that _____ at the Icarus Publishing Co. warehouse.
  a. breaks out
  b. will break out
  c. had broken out
  d. is breaking out

32. On November 4,. suspects Gary Talerino and Jennifer O'Brien were arrested on a charge of vandalism that _____ at the local high school.
  a. occurs
  b. will occur
  c. is occurring
  d. occurred

33. In many popular movies today, the heroes are _____ armed than the villains.
  a. more heavily
  b. more heavy
  c. heavier
  d. more heavier

34. That fine circus elephant now belongs to my sister and _____.
  a. I
  b. me
  c. mine
  d. myself

35. The person _____ made these delicious candied figs has my vote.
  a. that
  b. whom
  c. who
  d. whose

Answer questions 36–37 by choosing the sentence that best combines the underlined sentences into one.

36. Maya is an intelligent woman.
Maya cannot read or write.
   a. Maya cannot read or write, while she is an intelligent woman.
   b. Maya cannot read or write and is an intelligent woman.
   c. Although Maya cannot read or write, she is an intelligent woman.
   d. Being an intelligent woman, Maya cannot read or write.

37. Bernice and I do not like kumquats.
They have a strange taste.
   a. Bernice and I do not like kumquats whereas they have a strange taste.
   b. Bernice and I do not like kumquats; consequently, they have a strange taste.
   c. Bernice and I do not like kumquats because they have a strange taste.
   d. Bernice and I do not like kumquats; however, they have a strange taste.

Answer questions 38–44 by choosing the sentences that use verbs correctly.

38. a. Recession, as well as budget cuts, is hard on the ordinary citizen.
   b. Recession and budget cuts is hard on the ordinary citizen.
   c. Recession, as well as budget cuts, are hard on the ordinary citizen.
   d. Budget cuts, as well as the recession, is hard on the ordinary citizen.

39. a. Jury members become impatient with both prosecution and defense when they were sequestered for months.
   b. When jury members are sequestered for months, they are becoming impatient with both prosecution and defense.
   c. Jury members became impatient with both prosecution and defense when they are sequestered for months.
   d. When jury members are sequestered for months, they become impatient with both prosecution and defense.

40. a. All the children got out their rugs and took a nap.
   b. All the children have gotten out their rugs and took a nap.
   c. All the children got out their rugs and have taken a nap.
   d. All the children gotten out their rugs and taken a nap.

41. a. At first I was liking the sound of the wind, but later it got on my nerves.
   b. At first I liked the sound of the wind, but later it has gotten on my nerves.
   c. At first I like the sound of the wind, but later it got on my nerves.
   d. At first I liked the sound of the wind, but later it got on my nerves.

42. a. I became ill from eaten too many fried clams.
   b. I became ill from eating too many fried clams.
   c. I ate too many fried clams and becoming ill.
   d. I ate too many fried clams and become ill.

43. a. When we arrive in Singapore, it is raining.
b. When we arrived in Singapore, it were raining.
c. When we arrived in Singapore, it will be raining.
d. When we arrive in Singapore, it was raining.

44. a. They finished cleaning up, left the building, and return home.
b. They finished cleaning up, left the building, and returns home.
c. They finished cleaning up, left the building, and returned home.
d. They finished cleaning up, left the building, and returning home.

Answer questions 45–50 by choosing the sentences that are correctly written.

45. a. Searching for evidence, police officers, must be mindful of the Fourth Amendment.
b. Searching for evidence. Police officers must be mindful of the Fourth Amendment.
c. When searching for evidence. Police officers, must be mindful of the Fourth Amendment.
d. When searching for evidence, police officers must be mindful of the Fourth Amendment.

46. a. Of all the dogs in the K-9 Corps, Zelda is the most bravest.
b. Of all the dogs in the K-9 Corps, Zelda is the bravest.
c. Of all the dogs in the K-9 Corps, Zelda is the braver.
d. Of all the dogs in the K-9 Corps, Zelda is the more brave.

47. a. When her workday is over, Doctor Beasley likes to watch TV, preferring sitcoms to hospital shows.
b. When her workday is over. Doctor Beasley likes to watch TV, preferring sitcoms to hospital shows.
c. When her workday is over, Doctor Beasley likes to watch TV. Preferring sitcoms to hospital shows.
d. When her workday is over, Doctor Beasley likes to watch TV, preferring sitcoms. To hospital shows.

48. a. All day the exhausted volunteers had struggled through snake-ridden underbrush. In search of the missing teenagers, who still had not been found.
b. All day the exhausted volunteers had struggled through snake-ridden underbrush in search of the missing teenagers, who still had not been found.
c. All day the exhausted volunteers had struggled through snake-ridden underbrush in search of the missing teenagers. Who still had not been found.
d. All day the exhausted volunteers had struggled through snake-ridden underbrush. In search of the missing teenagers. Who still had not been found.

49. a. My roommate Rosie and I, we did not like each other at first, but now we get along fine.
b. My roommate Rosie and I did not like each other at first, but now her and I get along fine.
c. My roommate Rosie and me did not like each other at first, but now she and I get along fine.
d. My roommate Rosie and I did not like each other at first, but now we get along fine.

50. a. The TV show *Colombo* is said to have been inspired in part of the classic Russian novel, *Crime and Punishment.*
   b. The TV show *Colombo* is said to have been inspired in part by the classic Russian novel, *Crime and Punishment.*
   c. The TV show *Colombo* is said to have been inspired in part off of the classic Russian novel, *Crime and Punishment*
   d. The TV show *Colombo* is said to have been inspired in part from the classic Russian novel, *Crime and Punishment.*

PART THREE: MATHEMATICS

51. What is another way to express 20,706?
   a. 200 + 70 + 6
   b. 2000 + 700 + 6
   c. 20,000 + 70 + 6
   d. 20,000 + 700 + 6

52. If a car travels at the speed of 62 mph for 15 minutes, how far will it travel? (Distance = Rate × Time)
   a. 9.3 miles
   b. 15.5 miles
   c. 16 miles
   d. 24.8 miles

53. Fire pumper truck A pumps water at a rate of 500 gallons per minute. Fire pumper truck B pumps at a rate of 425 gallons per minute. If both trucks begin pumping at the same time, how many more gallons of water will truck A pump in 12 minutes than will truck B?
   a. 75
   b. 600
   c. 900
   d. 1,500

54. The cost of a list of supplies for an insurance office is as follows: $19.98 for printer ribbons; $52.20 for paper; $12.64 for ball-point pens; and $7.79 for staples. What is the total cost of the supplies?
   a. $92.61
   b. $91.30
   c. $93.60
   d. $93.61

55. Nationwide, in one year there were about 21,500 residential fires associated with furniture. Of these, 11,350 were caused by smoking materials. About what percent of the residential fires were smoking related?
   a. 47%
   b. 49%
   c. 51%
   d. 53%

56. A firefighter checks the gauge on a cylinder that normally contains 45 cubic feet of air and finds that the cylinder has only 10 cubic feet of air. The gauge indicates that the cylinder is
   a. $\frac{1}{4}$ full
   b. $\frac{2}{9}$ full
   c. $\frac{1}{3}$ full
   d. $\frac{4}{5}$ full

57. A gardener on a large estate determines that the length of garden hose needed to reach from the water spigot to a particular patch of prize-winning roses is 175 feet. If the available garden hoses are 45 feet long, how many sections of hose, when connected together, will it take to reach the roses?
   a. 4
   b. 2
   c. 5
   d. 3

58. A small-town emergency room admits a patient on August 3 at 10:42 p.m. and another patient at 1:19 a.m. on August 4. How much time has elapsed between admissions?
a. 1 hour 37 minutes
b. 2 hours 23 minutes
c. 2 hours 37 minutes
d. 3 hours 23 minutes

Use the information in the following passage to answer questions 59–61.

The cost of movie theater tickets is $7.50 for adults and $5 for children ages 12 and under. On Saturday and Sunday afternoons until 4:00 p.m., there is a matinee price: $5.50 for adults and $3 for children ages 12 and under. Special group discounts are available for groups of 30 or more people.

59. Which of these can be determined from the information given in the passage?
a. how much it will cost a family of 4 to buy movie theater tickets on Saturday afternoon
b. the difference between the cost of two movie theater tickets on Tuesday night and the cost of one ticket on Sunday at 3:00 p.m.
c. how much movie theater tickets will cost each person if he or she is part of a group of 40 people
d. the difference between the cost of a movie theater ticket for an adult on Friday night and a movie theater ticket for a 13-year-old on Saturday afternoon at 1:00 p.m.

60. How much will movie theater tickets cost for two adults, one 15-year-old child and one 10-year-old child at 7:00 p.m. on a Sunday night?
a. $17.00
b. $19.50
c. $25.00
d. $27.50

61. How can you find the difference in price between a movie theater ticket for an adult and a movie theater ticket for a child under the age of 12 if the tickets are for a show at 3:00 p.m. on a Saturday afternoon?
a. subtract $3.00 from $5.50
b. subtract $5.00 from $7.50
c. subtract $7.50 from $5.50
d. add $5.50 and $3.00 and divide by 2

62. Each sprinkler head in an office sprinkler system sprays water at an average of 16 gallons per minute. If 5 sprinkler heads are flowing at the same time, how many gallons of water will be released in 10 minutes?
a. 80
b. 160
c. 800
d. 1650

63. Which of these is equivalent to 35°C?
$(F = \frac{9}{5} C + 32)$
a. 105°F
b. 95°F
c. 63°F
d. 19°F

64. What is the volume of a pyramid that has a rectangular base 5 feet by 3 feet and a height of 8 feet? ($V = \frac{1}{3} lwh$)
a. 40 cubic feet
b. 16 cubic feet
c. 30 cubic feet
d. 120 cubic feet

65. How many feet of ribbon will a theatrical company need to tie off a performance area that is 34 feet long and 20 feet wide?
a. 54
b. 88
c. 108
c. 680

66. About how many liters of water will a 5-gallon container hold? 1 liter = 1.06 quarts.
a. 5
b. 19
c. 20
d. 21

67. A locked ammunition box is about $2\frac{1}{2}$ centimeters thick. About how thick is this box in inches? 1 cm = 0.39 inches.
a. $\frac{1}{4}$ inch
b. 1 inch
c. 2 inches
d. 5 inches

68. What is the approximate total weight of four security guards who weigh 152 pounds, 168 pounds, 182 pounds, and 201 pounds?
a. 690 pounds
b. 700 pounds
c. 710 pounds
c. 750 pounds

69. Which of these angle measures form a right triangle?
a. 40°, 50°, 90°
b. 45°, 50°, 85°
c. 40°, 40°, 100°
d. 20°, 30°, 130°

70. If the diameter of a metal spool is 3.5 feet, how many times will a 53-foot hose wrap completely around it? $C = \pi D; \pi = \frac{22}{7}$.
a. 2
b. 3
c. 4
d. 5

PART FOUR: VOCABULARY AND SPELLING

Answer questions 71–73 by choosing the word or phrase that means the *same* or nearly the same as the underlined word.

71. expedite the process
a. accelerate
b. evaluate
c. reverse
d. justify

72. giving an ultimatum
a. earnest plea
b. formal petition
c. solemn promise
d. non-negotiable demand

73. meticulous examination
a. painstaking
b. delicate
c. responsible
d. objective

Answer questions 74–76 by choosing the word that most nearly means the *opposite* of the underlined word.

74. impartial jury
   a. complete
   b. prejudiced
   c. unbiased
   d. erudite

75. judicious decision
   a. partial
   b. litigious
   c. imprudent
   d. unrestrained

76. lucid explanation
   a. ordinary
   b. turbulent
   c. implausible
   d. unclear

Answer questions 77–78 by choosing the word that means the same as *both* of the underlined phrases.

77. a military meal and clutter
   a. mess
   b. repast
   c. taunt
   d. mass

78. to equip with a weapon and a part of the human body
   a. member
   b. limb
   c. arm
   d. bow

Answer questions 79–80 by choosing the word or phrase that means the same or nearly the same as the underlined prefix or suffix.

79. redo, reelect
   a. above
   b. after
   c. before
   d. again

80. redden, harden
   a. to redo
   b. to undo
   c. to become
   d. to allow

Answer questions 81–85 by choosing the word that best fills the blank in the following sentences.

81. When I bought my fancy car, I didn't stop to _____ how I'd pay for it.
   a. consider
   b. promote
   c. require
   d. adjust

82. Kamala was the most intelligent person in the group, even though she had never had the _____ to attend college.
   a. sensitivity
   b. arrogance
   c. opportunity
   d. marketability

83. We knew nothing about Betty, because she was so _____.
   a. expressive
   b. secretive
   c. emotional
   d. artistic

84. My computer was state-of-the-art when I bought it five years ago, but now it is _____ .
a. current
b. dedicated
c. unnecessary
d. outmoded

85. The star's _____ remarks about other actors he had worked with made the whole company careful about what they said in front of him.
a. spiteful
b. changeable
c. approving
d. convoluted

Answer questions 86–100 by choosing the word that is spelled correctly and best completes the sentence.

86. It is my _____ that dinner is ready.
a. beleif
b. bilief
c. belief
d. bilief

87. She seems to have no _____ into that particular problem.
a. insite
b. incite
c. ensight
d. insight

88. He is too _____ for his own good.
a. sinsitive
b. sensitive
c. sensative
d. sinsative

89. My sister is going to be on the cover of *People* _____ .
a. magizine
b. magazene
c. magezine
d. magazine

90. My husband, Mysterious Marvin, performs in _____ shows all around the country.
a. magic
b. magick
c. magek
d. maggic

91. Because of a little misunderstanding with the IRS, I do not have _____ to my bank account.
a. acces
b. access
c. acess
d. excess

92. Sandra is a _____ attorney in town, but she's still my baby sister.
a. prominent
b. promanent
c. prominant
d. promenent

93. The tip came from an _____ source.
a. anynonimous
b. anonimous
c. anounymous
d. anonymous

94. Putting together a project proposal requires an _____ amount of paperwork.
  a. extraordinary
  b. extraordinery
  c. extrordinary
  d. ecstraordinary

95. The student gave his _____ that the report would be completed on time.
  a. asurrance
  b. assurance
  c. assurence
  d. assureance

96. The purpose of the new procedures was debated _____.
  a. frequently
  b. frequintly
  c. frequentlly
  d. frequentley

97. The _____ was placed on getting the work done on time.
  a. enphasis
  b. emphisis
  c. emphasis
  d. emfasis

98. The governor pointed to the _____ economic statistics.
  a. encouredging
  b. encouraging
  c. incurraging
  d. incouraging

99. The patient will have a _____ hearing on Friday.
  a. commitment
  b. committment
  c. comittment
  d. comitment

100. The teenager's excuse seemed _____ on the face of it.
  a. rediculous
  b. rediculus
  c. ridiculous
  d. ridiculus

ANSWERS

PART ONE: READING COMPREHENSION

1. **c.** The passage mentions only in passing the popularity of greyhound racing and the issue of housebreaking a puppy. It does not mention veterinarian services at all.

2. **d.** See the last paragraph. The passage does not mention choices **b** or **c**. Choice **a** is clearly wrong; the passage states the opposite.

3. **a.** See in the first paragraph. The other choices are not discussed in the passage.

4. **a.** See the last paragraph. Choices **b** and **d** are contradicted in paragraphs two and three, and choice **c** is not mentioned in the passage.

5. **d.** The whole passage seems to be encouraging people to adopt retired greyhounds. Choice **b** is not mentioned, while choices **a** and **c** are inaccurate according to the information in the passage.

6. **b.** See the end of the second paragraph.

7. **a.** The passage states that the events it describes happened in 1956; this rules out choice **c**. The purpose of the passage is to explain a historical event, so choices **b** and **d** are clearly wrong.

8. **b.** See the first paragraph. Choice **a** is contradicted in the first paragraph, and the passage does not discuss Lucy's later profession (choice **c**) or her major (choice **d**).

9. **b.** The last paragraph refers to Lucy's courage.

10. **a.** According to the first paragraph, Lucy was surprised not to be noticed.

11. **d.** See the second paragraph.

12. **c.** The other answers are all contrary to information in the passage.

13. **c.** The passage is mainly about how the flame retardant failed to work.

14. **d.** This is clearly stated in the first paragraph. The other choices are not mentioned in the passage.

15. **a.** The answer can be found in the last sentence of the passage.

16. **a.** See the last sentence of the second paragraph.

17. **b.** See the first sentence of the third paragraph.

18. **c.** Choice **a** is incorrect because the first sentence suggests that becoming hardened is unavoidable. Choice **b** is mentioned in the passage but is not the main idea. Choice **d** is implied in the passage but only as an example to support the main idea, not as the main idea itself.

19. **b.** See the first two sentences of the passage.

20. **c.** The passage claims that becoming jaded is inevitable.

21. **c.** The baby bird is an example of an orphaned or wounded creature.

22. **b.** This is the first step in the procedure described.

23. **d.** This is the next step in the procedure described.

24. **d.** This is clearly stated in the last paragraph (*first aid measures should be directed at cooling the body quickly*). The other responses are first aid for heat exhaustion victims.

25. **b.** This is clearly stated in the first sentence of the second paragraph. Choices **a** and **c** are symptoms of heat stroke. Choice **d** is not mentioned.

26. **d.** Heat stroke victims have a *blocked sweating mechanism*, as stated in the third paragraph.

27. **a.** This is an inference from the information given in the second paragraph: If the victim still suffers from the symptoms listed in the first sentence of the paragraph, the victim needs more water and salt to help with the *inadequate intake of water and the loss of fluids* that caused those symptoms.

28. b. The second sentence of the passage indicates that sanitation workers will be cleaning the trucks.

29. a. The third sentence of the passage indicates that routes vary in the length of time they take to complete.

30. c. According to the last sentence of the passage, in the past sanitation workers usually drove the same truck each day.

PART TWO: GRAMMAR

31. c. The sentence requires that the verb be in the past tense, *had broken out*.

32. d. The sentence requires that the verb be in the past tense, *occurred*.

33. a. The missing phrase modifies the verb *are armed*, so you need a comparative form of the adverb, *more heavily*.

34. b. The correct form of the pronoun is the objective case, *me*.

35. c. This is correct because it is the subject form, and *who* is doing something, making candied figs. Choices **b** and **d**, *whom* and *whose*, represent the objective and possessive forms, and choice **a**, *that*, is incorrect because the pronoun refers to a person rather than a thing.

36. c. The transitional word *although* correctly establishes a contrast.

37. c. The transitional conjunction *because* correctly establishes a causal relationship.

38. a. The subject *recession* agrees in number with its verb *is*; in answers **b**, **c**, and **d** the subjects and verbs do not agree.

39. d. The verbs *are sequestered* and *become* are consistently in the present tense; in **a**, **b**, and **c** there are unnecessary shifts in tense.

40. a. The verbs *got* and *took* agree in tense.

41. d. The verbs *liked* and *got* agree in tense.

42. b. *Became* and *eating* agree in tense.

43. a. The verbs *arrive* and *is* agree in tense. In the other sentences, the verbs do not agree.

44. c. This sentence is the only one that uses proper parallel structure in which the verbs agree; the word *returned* is in the past tense, as are *finished* and *left*.

45. d. Choice **a** is incorrect because no comma should separate subject and verb—i.e., *police officers* from *must*. Choices **b** and **c** contain sentence fragments.

46. b. *Bravest* is the correct form of the adjective.

47. a. The other choices contain sentence fragments.

48. b. The other choices contain sentence fragments.

49. d. In this choice, the correct pronoun case forms are used. Answer **a** contains a redundant subject (*My partner Rosie and I, we . . .*); **b** and **c** contain incorrect pronoun case forms.

50. b. The correct preposition is *by*. Answers **a**, **c**, and **d** contain incorrect prepositions: *of, off of*, and *from*.

PART THREE: MATHEMATICS

51. d. Choice **a** reads 276; **b** reads 2,706; **c** reads 20,076.

52. b. Solving this problem requires converting 15 minutes to 0.25 hour, which is the time, then using the formula: 62 mph times 0.25 hour is 15.5 miles.

53. c. The simplest way to solve this problem is to first subtract 425 from 500. The remainder of 75 is the number of gallons per minute more that Truck A is pumping. The second step is to multiply 75 by 12 minutes for a total of 900 gallons.

54. a. You simply add all the numbers together to solve this problem.

55. d. Division is used to arrive at a decimal, which can then be rounded to the nearest hundredth and converted to a percentage: 11,350 divided by

21,500 is 0.5279. 0.5279 rounded to the nearest hundredth is 0.53, or 53%.

56. b. Because the answer is a fraction, the best way to solve the problem is to convert the known to a fraction: $\frac{10}{45}$ of the cylinder is full. By dividing both the numerator and the denominator by 5, you can reduce the fraction to $\frac{2}{9}$.

57. a. The answer is arrived at by first dividing 175 by 45. Since the answer is 3.89, not a whole number, the gardener needs 4 sections of hose. Three sections of hose would be too short.

58. c. Subtraction and addition will solve this problem. From 10:42 to 12:42, two hours have elapsed. From 12:42 to 1:00, another 18 minutes have elapsed ($60 - 42 = 18$). Then from 1:00 to 1:19, there is another 19 minutes.

59. d. Choices **a** and **b** can both be ruled out because there is no way to determine how many tickets are for adults or for children. Answer **c** can be ruled out because the price of group tickets is not given.

60. d. Because the 15-year-old requires an adult ticket, there are 3 adult tickets at $7.50 each and one child's ticket at $5.

61. a. The adult price on Saturday afternoon is $5.50; the child's price is $3.00.

62. c. Multiply 16 times 5 to find out how many gallons all five sprinklers will release in one minute. Then multiply the result (80 gallons per minute) by the number of minutes (10) to get 800 gallons.

63. b. Use 35 for C. F = $(\frac{9}{5} \times 35) + 32$. Therefore F = $63 + 32$, or 95.

64. a. 5 times 3 times 8 is 120. 120 divided by 3 is 40.

65. c. There are two sides 34 feet long and two sides 20 feet long. Therefore, you should multiply 34 times 2 and 20 times 2, and then add the results: $68 + 40 = 108$.

66. b. There are four quarts to a gallon. There are therefore 20 quarts in a 5-gallon container. Divide 20 by 1.06 quarts per liter to get 18.86 liters and then round off to 19.

67. b. The problem is solved by first converting a fraction to a decimal, then multiplying $2.5 \times 0.39 = 0.975$, which is rounded to 1.

68. b. Add all four weights for a total of 703. 703 rounded to the nearest ten is 700.

69. a. This is the only choice that includes a 90° angle.

70. c. Solving this problem requires determining the circumference of the spool by multiplying $\frac{22}{7}$ by $3\frac{1}{2}$, or $\frac{7}{2}$. Divide the product (11) into 53. The answer is 4.8, so the hose will completely wrap only 4 times.

PART FOUR: VOCABULARY AND SPELLING

Use a dictionary to help you if you are not sure why the answers in Part Four are correct.

71. a.
72. d.
73. a.
74. b.
75. c.
76. d.
77. a.
78. c.
79. d.
80. c.
81. a.
82. c.
83. b.
84. d.
85. a.
86. c.

87. d.

88. b.

89. d.

90. a.

91. b.

92. a.

93. d.

94. a.

95. b.

96. a.

97. c.

98. b.

99. a.

100. c.

SCORING

The first step in determining your score is to find out how many questions you got right in each section, and then add up your score for each section for your total score. So fill in the blanks below by counting the questions you answered correctly in each section. Questions you didn't answer or got wrong don't count; only count the questions you got right.

Part One: _____ out of 30
Part Two: _____ out of 20
Part Three: _____ out of 20
Part Four: _____ out of 30
Total: _____ out of 100

The next step is to determine percentages for each section, so that you'll be able to compare your score from one section to another. Finding the percentage will be good practice for the kind of math you'll need for most civil service exams: divide the number you got right by the total number of questions in the section, and then move the decimal point to the right two places to get the percentage. For example, if you got 25 questions right in Part One, you would divide 25 by 30 (because there are 30 questions in Part One) for a total of 0.83. Move the decimal point to the right two places and you have the percentage, 83 percent. Follow this procedure for each of the four parts of the exam.

Your total percentage for the test is simply the number you got right. Most civil service exams have a passing score of 70 percent. However, if you're applying to one of the many agencies that use the written exam score to help determine your rank on the eligibility list, you need to do much better than 70 percent to have a chance of getting a job. In fact, you need the very best score you can possibly achieve.

To reach this goal, start by forgetting about total score—unless you got 100 percent, in which case you don't need the rest of this book! Your total score on this first practice exam doesn't matter nearly as much as your scores on the individual parts of the exam. These separate scores will help you see which areas you are strongest in and which need the most work. For instance, maybe you did pretty well on Part One, Reading Comprehension, but got a much lower percentage in grammar (Part Two) or math (Part Three). If that's the case, then you can spend less time brushing up your reading comprehension skills and more time on grammar or math—or whatever areas gave you the most trouble.

The chapters that follow this exam cover the four areas tested. Reading Comprehension (Part One) is in Chapter 9, Grammar (Part Two) in Chapter 10, Math (Part Three) in Chapter 12, and Vocabulary and Spelling (Part Four) in Chapter 11. Depending on your score on each part, you might breeze through a given chapter or really knuckle down and study hard. In either case, these chapters will give you what you need to score your best. When you finish studying these chapters, take the second practice exam in Chapter 13 to see how much you've improved.

C·H·A·P·T·E·R

READING COMPREHENSION

9

CHAPTER SUMMARY

Because reading is such a vital skill, most civil service exams include a reading comprehension section that tests your ability to understand what you read. The tips and exercises in this chapter will help you improve your comprehension of written passages as well as of tables, charts, and graphs, so that you can increase your score in this area.

emos, policies, procedures, reports—these are all things you'll be expected to understand if you become a civil servant. Understanding written materials is part of almost any job. That's why most civil service tests attempt to measure how well applicants understand what they read.

Reading comprehension tests are usually in a multiple-choice format and ask questions based on brief passages, much like the standardized tests that are offered in schools. For that matter, almost all standardized test questions test your reading skill. After all, you can't answer the question if you can't read it! Similarly, you can't study your training materials or learn new procedures once you're on the job if you can't read well. So reading comprehension is vital not only on the test but also for the rest of your career.

TYPES OF READING COMPREHENSION QUESTIONS

You have probably encountered reading comprehension questions before, where you are given a passage to read and then have to answer multiple-choice questions about it. This kind of question has two advantages for you as a test taker:

1. You don't have to know anything about the topic of the passage because
2. You're being tested only on the information the passage provides.

But the disadvantage is that you have to know where and how to find that information quickly in an unfamiliar text. This makes it easy to fall for one of the wrong answer choices, especially since they're designed to mislead you.

The best way to do well on this passage/question format is to be very familiar with the kinds of questions that are typically asked on the test. Questions most frequently ask you to:

1. identify a specific **fact or detail** in the passage
2. note the **main idea** of the passage
3. make an **inference** based on the passage
4. define a **vocabulary** word from the passage

In order for you to do well on a reading comprehension test, you need to know exactly what each of these questions is asking. **Facts and details** are the specific pieces of information that support the passage's **main idea**. The main idea is the thought, opinion, or attitude that governs the whole passage. Generally speaking, facts and details are indisputable—things that don't need to be proven, like statistics (18 million people) or descriptions (a green overcoat). Let's say, for example, you read a sentence that says *"After the department's reorganization, workers were 50% more productive."* A sentence like this, which gives you the **fact** that 50% of workers were more productive, might support a **main idea** that says, *"Every department should be reorganized."* Notice that this main idea is not something indisputable; it is an opinion. The writer thinks all departments should be reorganized, and because this is his opinion (and not everyone shares it), he needs to support his opinion with facts and details.

An **inference**, on the other hand, is a conclusion that can be drawn based on fact or evidence. For example, you can infer—based on the fact that workers became 50% more productive after the reorganization, which is a dramatic change—that the department had not been efficiently organized. The fact sentence, *"After the department's reorganization, workers were 50% more productive,"* also implies that the reorganization of the department was the reason workers became more productive. There may, of course, have been other reasons, but we can infer only one from this sentence.

As you might expect, **vocabulary** questions ask you to determine the meaning of particular words. Often, if you've read carefully, you can determine the meaning of such words from their context, that is, how the word is used in the sentence or paragraph.

PRACTICE PASSAGE 1: USING THE FOUR QUESTION TYPES

The following is a sample test passage, followed by four questions. Read the passage carefully, and then answer the questions, based on your reading of the text, by circling your choice. Then refer to the list above and note under your answer which type of question has been asked. Correct answers appear immediately after the questions.

Community policing has been frequently touted as the best way to reform urban law enforcement. The idea of putting more officers on foot patrol in high crime areas, where relations with police have frequently been strained, was initiated in Houston in 1983 under the leadership of then-Commissioner Lee Brown. He believed that officers should be accessible to the community at the street level. If officers were assigned to the same area over a period of time, those officers would eventually build a network of trust with neighborhood residents. That trust would mean that merchants and residents in the community would let officers know about criminal activities in the area and would support police intervention. Since then, many large cities have experimented with Community-Oriented Policing (COP) with mixed results. Some have found that police and citizens are grateful for the opportunity to work together. Others have found that unrealistic expectations by citizens and resistance from officers have combined to hinder the effectiveness of COP. It seems possible, therefore, that a good idea may need improvement before it can truly be considered a reform.

1. Community policing has been used in law enforcement since
   a. the late 1970s
   b. the early 1980s
   c. the Carter administration
   d. Lee Brown was New York City Police Commissioner

   Question type_____

2. The phrase "a network of trust" in this passage suggests that
   a. police officers can rely only on each other for support
   b. community members rely on the police to protect them
   c. police and community members rely on each other
   d. community members trust only each other

   Question type_____

3. The best title for this passage would be
   a. Community Policing: The Solution to the Drug Problem
   b. Houston Sets the Pace in Community Policing
   c. Communities and Cops: Partners for Peace
   d. Community Policing: An Uncertain Future

   Question type_____

4. The word "touted" in the first sentence of the passage most nearly means
   a. praised
   b. denied
   c. exposed
   d. criticized

   Question type_____

ANSWERS AND EXPLANATIONS FOR PRACTICE PASSAGE 1

Don't just look at the right answers and move on. The explanations are the most important part, so read them carefully. Use these explanations to help you understand how to tackle each kind of question the next time you come across it.

1. b. Question type: 1, fact or detail. The passage says that community policing began "in the last decade." A decade is a period of ten years. In addition, the passage identifies 1983 as the first large-scale use of community policing in Houston. Don't be misled by trying to figure out when Carter was president. Also, if you happen to know that Lee Brown was New York City's police commissioner, don't let that information lead you away from the information contained in the passage alone. Brown was commissioner in Houston when he initiated community policing.

2. c. Question type: 3, inference. The "network of trust" referred to in this passage is between the community and the police, as you can see from the sentence where the phrase appears. The key phrase in the question is *in this passage.* You may think that police can rely only on each other, or one of the other answer choices may appear equally plausible to you. But your choice of answers must be limited to the one suggested *in this passage.* Another tip for questions like this: Beware of absolutes! Be suspicious of any answer containing words like *only, always,* or *never.*

3. d. Question type: 2, main idea. The title always expresses the main idea. In this passage, the main idea comes at the end. The sum of all the details in the passage suggests that community policing is not without its critics and that therefore its

future is uncertain. Another key phrase is *mixed results,* which means that some communities haven't had full success with community policing.

4. a. Question type: 4, vocabulary. The word *touted* is linked in this passage with the phrase *the best way to reform.* Most people would think that a good way to reform something is praiseworthy. In addition, the next few sentences in the passage describe the benefits of community policing. Criticism or a negative response to the subject doesn't come until later in the passage.

Detail and Main Idea Questions

Main idea questions and fact or detail questions are both asking you for information that's right there in the passage. All you have to do is find it.

DETAIL OR FACT QUESTIONS

In detail or fact questions, you have to identify a specific item of information from the test. This is usually the simplest kind of question. You just have to be able to separate important information from less important information. However, the choices may often be very similar, so you must be careful not to get confused.

Be sure you read the passage and questions carefully. In fact, it is usually a good idea to read the questions first, *before* you even read the passage, so you'll know what details to look out for.

MAIN IDEA QUESTIONS

The main idea of a passage, like that of a paragraph or a book, is what it is *mostly* about. The main idea is like an umbrella that covers all of the ideas and details in the passage, so it is usually something general, not specific. For example, in Practice Passage 1, question 3 asked you what title would be best for the passage, and the correct answer was "Community Policing: An Uncertain Future." This is the best answer because it's the only one that includes both the positive and negative sides of community policing, both of which are discussed in the passage.

Sometimes the main idea is stated clearly, often in the first or last sentence of the passage—the main idea is expressed in the *last* sentence of Practice Passage 1, for example. The sentence that expresses the main idea is often referred to as the **topic sentence**.

At other times, the main idea is not stated in a topic sentence but is *implied* in the overall passage, and you'll need to determine the main idea by inference. Because there may be much information in the passage, the trick is to understand what all that information adds up to—the gist of what the author wants you to know. Often some of the wrong answers on main idea questions are specific facts or details from the passage. A good way to test yourself is to ask, "Can this answer serve as a *net* to hold the whole passage together?" If not, chances are you've chosen a fact or detail, not a main idea.

PRACTICE PASSAGE 2:
DETAIL AND MAIN IDEA QUESTIONS

Practice answering main idea and detail questions by working on the questions that follow this passage. Circle the answers to the questions, and then check your answers against the key that appears immediately after the questions.

There are three different kinds of burns: first degree, second degree, and third degree. It is important for firefighters to be able to recognize each of these types of burns so that they can be sure burn victims are given proper medical treatment. The least serious burn is the first-degree burn, which causes the skin to turn red but does not cause blistering. A mild sunburn is a good example of a first-degree burn, and, like a mild sunburn, first-degree burns generally do not require medical treatment other than a gentle cooling of the burned skin with ice or cold tap water.

Second-degree burns, on the other hand, do cause blistering of the skin and should be treated immediately. These burns should be immersed in warm water and then wrapped in a sterile dressing or bandage. (Do not apply butter or grease to these burns; despite the old wives' tale, butter does *not* help burns heal and actually increases chances of infection.) If second-degree burns cover a large part of the body, then the victim should be taken to the hospital immediately for medical care.

Third-degree burns are those that char the skin and turn it black, or burn so deeply that the skin shows white. These burns usually result from direct contact with flames and have a great chance of becoming infected. All third-degree burns should receive immediate hospital care. They should not be immersed in water, and charred clothing should not be removed from the victim. If possible, a sterile dressing or bandage should be applied to burns before the victim is transported to the hospital.

1. Which of the following would be the best title for this passage?
   a. Dealing with Third-Degree Burns
   b. How to Recognize and Treat Different Burns
   c. Burn Categories
   d. Preventing Infection in Burns

2. Second-degree burns should be treated with
   a. butter
   b. nothing
   c. cold water
   d. warm water

3. First-degree burns turn the skin
   a. red
   b. blue
   c. black
   d. white

4. Which of the following best expresses the main idea of the passage?
   a. There are three different types of burns.
   b. Firefighters should always have cold compresses on hand.
   c. Different burns require different types of treatment.
   d. Butter is not good for healing burns.

ANSWERS AND EXPLANATIONS FOR PRACTICE PASSAGE 2

1. **b.** A question that asks you to choose a title for a passage is a main idea question. This main idea is expressed in the second sentence, the topic sentence: "It is important for firefighters to be able to recognize each of these types of burns so that they can be sure burn victims are given proper treatment." Answer **b** expresses this idea and is the only title that encompasses all of the ideas expressed in the passage. Answer **a** is too limited; it deals only with one of the kinds of burns discussed in the passage. Likewise, answers **c** and **d** are also too limited. Answer **c** covers types of burns but not their treatment, and **d** deals only with preventing infection, which is only a secondary part of the discussion of treatment.

2. **d.** The answer to this fact question is clearly expressed in the sentence, "These burns should be immersed in warm water and then wrapped in a sterile dressing or bandage." The hard part is keeping track of whether "These burns" refers to the kind of burns in the question, which is second-

degree burns. It's easy to choose a wrong answer here because all of the answer choices are mentioned in the passage. You need to read carefully to be sure you match the right burn to the right treatment.

3. **a.** This is another fact or detail question. The passage says that a first-degree burn "causes the skin to turn red." Again, it's important to read carefully because all of the answer choices (except **b**, which can be eliminated immediately) are listed elsewhere in the passage.

4. **c.** Clearly this is a main idea question, and **c** is the only answer that encompasses the whole passage. Answers **b** and **d** are limited to *particular* burns or treatments, and answer **a** discusses only burns and not their treatment. In addition, the second sentence tells us that "It is important for firefighters to be able to *recognize each of these types of burns so that they can be sure burn victims are given proper medical treatment.*"

INFERENCE AND VOCABULARY QUESTIONS

Questions that ask you about the meaning of vocabulary words in the passage and those that ask what the passage *suggests* or *implies* (inference questions) are different from detail or main idea questions. In vocabulary and inference questions, you usually have to pull ideas from the passage, sometimes from more than one place in the passage.

INFERENCE QUESTIONS

Inference questions can be the most difficult to answer because they require you to draw meaning from the text when that meaning is implied rather than directly stated. Inferences are conclusions that we draw based on the clues the writer has given us. When you draw inferences, you have to be something of a detective, looking for such clues as word choice, tone, and specific details that suggest a certain conclusion, attitude, or point of view. You have to read between the lines in order to make a judgment about what an author was implying in the passage.

A good way to test whether you've drawn an acceptable inference is to ask, "What evidence do I have for this inference?" If you can't find any, you probably have the wrong answer. You need to be sure that your inference is logical and that it is based on something that is suggested or implied in the passage itself—not by what you or others might think. Like a good detective, you need to base your conclusions on evidence—facts, details, and other information—not on random hunches or guesses.

VOCABULARY QUESTIONS

Questions designed to test vocabulary are really trying to measure how well you can figure out the meaning of an unfamiliar word from its context. *Context* refers to the words and ideas surrounding a vocabulary word. If the context is clear enough, you should be able to substitute a nonsense word for the one being sought, and you would still make the right choice because you could determine meaning strictly from the sense of the sentence. For example, you should be able to determine the meaning of the italicized nonsense word below based on its context:

The speaker noted that it gave him great *terivinix* to announce the winner of the Outstanding Leadership Award.

In this sentence, *terivinix* most likely means

a. pain
b. sympathy
c. pleasure
d. anxiety

Clearly, the context of an award makes c, *pleasure*, the best choice. Awards don't usually bring pain, sympathy, or anxiety.

When confronted with an unfamiliar word, try substituting a nonsense word and see if the context gives you the clue. If you're familiar with prefixes, suffixes, and word roots, you can also use this knowledge to help you determine the meaning of an unfamiliar word.

You should be careful not to guess at the answer to vocabulary questions based on how you may have seen the word used before or what you *think* it means. Many words have more than one possible meaning, depending on the context in which they're used, and a word you've seen used one way may mean something else in a test passage. Also, if you don't look at the context carefully, you may make the mistake of confusing the vocabulary word with a similar word. For example, the vocabulary word may be *taut* (meaning *tight*), but if you read too quickly or don't check the context, you might think the word is *tout* (meaning *publicize* or *praise*) or *taunt* (meaning *tease*). Always make sure you read carefully and that what you think the word means fits into the context of the passage you're being tested on.

PRACTICE PASSAGE 3:
INFERENCE AND VOCABULARY QUESTIONS

The questions that follow this passage are strictly vocabulary and inference questions. Circle the answers to the questions, and then check your answers against the key that appears immediately after the questions.

Dealing with irritable patients is a great challenge for health-care workers on every level. It is critical that you do not lose your patience when confronted by such a patient. When handling irate patients, be sure to remember that they are not angry at you; they are simply projecting their anger at something else *onto* you. Remember that if you respond to these patients as irritably as they act with you, you will only increase their hostility, making it much more difficult to give them proper treatment. The best thing to do is to remain calm and ignore any imprecations patients may hurl your way. Such patients may be irrational and may not realize what they're saying. Often these patients will purposely try to anger you just to get some reaction out of you. If you react to this behavior with anger, they win by getting your attention, but you both lose because the patient is less likely to get proper care.

1. The word "irate" as it is used in the passage most nearly means
   a. irregular, odd
   b. happy, cheerful
   c. ill-tempered, angry
   d. sloppy, lazy

2. The passage suggests that health-care workers
   a. easily lose control of their emotions
   b. are better off not talking to their patients

   c. must be careful in dealing with irate patients because the patients may sue the hospital
   d. may provide inadequate treatment if they become angry at patients

3. An "imprecation" is most likely
   a. an object
   b. a curse
   c. a joke
   d. a medication

4. Which of the following best expresses the writer's views about irate patients?
   a. Some irate patients just want attention.
   b. Irate patients are always miserable.
   c. Irate patients should be made to wait for treatment.
   d. Managing irate patients is the key to a successful career.

ANSWERS AND EXPLANATIONS
FOR PRACTICE PASSAGE 3

1. **c.** This is a vocabulary question. *Irate* means *ill-tempered, angry*. It should be clear that **b**, *happy, cheerful*, is not the answer; dealing with happy patients is normally not "a great challenge." Patients that are **a**, *irregular, odd*, or **d**, *sloppy, lazy*, may be a challenge in their own way, but they aren't likely to rouse a health-care worker to anger. In addition, the passage explains that irate patients are not "*angry* at you," and *irate* is used as a synonym for *irritable*, which describes the patients under discussion in the very first sentence.

2. **d.** This is an inference question, as the phrase "the passage *suggests*" might have told you. The idea that angry health-care workers might give inadequate treatment is implied by the passage as a whole,

which seems to be an attempt to prevent angry reactions to irate patients. Furthermore, the last sentence in particular makes this inference possible: "If you react to this behavior with anger . . . you both lose because the patient is less likely to get proper care." Answer **c** is not correct, because while it may be true that some irate patients have sued the hospital in the past, there is no mention of suits anywhere in this passage. Likewise, answer **b** is incorrect; the passage does suggest ignoring patients' insults, but nowhere does it recommend not talking to patients—it simply recommends not talking angrily. And while it may be true that some health-care workers may lose control of their emotions, the passage does not provide any facts or details to support answer **a**, that they "*easily* lose control." Watch out for key works like *easily* that may distort the intent of the passage.

3. **b.** If you didn't know what an imprecation is, the context should reveal that it's something you can ignore, so neither **a**, an *object*, nor **d**, a *medication*, is a likely answer. Furthermore, **c** is not likely either, since an irate patient is not likely to be making jokes.

4. **a.** The writer seems to believe that some irate patients just want attention, as is suggested when the writer says, "Often these patients will purposely try to anger you just to get some reaction out of you. If you react to this behavior with anger, they win *by getting your attention*." It should be clear that **b** cannot be the answer, because it includes an absolute: "Irate patients are *always* miserable." Perhaps *some* of the patients are *often* miserable, but an absolute like *always* is almost always wrong. Besides, this passage refers to patients who may be irate in the hospital, but we have no indication of what these patients are like at other times, and *miserable* and *irate* are not exactly the same thing,

either. Answer **c** is also incorrect because the purpose of the passage is to ensure that patients receive "proper treatment" and that irate patients are not discriminated against because of their behavior. Thus, "irate patients should be made to wait for treatment" is not a logical answer. Finally, **d** cannot be correct because though it may be true, there is no discussion of career advancement in the passage.

REVIEW: PUTTING IT ALL TOGETHER

A good way to solidify what you've learned about reading comprehension questions is for *you* to write the questions. Here's a passage, followed by space for you to write your own questions. Write one question of each of the four types: fact or detail, main idea, inference, and vocabulary.

The "broken window" theory was originally developed to explain how minor acts of vandalism or disrespect can quickly escalate to crimes and attitudes that break down the entire social fabric of an area. It is a theory that can easily be applied to any situation in society. The theory contends that if a broken window in an abandoned building is not replaced quickly, soon all the windows will be broken. In other words, a small violation, if condoned, leads others to commit similar or greater violations. Thus, after all the windows have been broken, the building is likely to be looted and perhaps even burned down.

According to this theory, violations increase exponentially. Thus, if disrespect to a superior is tolerated, others will be tempted to be disrespectful as well. A management crisis could erupt literally overnight. For example, if one firefighter begins to disregard proper housewatch procedure by neglecting to keep

If English Isn't Your First Language

When non-native speakers of English have trouble with reading comprehension tests, it's often because they lack the cultural, linguistic, and historical frame of reference that native speakers enjoy. People who have not lived in or been educated in the U.S. often don't have the background information that comes from reading American newspapers, magazines, and textbooks.

A second problem for non-native English speakers is the difficulty in recognizing vocabulary and idioms (expressions like "chewing the fat") that assist comprehension. In order to read with good understanding, it's important to have an immediate grasp of as many words as possible in the text. Test takers need to be able to recognize vocabulary and idioms immediately so that the ideas those words express are clear.

The Long View

Read newspapers, magazines, and other periodicals that deal with current events and matters of local, state, and national importance. Pay special attention to articles related to the career you want to pursue.

Be alert to new or unfamiliar vocabulary or terms that occur frequently in the popular press. Use a highlighter pen to mark new or unfamiliar words as you read. Keep a list of those words and their definitions. Review them for 15 minutes each day. Though at first you may find yourself looking up a lot of words, don't be frustrated—you'll look up fewer and fewer as your vocabulary expands.

During the Test

When you are taking the test, make a picture in your mind of the situation being described in the passage. Ask yourself, "What did the writer mostly want me to think about this subject?"

Locate and underline the topic sentence that carries the main idea of the passage. Remember that the topic sentence—if there is one—may not always be the first sentence. If there doesn't seem to be one, try to determine what idea summarizes the whole passage.

up the housewatch administrative journal, and this firefighter is not reprimanded, others will follow suit by committing similar violations of procedure, thinking, "If he can get away with it, why can't I?" So what starts out as a small thing, a violation that may seem not to warrant disciplinary action, may actually ruin the efficiency of the entire firehouse, putting the people the firehouse serves at risk.

1. Detail question:_____
   a.
   b.
   c.
   d.

2. Main idea question:_____

    a.

    b.

    c.

    d.

3. Inference question:_____

    a.

    b.

    c.

    d.

4. Vocabulary question:_____

    a.

    b.

    c.

    d.

POSSIBLE QUESTIONS

Here is one question of each type based on the passage above. Your questions may be very different, but these will give you an idea of the kinds of questions that could be asked.

1. Detail question: According to the passage, which of the following could happen "overnight"?

    a. The building will be burned down.

    b. The firehouse may become unmanageable.

    c. A management crisis might erupt.

    d. The windows will all be broken.

2. Main idea question: Which of the following best expresses the main idea of the passage?

    a. Even minor acts of disrespect can lead to major problems.

    b. Broken windows must be repaired immediately.

    c. People shouldn't be disrespectful to their superiors.

    d. Housewatch procedures must be taken seriously.

3. Inference question: With which of the following statements would the author most like agree?

    a. The "broken window" theory is inadequate.

    b. Managers should demand respect from subordinates.

    c. Firefighters are lazy and disrespectful.

    d. People will get away with as much as they can.

4. Vocabulary question: In the first parapgraph, *condoned* most nearly means

    a. punished

    b. overlooked

    c. condemned

    d. applauded

Answers

1. c.

2. a.

3. d.

4. b.

READING TABLES, GRAPHS, AND CHARTS

Depending on what position you're testing for, civil service exams may also include a section testing your ability to read tables, charts, and graphs. These sections are really quite similar to regular reading comprehension exams, but instead of pulling information from a passage of text, you'll need to answer questions about a graphic representation of data. The types of questions asked about tables, charts, and graphs are actually quite similar to those about reading passages, though there usually aren't any questions on vocabulary. The main difference in reading tables, charts, or graphs is that you're "reading" or interpreting data represented in tabular (table) or graphic (picture) form rather than textual (sentence and paragraph) form.

Tables

Tables present data in rows and columns. Here's a very simple table that shows the number of accidents reported in one county over a 24-hour period. Use it to answer the question that follows.

Time of Day	Number of Accidents
6:00 A.M.–9:00 A.M.	11
9:00 A.M.–12:00 P.M.	3
12:00 P.M.–3:00 P.M.	5
3:00 P.M.–6:00 P.M.	7
6:00 P.M.–9:00 P.M.	9
9:00 P.M.–12:00 A.M.	6
12:00 A.M.–3:00 A.M.	5
3:00 A.M.–6:00 A.M.	3

1. Based on the information provided in this table, at what time of day do the most accidents occur?
    a. noon
    b. morning rush hour
    c. evening rush hour
    d. midnight

The correct answer, of course, is **b**, morning rush hour. You can clearly see that the highest number of accidents (11) occurred between 6:00 A.M. and 9:00 A.M.

Graphs

Now, here's the same information presented as a graph. A graph uses two axes rather than columns and rows to create a visual picture of the data:

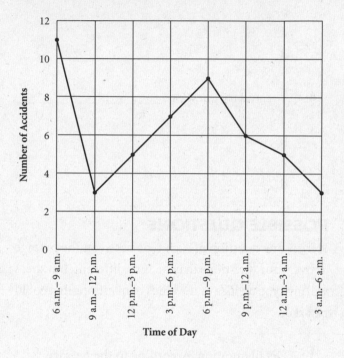

Here you can actually see the time of greatest number of accidents represented by a line that corresponds to the time of day and number. These numbers can also be represented by a box in a bar graph, as shown on the next page.

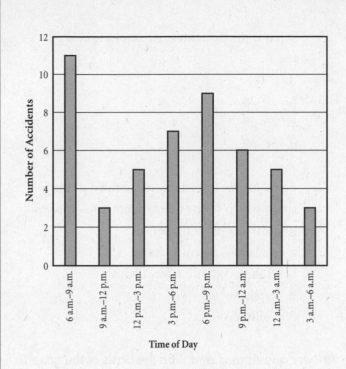

Time of Day

The key to "reading" graphs is to be sure that you know exactly what the numbers on each axis represent. Otherwise, you're likely to grossly misinterpret the information. Here, you see that the horizontal axis represents the time of day and the vertical axis represents the number of accidents that occurred. Thus, the tallest bar shows the time of day with the most accidents.

Like regular reading comprehension questions, questions on tables, charts, and graphs may also ask you to make inferences or even do basic math using the information and numbers the table, chart, or graph supplies. For example, you may be asked questions like the following on the information presented in the table, line graph, or bar graph above. The answers follow immediately after the questions.

2. What is the probable cause for the high accident rate between 6 A.M. and 9 A.M.?
   a. People haven't had their coffee yet.
   b. A lot of drivers are rushing to work.
   c. Sun glare.
   d. Construction.

3. What is the total number of accidents?
   a. 48
   b. 51
   c. 49
   d. 53

2. **b.** A question like this tests your common sense as well as your ability to read the graph. Though there may indeed be sun glare and though many drivers may not have had their coffee, these items are too variable to account for the high number of accidents. In addition, **d**, construction, is not logical because construction generally slows traffic down. Answer **b** is the best answer, because from 6:00 to 9:00 A.M. there is consistently a lot of rush hour traffic. In addition, many people do *rush*, and this increases the likelihood of accidents.

3. **c.** This question, of course, tests your basic ability to add. To answer this question correctly, you need to determine the value of each bar and then add those numbers together.

Charts

Finally, you may be presented information in the form of a chart like the pie chart on the next page. Here the accident figures have been converted to percentages. In this figure you don't see the exact number of accidents, but you see how accidents for each time period compare to the others.

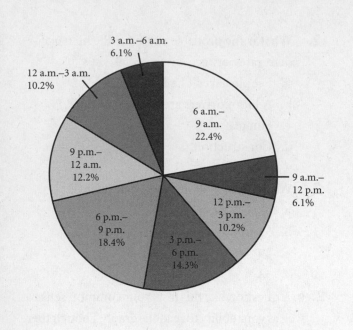

3 a.m.–6 a.m.
6.1%

12 a.m.–3 a.m.
10.2%

6 a.m.–
9 a.m.
22.4%

9 p.m.–
12 a.m.
12.2%

9 a.m.–
12 p.m.
6.1%

6 p.m.–
9 p.m.
18.4%

12 p.m.–
3 p.m.
10.2%

3 p.m.–
6 p.m.
14.3%

1. What is the percentage of smoking-related fires?
   a. 5–8
   b. 10–26
   c. 26–58
   d. 58–62

2. Based on the information provided in the chart, which of the following reasons applies to the majority of these fires?
   a. malicious intent to harm
   b. violation of fire safety codes
   c. carelessness
   d. faulty products

PRACTICE

Try the following questions to hone your skill at reading tables, graphs, and charts.

Answer questions 1 and 2 on the basis of the graph shown below.

Causes of household fires, in percentages

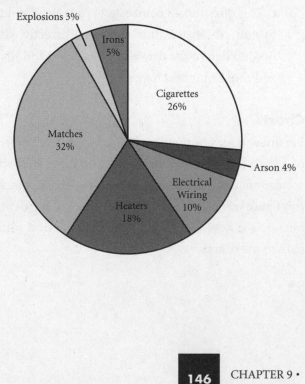

Explosions 3%

Irons
5%

Cigarettes
26%

Matches
32%

Arson 4%

Electrical
Wiring
10%

Heaters
18%

Answer questions 3 and 4 on the basis of the graph shown below.

Number of sick days per year of employment

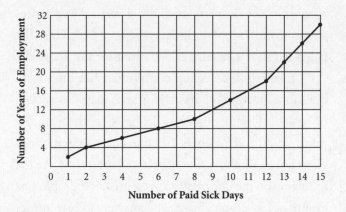

Number of Years of Employment

Number of Paid Sick Days

3. At what point does the rate of increase of sick days change?
   a. 4 years of employment
   b. 10 years of employment
   c. 8 years of employment
   d. 12 years of employment

4. During what years of employment are the number of sick days equal to double the number of years of employment?

- a. 1, 4, and 12
- b. 13, 14, and 15
- c. 1, 2, and 15
- d. 2, 4, and 10

ANSWERS AND EXPLANATIONS TO PRACTICE EXERCISE

1. c. Of the causes presented in the chart, both cigarettes (26 percent) and matches (32 percent) are related to smoking. But not all match fires are necessarily smoking related. Thus, the best answer allows for a range between 26 percent and 58 percent.

2. c. Fires from cigarettes, heaters, irons, and matches—81 percent in total—are generally the result of carelessness. Only 4 percent of fires are arsons, so **a** cannot be correct. Electrical, heater, and explosion fires *may* be the result of fire safety code violations, but even so, they total only 31 percent. Finally, there's no indication in this chart that there were faulty products involved.

3. b. In the first nine years, employees gain an additional two sick days every two years. At ten years of employment, however, the gain increases from two days every two years to four days, that is, from ten days in the eighth year to fourteen days in the tenth year.

4. c. In the first year, the number of sick days is two; in the second, four; and not until the fifteenth year does the number of sick days (thirty) again double the number of years of employment.

ADDITIONAL RESOURCES

Here are some other ways you can build the vocabulary and knowledge that will help you do well on reading comprehension questions.

- Practice asking the four sample question types about passages you read for information or pleasure.
- If you belong to a computer network such as America Online or Compuserve, search out articles related to the career you'd like to pursue. Exchange views with others on the Internet. All of these exchanges will help expand your knowledge of job-related material that may appear in a passage on the test.
- Use your library. Many public libraries have sections, sometimes called "Lifelong Learning Centers," that contain materials for adult learners. In these sections you can find books with exercises in reading and study skills. It's also a good idea to enlarge your base of information by reading related books and articles. Many libraries have computer systems that allow you to access information quickly and easily. Library personnel will show you how to use the computers and microfilm and microfiche machines.
- Begin now to build a broad knowledge of your potential profession. Get in the habit of reading articles in newspapers and magazines on job-related issues. Keep a clipping file of those articles. This will help keep you informed of trends in the profession and familiarize you with pertinent vocabulary.

- Consider reading or subscribing to professional journals. They are usually available for a reasonable annual fee. They may also be available in your public library.

- If you need more help building your reading skills and taking reading comprehension tests, consider *Reading Comprehension in 20 Minutes a Day* by Elizabeth Chesla, and *501 Reading Comprehension Questions*, both published by LearningExpress.

C·H·A·P·T·E·R

GRAMMAR

10

CHAPTER SUMMARY

This chapter reviews the sentence-level writing skills often tested on multiple-choice exams, including complete sentences, capitalization, punctuation, subject-verb agreement, verb tenses, pronouns, and confusing word pairs. It also shows you how to choose the answer choice that is most clearly written.

 nowing how to use written language is vital, not just for the exam, but for your civil service career. Almost every civil service job involves at least some writing. So civil service exams often include questions that test your grammar and your ability to tell a well-written sentence from a poorly written one.

COMPLETE SENTENCES

Sentences are the basic unit of written language. Most writing is done using complete sentences, so it's important to distinguish sentences from fragments. A sentence expresses a complete thought, while a fragment requires something more to express a complete thought.

Look at the following pairs of word groups. The first in each pair is a sentence fragment; the second is a complete sentence.

COMPLETE SENTENCES

Fragment	Complete Sentence
The dog walking down the street.	The dog was walking down the street.
Exploding from the bat for a home run.	The ball exploded from the bat for a home run.

These examples show that a sentence must have a subject and a verb to complete its meaning. The first fragment has a subject, but not a verb. *Walking* looks like a verb, but it is actually an adjective describing *dog*. The second fragment has neither a subject nor a verb. *Exploding* looks like a verb, but it too is an adjective describing something not identified in the word group.

Now look at the next set of word groups. Mark those that are complete sentences.

1.

    a. We saw the tornado approaching.

    b. When we saw the tornado approaching.

2.

    a. Before the house was built in 1972.

    b. The house was built in 1972.

3.

    a. Since we are leaving in the morning.

    b. We are leaving in the morning.

If you chose **1.a.**, **2.b.**, and **3.b.**, you were correct. You may have noticed that the groups of words are the same, but the fragments have an extra word at the beginning. These words are called subordinating conjunctions. If a group of words that would normally be a complete sentence is preceded by a subordinating conjunction, something more is needed to complete the thought.

- When we saw the tornado approaching, we headed for cover.
- Before the house was built in 1972, the old house was demolished.
- Since we were leaving in the morning, we went to bed early.

Here is a list of words that can be used as subordinating conjunctions.

after	that
although	though
as	unless
because	until
before	when
if	whenever
once	where
since	wherever
than	while

If you can tell when a group of words isn't a sentence, then you can tell when one or more sentences have been run together, sometimes with a comma in between. Some tests will ask you to find run-on sentences. Each of the sentences below is a run-on sentence. Can you find where to put a period and begin a new sentence?

1. We went to the beach, we had a good time.

2. Without exception, the prisoners conformed to the new ruling they kept their cells clean.

3. The defense needed time to examine the new evidence, the lawyer asked for an extension.

If you noticed that a new sentence begins after *beach* in the first sentence, after *ruling* in the second, and after *evidence* in the third, you were right. Generally, you can tell whether you're looking at a run-on by covering the second half of the sentence and asking yourself whether the first half by itself is a sentence. Then cover the first half. Is the second half a sentence by itself? If your answer to the first and/or second question is *no*, then the sentence is fine. If you answered both questions *yes*—both halves of the sentence could be sentences by themselves—then you've got a run-on, unless there happens to be a semicolon (;) between the two halves.

Some of the questions on a civil service exam may test your ability to distinguish a sentence from a fragment or a run-on. Check for a subject and a verb, as well as for subordinating conjunctions. Check yourself with the following sample questions. The answers are at the end of this chapter.

1. Which of the following groups of words is a complete sentence?
   a. The treasure buried beneath the floorboards beside the furnace.
   b. After we spent considerable time examining all of the possibilities before making a decision.
   c. In addition to the methods the doctor used to diagnose the problem.
   d. The historical account of the incident bore the most resemblance to fact.

2. Which of the following groups of words is a complete sentence?
   a. This was fun to do.
   b. We looking.
   c. Before the door opened.
   d. If we ever see you again.

3. Which of the following groups of words is a run-on?
   a. Whenever I see the moon rise, I am awed by the deep orange color.

   b. The special services unit completed its work and made its report to the chief.
   c. Unless we hear from the directors of the board before the next meeting, we will not act on the new proposal.
   d. We slept soundly we never heard the alarm.

CAPITALIZATION

You may encounter questions that test your ability to capitalize correctly. Here is a quick review of the most common capitalization rules.

- Capitalize the first word of a sentence. If the first word is a number, write it as a word.
- Capitalize the pronoun *I*.
- Capitalize the first word of a quotation: I said, "What's the name of your dog?" Do not capitalize the first word of a partial quotation: He called me "the worst excuse for a student" he had ever seen.
- Capitalize proper nouns and proper adjectives.

See the table on the next page.

The following passage contains no capitalized words. Circle those letters that should be capitalized.

when I first saw the black hills on january 2, 2000, i was shocked by their beauty. we had just spent new year's day in sioux falls, south dakota, and had headed west toward our home in denver, colorado. as we traveled along interstate 90, i could see the black hills rising slightly in the distance. president calvin coolidge had called them "a wondrous sight to behold." i understood why. after driving through the badlands and stopping at wall drug in wall, south

CAPITALIZATION

Category	Example (Proper nouns)
days of the week, months of the year	Friday, Saturday; January, February
holidays, special events	Christmas, Halloween; Two Rivers Festival, Dilly Days
names of individuals	John Henry, George Billeck
names of structures, buildings	Lincoln Memorial, Principal Building
names of trains, ships, aircraft	Queen Elizabeth, Chicago El
product names	Corn King hams, Dodge Intrepid
cities and states	Des Moines, Iowa; Juneau, Alaska
streets, highways, roads	Grand Avenue, Interstate 29, Deadwood Road
landmarks, public areas	Continental Divide, Grand Canyon, Glacier National Park
bodies of water	Atlantic Ocean, Mississippi River
ethnic groups, languages, nationalities	Asian-American, English, Arab
official titles	Mayor Daley, President Johnson
institutions, organizations, businesses	Dartmouth College, Lions Club, Chrysler Corporation
proper adjectives	English muffin, Polish sausage

dakota, we liked the way the evergreen-covered hills broke the barren monotony of the landscape. my oldest daughter said, "dad, look! there's something that's not all white." we could see why the lakota sioux regarded them as a native american holy ground. we saw mount rushmore and custer state park, the home of the largest herd of buffalo in north america. we also drove the treacherous spearfish canyon road. fortunately, our jeep cherokee had no trouble with the ice and snow on the winding road.

Check your circled version against the corrected version of the passage below.

When I first saw the Black Hills on January 2, 2000, I was shocked by their beauty. We had just spent New Year's Day in Sioux Falls, South Dakota, and had headed west toward our home in Denver, Colorado. As we traveled along Interstate 90, I could see the Black Hills rising slightly in the distance. President Calvin Coolidge had called them "a wondrous sight to behold." I understood why. After driving through the Badlands and stopping at Wall Drug in Wall, South Dakota, we liked the way the evergreen-covered hills broke the barren monotony of the landscape. My oldest daughter said, "Dad, look! There's something that's not all white." We could see why the Lakota Sioux regarded them as a Native American holy ground. We saw Mount Rushmore and Custer State Park, the home of the largest herd of buffalo in North America. We also drove the treacherous Spearfish Canyon Road. Fortunately, our Jeep Cherokee had no trouble with the ice and snow on the winding road.

Now try these sample questions. Choose the option that is capitalized correctly. Answers are at the end of the chapter.

4.

   a. This year we will celebrate christmas on Tuesday, December 25 in Manchester, Ohio.

   b. This year we will celebrate Christmas on Tuesday, December 25 in manchester, Ohio.

   c. This year we will celebrate Christmas on Tuesday, December 25 in Manchester, Ohio.

   d. This year we will celebrate christmas on Tuesday, December 25 in manchester, Ohio.

5.

   a. Abraham Adams made an appointment with Mayor Burns to discuss the building plans.

   b. Abraham Adams made an appointment with Mayor Burns to discuss the Building Plans.

   c. Abraham Adams made an appointment with mayor Burns to discuss the building plans.

   d. Abraham Adams made an appointment with mayor Burns to discuss the Building Plans.

6.

   a. Ms. Abigal Dornburg, M.D., was named head of the review board for Physicians Mutual.

   b. Ms. Abigal Dornburg, M.D., was named Head of the Review Board for Physicians Mutual.

   c. Ms. Abigal Dornburg, m.d. Was named head of the review board for Physicians mutual.

   d. Ms. Abigal dornburg, M.D., was named head of the review board for Physicians Mutual.

PUNCTUATION

PERIODS

Here is a quick review of the rules regarding the use of a period.

- Use a period at the end of a sentence that is not a question or an exclamation.
- Use a period after an initial in a name: Millard K. Furham
- Use a period after an abbreviation, unless the abbreviation is an acronym.
  Abbreviations: Mr., Ms., Dr., A.M., General Motors Corp., Allied Inc.
  Acronyms: NASA, AIDS
- If a sentence ends with an abbreviation, use only one period. (We brought food, tents, sleeping bags, etc.)

COMMAS

Using commas correctly can make the difference between presenting information clearly and distorting the facts. The following chart demonstrates the necessity of commas in written language. How many people are listed in the sentence?

COMMAS AND MEANING

Number undetermined	My sister Diane John Carey Melissa and I went to the fair.
Four people	My sister Diane, John Carey, Melissa, and I went to the fair.
Five people	My sister, Diane, John Carey, Melissa, and I went to the fair.
Six people	My sister, Diane, John, Carey, Melissa, and I went to the fair.

Here is a quick review of the most basic rules regarding the use of commas.

- Use a comma before *and, but, or, for, nor,* and *yet* when they separate two groups of words that could be complete sentences.
  Example: The coaches laid out the game plan, and the team executed it to perfection.
- Use a comma to separate items in a series.
  Example: The student driver stopped, looked, and listened when she got to the railroad tracks.
- Use a comma to separate two or more adjectives modifying the same noun.
  Example: The hot, black, rich coffee tasted great after an hour in below-zero weather. [Notice that there is no comma between *rich* (an adjective) and *coffee* (the noun *rich* describes)].
- Use a comma after introductory words, phrases, or clauses in a sentence.

Examples: Usually, the class begins with a short writing assignment. [Word]
Racing down the street, the yellow car ran a stoplight. [Phrase]
After we found the source of the noise, we relaxed and enjoyed the rest of the evening. [Clause]

- Use a comma after a name followed by Jr., Sr., or some other abbreviation.
  Example: The class was inspired by the speeches of Martin Luther King, Jr.
- Use a comma to separate items in an address.
  Example: The car stopped at 1433 West G Avenue, Orlando, Florida 36890.
- Use a comma to separate a day and a year, as well as after the year.
  Example: I was born on July 21, 1954, during a thunderstorm.
- Use a comma after the greeting of a friendly letter and after the closing of any letter.
  Example: Dear Uncle Jon,
  Sincerely yours,
- Use a comma to separate contrasting elements in a sentence.
  Example: Your essay needs strong arguments, not strong opinions, to convince me.
- Use commas to set off appositives (words or phrases that explain or identify a noun).
  Example: My cat, a Siamese, is named Ron.

The following passage contains no commas or periods. Add commas and periods as needed.

Dr Newton Brown Jr a renowned chemist has held research positions for OPEC Phillips Petroleum Inc Edward L Smith Chemical Designs and R J Reynolds Co His thorough exhaustive research is recognized in academic circles as well as in the business community as the most well-designed reliable data available Unfortunately on July 6 1998 he retired after a brief but serious illness He lives in a secluded retirement community at 2401 Beach Sarasota Springs Florida

Check your version against the corrected version below.

Dr. Newton Brown, Jr., a renowned chemist, has held research positions for OPEC, Phillips Petroleum Inc., Edward L. Smith Chemical Designs, and R. J. Reynolds Co. His thorough, exhaustive research is recognized in academic circles, as well as in the business community, as the most well-designed, reliable data available. Unfortunately, on July 6, 1998, he retired after a brief, but serious illness. He lives in a secluded retirement community at 2401 Beach, Sarasota Springs, Florida.

APOSTROPHES

Apostrophes communicate important information in written language. Here is a quick review of the two most important rules regarding the use of apostrophes.

- Use an apostrophe to show that letters have been omitted from a word to form a contraction.

Examples: do not = don't; national = nat'l; I will = I'll; it is = it's

- Use an apostrophe to show possession.

Check yourself with these sample test questions. Choose which of the four options is punctuated correctly. Answers are at the end of the chapter.

7.
   a. Although it may seem strange, my partners purpose in interviewing Dr. E. S. Sanders Jr. was to eliminate him as a suspect in the crime.
   b. Although it may seem strange my partner's purpose in interviewing Dr. E. S. Sanders, Jr. was to eliminate him, as a suspect in the crime.
   c. Although it may seem strange, my partner's purpose in interviewing Dr. E. S. Sanders, Jr., was to eliminate him as a suspect in the crime.
   d. Although it may seem strange, my partner's purpose in interviewing Dr. E. S. Sanders, Jr. was to eliminate him, as a suspect in the crime.

APOSTROPHES TO SHOW POSSESSION

Singular nouns (add 's)	Plural nouns ending in s (add ')	Plural nouns not ending in s
boy's	boys'	men's
child's	kids'	children's
lady's	ladies'	women's

8.

a. After colliding with a vehicle at the intersection of Grand, and Forest Ms. Anderson saw a dark hooded figure crawl through the window, reach back and grab a small parcel, and run north on Forest.

b. After colliding with a vehicle at the intersection of Grand, and Forest, Ms. Anderson saw a dark hooded figure crawl through the window, reach back and grab a small parcel, and run north on Forest.

c. After colliding with a vehicle at the intersection of Grand and Forest Ms. Anderson saw a dark, hooded figure crawl through the window, reach back and grab a small parcel, and run north on Forest.

d. After colliding with a vehicle at the intersection of Grand and Forest, Ms. Anderson saw a dark, hooded figure crawl through the window, reach back and grab a small parcel, and run north on Forest.

9.

a. When we interviewed each of the boys and the fathers, we determined that the men's stories did not match the boy's versions.

b. When we interviewed each of the boys and the fathers, we determined that the men's stories did not match the boys' versions.

c. When we interviewed each of the boys and the fathers, we determined that the mens' stories did not match the boys' versions.

d. When we interviewed each of the boys' and the fathers', we determined that the men's stories did not match the boys' versions.

VERBS

SUBJECT-VERB AGREEMENT

In written language a subject must agree with its verb in number. In other words, if a subject is singular, the verb must be singular. If the subject is plural, the verb must be plural. If you are unsure whether a verb is singular or plural, apply this simple test. Fill in the blanks in the two sentences below with the matching form of the verb. The verb form that best completes the first sentence is singular. The verb form that best completes the second sentence is plural.

One person _____. [Singular]
Two people _____. [Plural]

Look at these examples using the verbs *speak* and *do*. Try it yourself with any verb that confuses you.

One person *speaks*.   One person *does*.
Two people *speak*.   Two people *do*.

Pronoun Subjects

Few people have trouble matching noun subjects and verbs, but pronouns are sometimes difficult for even the most sophisticated speakers of English. Some pronouns are always singular, others are always plural, still others can be both singular and plural.

These pronouns are always singular.

each	everyone
either	no one
neither	nobody
anybody	one
anyone	somebody
everybody	someone

The indefinite pronouns *each, either*, and *neither* are the ones most often misused. You can avoid a mismatch by mentally adding the word *one* after the pronoun and removing the other words between the pronoun and the verb. Look at the following examples.

Each **of the men** wants his own car.
Each **one** wants his own car.

Either **of the salesclerks** knows where the sale merchandise is located.
Either **one** knows where the sale merchandise is located.

These sentences may sound awkward because many speakers misuse these pronouns, and you are probably used to hearing them used incorrectly. Despite that, the substitution trick (*one* for the words following the pronoun) will help you avoid this mistake.

Some pronouns are always plural and require a plural verb:

both   many
few   several

Other pronouns can be either singular or plural:

all   none
any   some
most

The words or prepositional phrases following them determine whether they are singular or plural. If what follows the pronouns is plural, the verb must be plural. If what follows is singular, the verb must be singular.

All of the **work is** finished.
All of the **jobs are** finished.

Is any of the **pizza** left?
Are any of the **pieces** of pizza left?

None of the **time was** wasted.
None of the **minutes were** wasted.

Subjects Joined by *and*

If two nouns or pronouns are joined by *and*, they require a plural verb.

He and she want to buy a new house.
Jack and Jill want to buy a new house.

Subjects Joined by *or* or *nor*

If two nouns or pronouns are joined by *or* or *nor*, they require a singular verb. Think of them as two separate sentences and you'll never make a mistake in agreement.

He or she wants to buy a new house.
    He wants to buy a new house.
    She wants to buy a new house.

Neither Jack nor Jill wants to buy a new house.
    Jack wants not to buy a new house.
    Jill wants not to buy a new house.

Circle the correct verb in each of the following sentences. Answers are at the end of the chapter.

10. Every other day either Bert or Ernie (takes, take) out the trash.

11. A woman in one of my classes (works, work) at the Civic Center box office.

12. A good knowledge of the rules (helps, help) you understand the game.

13. Each of these prescriptions (causes, cause) bloating and irritability.

14. (Have, Has) either of them ever arrived on time?

VERB TENSE

The tense of a verb tells a reader when the action occurs. Present tense verbs tell the reader to imagine that action happening as it is being read, while past tense verbs tell the reader the action has already happened. Read the following two paragraphs. The first one is written in the present tense, the second in the past tense. Notice the difference in the verbs. They are highlighted to make them easier to locate.

As Horace **opens** the door, he **glances** around cautiously. He **sees** signs of danger everywhere. The centerpiece and placemats from the dining room table **are scattered** on the floor next to the table. An end table in the living room **is lying** on its side. He **sees** the curtains flapping and **notices** glass on the carpet in front of the window.

As Horace **opened** the door, he **glanced** around cautiously. He **saw** signs of danger everywhere. The centerpiece and placemats from the dining room table **were scattered** on the floor next to the table. An end table in the living room **was lying** on its side. He **saw** the curtains flapping and **noticed** glass on the carpet in front of the window.

It's easy to distinguish present tense from past tense by simply fitting the verb into a sentence.

VERB TENSE	
Present tense (Today, I ___ . . .)	**Past tense (Yesterday, I ___ . . .)**
drive	drove
think	thought
rise	rose
catch	caught

The important thing to remember about verb tense is to keep it consistent. If a passage begins in the present tense, keep it in the present tense unless there is a specific reason to change—to indicate that some action occurred in the past, for instance. If a passage begins in the past tense, it should remain in the past tense. Verb tense should never be mixed as it is in the following sentence.

Wrong: Terry **opens** the door and **saw** the crowd.
Correct: Terry **opens** the door and **sees** the crowd.
Terry **opened** the door and **saw** the crowd.

However, sometimes it is necessary to use a different verb tense in order to clarify when an action occurred. Read the following sentences and the explanations following them.

The game warden **sees** the fish that you **caught**. [The verb **sees** is in the present tense, indicating that the action is occurring in the present. However, the verb **caught** is in the past tense, indicating that the fish were caught at some earlier time.]

The house that **was built** over a century ago **sits** on top of the hill. [The verb phrase **was built** is in the past tense, indicating that the house was built in the past. However, the verb **sits** is in the present tense, indicating that the action is still occurring.]

Check yourself with these sample questions. Choose the option that uses verb tense correctly. Answers are at the end of the chapter.

15.
  a. When I cry, I always get what I want.
  b. When I cry, I always got what I want.
  c. When I cried, I always got what I want.
  d. When I cried, I always get what I wanted.

16.
  a. It all started after I came home and am in my room studying for a big test.
  b. It all started after I came home and was in my room studying for a big test.
  c. It all starts after I come home and was in my room studying for a big test.
  d. It all starts after I came home and am in my room studying for a big test.

17.
  a. The child became excited and dashes into the house and slams the door.
  b. The child becomes excited and dashed into the house and slammed the door.
  c. The child becomes excited and dashes into the house and slammed the door.
  d. The child became excited and dashed into the house and slammed the door.

PRONOUNS

PRONOUN CASE

Most of the time, a single pronoun in a sentence is easy to use correctly. In fact, most English speakers would readily identify the mistakes in the following sentences.

> **Me** went to the movie with **he**.
> My teacher gave **she** a ride to school.

Most people know that **Me** in the first sentence should be I and that **he** should be **him**. They would also know that **she** in the second sentence should be **her**. Such errors are easy to spot when the pronouns are used alone in a sentence. The problem occurs when a pronoun is used with a noun or another pronoun. See if you can spot the errors in the following sentences.

> The director rode with Jerry and **I**.
> Belle and **him** are going to the ice arena.

The errors in these sentences are not as easy to spot as those in the sentences with a single pronoun. The easiest way to attack this problem is to turn the sentence with two pronouns into two separate sentences. Then the error once again becomes very obvious.

> The director rode with Jerry.
> The director rode with **me** (not I).

> Belle is going to the ice arena. [Notice the singular verb *is* in place of *are*.]
> **He** (not him) is going to the ice arena.

PRONOUN AGREEMENT

Another common error in using pronouns involves singular and plural pronouns. Like subjects and verbs, pronouns must match the number of the nouns they represent. If the noun a pronoun represents is singular, the pronoun must be singular. On the other hand, if the noun a pronoun represents is plural, the pronoun must be plural. Sometimes a pronoun represents another pronoun. If so, either both pronouns must be singular or both pronouns must be plural. Consult the list of singular and plural pronouns you saw earlier in this chapter.

> The **doctor** must take a break when **she** (or **he**) is tired. [singular]
> **Doctors** must take breaks when **they** are tired. [plural]

> **One** of the girls misplaced **her** purse. [singular]
> **All** of the girls misplaced **their** purses. [Plural]

If two or more singular nouns or pronouns are joined by *and,* use a plural pronoun to represent them.

> **Buddha and Muhammad** built religions around **their** philosophies.
> If **he and she** want to know where I was, **they** should ask me.

If two or more singular nouns or pronouns are joined by *or,* use a singular pronoun. If a singular and a plural noun or pronoun are joined by *or,* the pronoun agrees with the closest noun or pronoun it represents.

> **Matthew or Jacob** will loan you **his** calculator.
> **The elephant or the moose** will furiously protect **its** young.

> Neither **the soldiers** nor **the sergeant** was sure of **his** location.
> Neither **the sergeant** nor **the soldiers** were sure of **their** location.

Circle the correct pronoun in the following sentences. Answers are at the end of the chapter.

18. Andy or Arvin will bring (his, their) camera so (he, they) can take pictures of the party.

19. One of the file folders isn't in (its, their) drawer.

20. The NAPA store sent Bob and Ray the parts (he, they) had ordered.

21. Benny and (he, him) went to the movies with Bonnie and (I, me).

22. Neither my cousins nor my uncle knows what (he, they) will do tomorrow.

EASILY CONFUSED WORD PAIRS

The following words pairs are often misused in written language. By reading the explanations and looking at the examples, you can learn to use them correctly every time.

Its/it's

Its is a possessive pronoun that means "belonging to it." *It's* is a contraction for *it is* or *it has.* The only time you will ever use *it's* is when you can also substitute the words *it is* or *it has.*

Who/that

Who refers to people. *That* refers to things.

> There is the man **who** helped me find a new pet.
> The woman **who** invented the copper-bottomed kettle died in 1995.

This is the house **that** Harold bought.

The magazine **that** I needed was no longer in print.

There/their/they're

Their is a possessive pronoun that shows ownership. *There* is an adverb that tells where an action or item is located. *They're* is a contraction for the words *they are.* Here is an easy way to remember these words.

- *Their* means "belonging to them." Of the three words, *their* can be most easily transformed into the word *them.* Extend the *r* on the right side and connect the *i* and the *r* to turn *their* into *them.* This clue will help you remember that *their* means "belonging to them."
- If you examine the word *there,* you can see from the way it's written that it contains the word *here.* Whenever you use *there,* you should be able to substitute *here.* The sentence should still make sense.
- Imagine that the apostrophe in *they're* is actually a very small letter *a.* Use *they're* in a sentence only when you can substitute *they are.*

Your/you're

Your is a possessive pronoun that means "belonging to you." *You're* is a contraction for the words *you are.* The only time you will ever use *you're* is when you can also substitute the words *you are.*

To/too/two

To is a preposition or an infinitive.

- As a preposition: to the mall, to the bottom, to my church, to our garage, to his school, to his hideout, to our disadvantage, to an open room, to a ballad, to the gymnasium

- As an infinitive (*to* followed by a verb, sometimes separated by adverbs): to walk, to leap, to see badly, to find, to advance, to read, to build, to want sorely, to misinterpret badly, to peruse carefully

Too means "also." Whenever you use the word *too,* substitute the word *also.* The sentence should still make sense.

Two is a number, as in one, two. If you give it any thought at all, you'll never misuse this form.

The key is to think consciously about these words when you see them in written language. Circle the correct form of these easily confused words in the following sentences. Answers are at the end of the chapter.

23. (Its, It's) (to, too, two) late (to, too, two) remedy the problem now.

24. This is the man (who, that) helped me find the book I needed.

25. (There, Their, They're) going (to, too, two) begin construction as soon as the plans are finished.

26. We left (there, their, they're) house after the storm subsided.

27. I think (your, you're) going (to, too, two) win at least (to, too, two) more times.

28. The corporation moved (its, it's) home office.

ANSWERING MULTIPLE-CHOICE QUESTIONS ON GRAMMAR IN SENTENCES

As you take the portion of the test that assesses your writing skills, apply what you know about the rules of grammar:

- Look for complete sentences.
- Check for endmarks, commas, and apostrophes.
- Look for subject-verb agreement and consistency in verb tense.
- Check the pronouns to make sure the correct form is used and that the number (singular or plural) is correct.
- Check those easily confused pairs of words.

CLEAR SENTENCES

Some civil service exams may ask you to read two or more written versions of the same information and to choose the one that most *clearly* presents accurate information. It may be that all the choices are more or less correct grammatically, but some of them are so poorly written that they're hard to understand. You want the *best* option, the one that's clearest and most accurate. Check for accuracy first. If the facts are wrong, the answer is wrong, no matter how well-written the answer choice is. If the facts are accurately represented in several of the answer choices, then you must evaluate the writing itself. Here are a few tips for choosing the **best** answer.

1. The **best** answer will be written in plain English in such a way that most readers can understand it the first time through. If you read through an answer choice and find you need to reread it to understand what it says, look for a better option.
2. The **best** option will present the information in logical order, usually chronological order. If the order

seems questionable or is hard to follow, look for a better option.
3. The **best** option will be written with active rather than passive verbs. Answer choices written with passive verbs sound formal and stuffy. Look for an option that sounds like normal conversation. Here's an example.

Passive Voice

At 8:25 p.m., Officer Sanchez was dispatched to 18 Grand, an apartment complex, where a burglary had been reported by Milo Andrews, the manager.

Active Voice

At 8:25 p.m., Officer Sanchez responded to a burglary reported by Milo Andrews, the manager of an apartment complex at 18 Grand.

The first version uses the passive verbs "was dispatched" and "had been reported" rather than active verbs. Example 2 uses the active verb "responded."

4. The **best** answer contains clearly identified pronouns.

Unclear

Ann Dorr and the officer went to the precinct house, where she made her report.

Bob reminded his father that he had an appointment.

Clear

Ann Dorr and the officer went to the precinct house, where the officer made her report.

Bob reminded his father that Bob had an appointment.

An answer choice with clearly identified pronouns is a better choice than one with uncertain pronoun references. Sometimes the noun must be repeated to make the meaning clear.

5. The **best** option will use words clearly. Watch for unclear modifying words or phrases such as the ones in the following sentences. Misplaced and dangling modifiers can be hard to spot because your brain tries to make sense of things as it reads. In the case of misplaced or dangling modifiers, you may make a logical connection that is not present in the words.

Dangling Modifiers

Nailed to the tree, Cedric saw a "No Hunting" sign.

Waddling down the road, we saw a skunk.

Clear Modifiers

Cedric saw a "No Hunting" sign nailed to a tree.

We saw a skunk waddling down the road.

In the first version of the sentences, it sounds like *Cedric* was nailed to a tree and *we* were waddling down the road. The second version probably represents the writer's intentions: the *sign* was nailed to a tree and the *skunk* was waddling.

Misplaced Modifier

A dog followed the boy who was growling and barking.

George told us about safe sex in the kitchen.

Clear Modifiers

A dog who was growling and barking followed the boy.

In the kitchen, George told us about safe sex.

Do you think the boy was growling and barking? Did George discuss avoiding sharp knives and household poisons? The second version of each sentence represents the real situation.

6. Finally, the **best** option will use words efficiently. Avoid answer choices that are redundant (repeat unnecessarily) or wordy. Extra words take up valuable time and increase the chances that facts will be misunderstood. In the following examples, the italicized words are redundant or unnecessary. Try reading the sentences without the italicized words.

Redundant

They refunded our money *back to us*.

We can proceed *ahead* with the plan we made *ahead of time*.

The car was red *in color*.

Wordy

The reason he pursued the car *was* because it ran a stoplight.

We didn't know what *it was* we were doing.

There are many citizens *who* obey the law.

In each case, the sentence is simpler and easier to read without the italicized words. When you find an answer choice that uses unnecessary words, look for a better option.

The BEST Option:

- Is ACCURATE
- Is written in plain English
- Presents information in a logical order
- Uses active verbs
- Has clearly identified pronouns
- Uses words clearly
- Uses words efficiently

Here are four sample multiple-choice questions. By applying the principles explained in this section, choose the best version of each of the four sets of sentences. The answers and a short explanation for each question are at the end of the chapter.

29.

a. Vanover caught the ball. This was after it had been thrown by the shortstop. Vanover was the first baseman who caught the double-play ball. The shortstop was Hennings. He caught a line drive.

b. After the shortstop Hennings caught the line drive, he threw it to the first baseman Vanover for the double play.

c. After the line drive was caught by Hennings, the shortstop, it was thrown to Vanover at first base for a double play.

d. Vanover the first baseman caught the flip from shortstop Hennings.

30.

a. This writer attended the movie *Casino* starring Robert DeNiro.

b. The movie *Casino* starring Robert DeNiro was attended by me.

c. The movie *Casino* starring Robert DeNiro was attended by this writer.

d. I attended the movie *Casino* starring Robert DeNiro.

31.

a. They gave cereal boxes with prizes inside to the children.

b. They gave cereal boxes to children with prizes inside.

c. Children were given boxes of cereal by them with prizes inside.

d. Children were given boxes of cereal with prizes inside by them.

32.

  a. After playing an exciting drum solo, the crowd rose to its feet and then claps and yells until the band plays another cut from their new album.

  b. After playing an exciting drum solo, the crowd rose to its feet and then clapped and yelled until the band played another cut from their new album.

  c. After the drummer's exciting solo, the crowd rose to its feet and then claps and yells until the band plays another cut from their new album.

  d. After the drummer's exciting solo, the crowd rose to its feet and then clapped and yelled until the band played another cut from their new album.

ADDITIONAL RESOURCES

This has been a very fast review of only a few aspects of written English. For more help with these aspects and more, here are some books you can consult.

FOR NON-NATIVE SPEAKERS OF ENGLISH

- *English Made Simple* by Arthur Waldhorn and Arthur Ziegler (Made Simple Books)
- *Errors in English and How to Correct Them* by Harry Shaw (HarperCollins)
- *Living Language English for New Americans* by Carol Pineiro, Carol Houser, and Ana Suffredini (Living Language)

FOR EVERYONE

- *501 Grammar and Writing Questions* (LearningExpress)
- *Writing Skills in 20 Minutes a Day* by Judith Olson (LearningExpress, order information at the back of this book)
- *1001 Pitfalls in English Grammar* by Vincent Foster Hopper (Barron's)
- *Better English* by Norman Lewis (Dell)
- *Action Grammar* by Joanne Feierman (Fireside)

ANSWERS

1. d.
2. a.
3. d.
4. c.
5. a.
6. a.
7. c.
8. d.
9. b.
10. takes
11. works
12. helps
13. causes
14. Has
15. a.
16. b.
17. d.
18. his, he
19. its
20. they
21. he, me
22. he

23. It's, too, to
24. who
25. They're, to
26. their
27. you're, to, two
28. its
29. b. Answer **a** is unnecessarily wordy and the order is not logical. Answer **c** is written using passive voice verbs. Answer **d** omits a piece of important information.
30. d. Both answers **a** and **c** use the stuffy-sounding *this writer.* Answer **d** is best because it uses an active verb.
31. a. In both answers **b** and **c** the modifying phrase *with prizes inside* is misplaced. Both answers **c** and **d** are written in passive rather than active voice.
32. d. Both answers **a** and **b** contain a dangling modifier, stating that the crowd played an exciting drum solo. Both answers **b** and **c** mix past and present verb tense. Only answer **d** has clearly written modifiers and a consistent verb tense.

C·H·A·P·T·E·R

VOCABULARY AND SPELLING

11

CHAPTER SUMMARY

Vocabulary and spelling are tested, at least indirectly, on most civil service exams. This chapter provides tips and exercises to help you improve your score in both areas.

 person's vocabulary is seen as a measure of an ability to express ideas clearly and precisely. For almost any job, you must know the working vocabulary of the profession or have the tools for acquiring that vocabulary quickly. Spelling is regarded as a measure of a person's accuracy in presenting information. Most civil servants have to be able to write correctly in order to communicate clearly. In addition, accurate spelling and a wide and flexible vocabulary are seen as the marks of thoughtful and well-educated people.

VOCABULARY

Many civil service exams test vocabulary. There are three basic kinds of questions.

- Synonyms and antonyms: Identifying words that mean the same as or the opposite of given words

- Context: Determining the meaning of a word or phrase by noting how it is used in a sentence or paragraph
- Word parts: Choosing the meaning suggested by a part of the word, such as a prefix or suffix

SYNONYM AND ANTONYM QUESTIONS

A word is a *synonym* of another word if it has the same or nearly the same meaning as the other word. *Antonyms* are words with opposite meanings. Test questions often ask you to find the synonym or antonym of a word. If you're lucky, the word will be surrounded by a sentence that helps you guess what the word means. If you're less lucky, you'll just get the word, and then you have to figure out what the word means without any help.

Questions that ask for synonyms and antonyms can be tricky because they require you to recognize the meaning of several words that may be unfamiliar—not only the words in the questions but also the answer choices. Usually the best strategy is to *look* at the structure of the word and to *listen* for its sound. See if a part of a word looks familiar. Think of other words you know that have similar key elements. How could those words be related?

Synonym Practice

Try your hand at identifying the word parts and related words in these sample synonym questions. Circle the word that means the same or about the same as the underlined word. Answers and explanations appear right after the questions.

1. a set of <u>partial</u> prints
   a. identifiable
   b. incomplete
   c. visible
   d. enhanced

2. <u>substantial</u> evidence
   a. inconclusive
   b. weighty
   c. proven
   d. alleged

3. <u>corroborated</u> the statement
   a. confirmed
   b. negated
   c. denied
   d. challenged

4. <u>ambiguous</u> questions
   a. meaningless
   b. difficult
   c. simple
   d. vague

Answers to Synonym Questions

The explanations are just as important as the answers, because they show you how to go about choosing a synonym if you don't know the word.

1. **b.** *Partial* means *incomplete.* The key part of the word here is *part.* A partial print is only part of the whole.
2. **b.** *Substantial* evidence is *weighty.* The key part of the word here is *substance.* Substance has weight.
3. **a.** *Corroboration* is *confirmation.* The key part of the word here is the prefix *co-,* which means *with* or *together.* Corroboration means that one statement fits with another.
4. **d.** *Ambiguous* questions are *vague* or uncertain. The key part of this word is *ambi-,* which means *two* or *both.* An ambiguous question can be taken two ways.

Antonym Practice

The main danger in answering questions with antonyms is forgetting that you are looking for *opposites* rather than synonyms. Most questions will include one or more synonyms as answer choices. The trick is to keep your mind on the fact that you are looking for the opposite of the word. If you're allowed to mark in the books or on the test papers, circle the word *antonym* or *opposite* in the directions to help you remember.

Otherwise, the same tactics that work for synonym questions work for antonyms as well: try to determine the meaning of part of the word or to remember a context where you've seen the word before.

Circle the word that means the *opposite* of the underlined word in the sentences below. Answers are immediately after the questions.

5. <u>zealous</u> pursuit
   a. envious
   b. eager
   c. idle
   d. comical

6. <u>inadvertently</u> left
   a. mistakenly
   b. purposely
   c. cautiously
   d. carefully

7. <u>exorbitant</u> prices
   a. expensive
   b. unexpected
   c. reasonable
   d. outrageous

8. <u>compatible</u> workers
   a. comfortable
   b. competitive
   c. harmonious
   d. experienced

9. <u>belligerent</u> attitude
   a. hostile
   b. reasonable
   c. instinctive
   d. ungracious

Answers to Antonym Questions

Be sure to read the explanations as well as the right answers.

5. c. *Zealous* means *eager*, so *idle* is most nearly opposite. Maybe you've heard the word *zeal* before. One trick in this question is not to be misled by the similar sounds of *zealous* and *jealous*. The other is not to choose the synonym, *eager*.

6. b. *Inadvertently* means *by mistake*, so *purposely* is the antonym. The key element in this word is the prefix *in-*, which usually means *not, the opposite of*. As usual, one of the answer choices (a) is a synonym.

7. c. The key element here is *ex-*, which means *out of* or *away from*. *Exorbitant* literally means "out of orbit." The opposite of an *exorbitant* or *outrageous* price would be a *reasonable* one.

8. b. The opposite of *compatible* is *competitive*. Here you have to distinguish among three words that contain the same prefix, *com-*, and to let the process of elimination work for you. The other choices are too much like synonyms.

9. b. The key element in this word is the root *belli-*, which means *warlike*. The synonym choices, then, are *hostile* and *ungracious*; the antonym is *reasonable*.

CONTEXT QUESTIONS

Context is the surrounding text in which a word is used. Most people use context to help them determine the meaning of an unknown word. A vocabulary question that gives you a sentence around the vocabulary word is usually easier to answer than one with little or no context. The surrounding text can help you as you look for synonyms for the specified words in the sentences.

The best way to take meaning from context is to look for key words in sentences or paragraphs that convey the meaning of the text. If nothing else, the context will give you a means to eliminate wrong answer choices that clearly don't fit. The process of elimination will often leave you with the correct answer.

Context Practice

Try these sample questions. Circle the word that best describes the meaning of the underlined word in the sentence.

10. The clerks in the store were <u>appalled</u> by the wild and uncontrolled behavior of the angry customer.
    a. horrified
    b. amused
    c. surprised
    d. dismayed

11. Despite the fact that he appeared to have financial resources, the client claimed to be <u>destitute</u>.
    a. wealthy
    b. ambitious
    c. solvent
    d. impoverished

12. Though she was <u>distraught</u> over the disappearance of her child, the woman was calm enough to give the officer her description.
    a. punished
    b. distracted
    c. composed
    d. anguished

13. The unrepentant embezzler expressed no <u>remorse</u> for his actions.
    a. sympathy
    b. regret
    c. reward
    d. complacency

Some tests may ask you to fill in the blank by choosing a word that fits the context. In the following questions, circle the word that best completes the sentence.

14. Professor Washington was a very_____ man known for his reputation as a scholar.
    a. stubborn
    b. erudite
    c. illiterate
    d. disciplined

15. His_____was demonstrated by his willingness to donate large amounts of money to worthy causes.
    a. honesty
    b. loyalty
    c. selfishness
    d. altruism

Answers to Context Questions

Check to see whether you were able to pick out the key words that help you define the target word, as well as whether you got the right answer.

10. a. The key words *wild* and *uncontrolled* signify *horror* rather than the milder emotions described by the other choices.

11. d. The key words here are *financial resources,* but this is a clue by contrast. The introductory *Despite the fact* signals that you should look for the opposite of the idea of having financial resources.

12. d. The key words here are *though* and *disappearance of her child,* signalling that you are looking for an opposite of *calm* in describing how the mother spoke to the officer. The only word strong enough to match the situation is *anguish.*

13. b. *Remorse* means *regret* for one's action. The part of the word here to beware of is the prefix *re-*. It doesn't signify anything in this word, though it often means *again* or *back.* Don't be confused by the two choices which also contain the prefix *re-*. The strategy here is to see which word sounds better in the sentence. The key words are *unrepentant* and *no,* indicating that you're looking for something that shows no repentance.

14. b. The key words here are *professor* and *scholarly.* Even if you don't know the word *erudite,* the other choices don't fit the description of the professor.

15. d. The key words here are *large amounts of money to worthy causes.* They give you a definition of the word you're looking for. Again, even if you don't know the word *altruism,* the other choices seem inappropriate to describe someone so generous.

QUESTIONS ABOUT WORD PARTS

Some tests may ask you to find the meaning of a part of a word: roots, which are the main part of the word; prefixes, which go before the root word; or suffixes, which go after. Any of these elements can carry meaning or change the use of a word in a sentence. For instance, the suffix *-s* or *-es* can change the meaning of a noun from singular to plural: *boy, boys.* The prefix *un-* can change the meaning of a root word to its opposite: *necessary, unnecessary.*

To identify most parts of words, the best strategy is to think of words you already know which carry the same root, suffix, or prefix. Let what you know about those words help you to see the meaning in words that are less familiar.

Word Part Practice

Circle the word or phrase below that best describes the meaning of the underlined portion of the word. Answers appear after the questions.

16. <u>pro</u>active
   a. after
   b. forward
   c. toward
   d. behind

17. <u>re</u>cession
   a. against
   b. see
   c. under
   d. back

18. <u>con</u>temporary
   a. with
   b. over
   c. apart
   d. time

19. etymo<u>logy</u>
   a. state of
   b. prior to
   c. study of
   d. quality of

20. vanda<u>lize</u>
   a. to make happen
   b. to stop

   c. to fill
   d. to continue

Answers to Word Part Questions

Even if the word in the question was unfamiliar, you might have been able to guess the meaning of the prefix or suffix by thinking of some other word that has the same prefix or suffix.

16. b. Think of *propeller*. A propeller sends an airplane *forward*.

17. d. Think of *recall*: Manufacturers *recall* or *bring back* cars that are defective; people *recall* or *bring back* past events in memory.

18. a. Think of *congregation*: a group of people gather *with* each other in a house of worship.

19. c. Think of *biology*, the *study of* life.

20. a. Think of *scandalize*: to *make* something shocking *happen*.

WORDS THAT ARE EASILY CONFUSED

Vocabulary tests of any kind often contain words that are easily confused with each other. A smart test taker will be aware of these easily mixed up words or phrases:

accept: to receive willingly	**except:** exclude or leave out
complement: to complete	**compliment:** to say something flattering
council: a group that makes decisions	**counsel:** to give advice
contemptuous: having an attitude of contempt	**contemptible:** worthy of contempt
continuous: without interruption	**continual:** from time to time
emigrate: to move from	**immigrate:** to move to
ingenious: something clever	**ingenuous:** guileless or naive
oral: pertaining to the mouth	**verbal:** pertaining to language
persecute: to oppress someone	**prosecute:** to bring a legal action against someone

How to Answer Vocabulary Questions

- The key to answering vocabulary questions is to **notice and connect** what you do know to what you may not recognize.
- **Know your word parts.** You can recognize or make a good guess at the meanings of words when you see some suggested meaning in a root word, prefix, or suffix.
- **Note directions very carefully.** Remember when you are looking for opposites rather than synonyms.
- **Use a process of elimination.** Think of how the word makes sense in the sentence.
- **Don't be confused by words that sound like other words,** but may have no relation to the word you need.

A List of Word Parts

On the next page are some of the word elements seen most often in vocabulary tests. Simply reading them and their examples five to ten minutes a day will give you the quick recognition you need to make a good association with the meaning of an unfamiliar word.

SPELLING

Generally spelling tests are in a multiple-choice format. You will be given several possible spellings for a word and asked to identify the one that is correct. Thus, you must be able to see very fine differences between word spellings. The best way to prepare for a spelling test is to have a good grasp of the spelling fundamentals and be able to recognize when those rules don't apply.

Remember that English is full of exceptions in spelling. You have to develop a good eye to spot the errors.

Even though there are so many variant spellings for words in English, civil service tests generally are looking to make sure that you know and can apply the basic rules. Here are some of those rules to review:

- *i* before *e*, except after *c*, or when *ei* sounds like *a*
  Examples: piece, receive, neighbor
- *gh* can replace *f* or be silent
  Examples: enough, night
- Double the consonant when you add an ending
  Examples: forget/forgettable, shop/shopping
- Drop the *e* when you add *ing*
  Example: hope/hoping
- The spelling of prefixes and suffixes generally doesn't change
  Examples: project, propel, proactive

SPELLING PRACTICE

Here are some examples of how spelling would appear on a civil service test. Choose the word that is spelled correctly in the following sentences. This time there's no answer key. Instead, use your dictionary to find the right answers.

21. We went to an _____ of early Greek art.
    a. exibition
    b. exhibition
    c. excibition
    d. exebition

word element	meaning	example
ama	love	amateur
ambi	both	ambivalent, ambidextrous
aud	hear	audition
bell	war	belligerent, bellicose
bene	good	benefactor
cid/cis	cut	homicide, scissor
cogn/gno	know	knowledge, recognize
curr	run	current
flu/flux	flow	fluid, fluctuate
gress	to go	congress, congregation
in	not, in	ingenious
ject	throw	inject, reject
luc/lux	light	lucid, translucent
neo	new	neophyte
omni	all	omnivorous
pel/puls	push	impulse, propeller
pro	forward	project
pseudo	false	pseudonym
rog	ask	interrogate
sub	under	subjugate
spec/spic	look, see	spectator
super	over	superfluous
temp	time	contemporary, temporal
un	not, opposite	uncoordinated
viv	live	vivid

22. We will _____ go to the movies tonight.
    a. probly
    b. probbaly
    c. probely
    d. probably

23. We took _____ of pictures on our vacation.
    a. allot
    b. alot
    c. a lot
    d. alott

24. The high scorer had the greatest number of
_____ answers.
  a. accurate
  b. acurate
  c. accuret
  d. acccurit

25. He was warned not to use _____
force.
  a. exessive
  b. excesive
  c. excessive
  d. excesive

USING SPELLING LISTS

Some test makers will give you a list to study before you take the test. If you have a list to work with, here are some suggestions.

- Divide the list into groups of three, five, or seven to study. Consider making flash cards of the words you don't know.
- Highlight or circle the tricky elements in each word.
- Cross out or discard any words that you already know for certain. Don't let them get in the way of the ones you need to study.
- Say the words as you read them. Spell them out in your mind so you can "hear" the spelling.

Here's a sample spelling list. These words are typical of the words that appear on exams. If you aren't given a list by the agency that's testing you, study this one.

achievement	doubtful	ninety
allege	eligible	noticeable
anxiety	enough	occasionally
appreciate	enthusiasm	occurred
asthma	equipped	offense
arraignment	exception	official
autonomous	fascinate	pamphlet
auxiliary	fatigue	parallel
brief	forfeit	personnel
ballistics	gauge	physician
barricade	grieve	politics
beauty	guilt	possess
beige	guarantee	privilege
business	harass	psychology
bureau	hazard	recommend
calm	height	referral
cashier	incident	recidivism
capacity	indict	salary
cancel	initial	schedule
circuit	innocent	seize
colonel	irreverent	separate
comparatively	jeopardy	specific
courteous	knowledge	statute
criticism	leisure	surveillance
custody	license	suspicious
cyclical	lieutenant	tentative
debt	maintenance	thorough
definitely	mathematics	transferred
descend	mortgage	warrant

How to Answer Spelling Questions

- **Sound out the word in your mind.** Remember that long vowels inside words usually are followed by single consonants: sofa, total. Short vowels inside words usually are followed by double consonants: dribble, scissors.
- **Give yourself auditory (listening) clues when you learn words.** Say "Wed-nes-day" or "lis-ten" or "bus-i-ness" to yourself so that you remember to add letters you do not hear.
- **Look at each part of a word**. See if there is a root, prefix or suffix that will always be spelled the same way. For example, in uninhabitable, un-, in-, and -able are always spelled the same. What's left is habit, a self-contained root word that's pretty easy to spell.

MORE PRACTICE IN VOCABULARY AND SPELLING

Here is a second set of practice exercises with samples of each kind of question covered in this chapter. Answers to all questions except spelling questions are at the end of the chapter. For spelling questions, use a dictionary.

Circle the word that means the same or nearly the same as the underlined word.

26. <u>convivial</u> company
    a. lively
    b. dull
    c. tiresome
    d. dreary

27. <u>conspicuous</u> behavior
    a. secret
    b. notable
    c. visible
    d. boorish

28. <u>meticulous</u> record-keeping
    a. dishonest
    b. casual
    c. painstaking
    d. careless

29. <u>superficial</u> wounds
    a. life-threatening
    b. bloody
    c. severe
    d. shallow

30. <u>impulsive</u> actions
    a. cautious
    b. imprudent
    c. courageous
    d. cowardly

Circle the word that is most nearly opposite in meaning to the underlined word.

31. <u>amateur</u> athlete
    a. professional
    b. successful
    c. unrivaled
    d. former

32. <u>lucid</u> opinions
    a. clear
    b. strong
    c. hazy
    d. heartfelt

33. traveling <u>incognito</u>
   a. unrecognized
   b. alone
   c. by night
   d. publicly

34. <u>incisive</u> reporting
   a. mild
   b. sharp
   c. dangerous
   d. insightful

35. <u>tactful</u> comments
   a. rude
   b. pleasant
   c. complimentary
   d. sociable

Using the context, choose the word that means the same or nearly the same as the underlined word.

36. Though he had little time, the student took <u>copious</u> notes in preparation for the test.
   a. limited
   b. plentiful
   c. illegible
   d. careless

37. Though flexible about homework, the teacher was <u>adamant</u> that papers be in on time.
   a. liberal
   b. casual
   c. strict
   d. pliable

38. The condition of the room after the party was <u>deplorable</u>.
   a. regrettable
   b. pristine
   c. festive
   d. tidy

Choose the word that best completes the following sentences.

39. Her position as a(n) _____ teacher took her all over the city.
   a. primary
   b. secondary
   c. itinerant
   d. permanent

40. Despite her promise to stay in touch, she remained _____ and difficult to locate.
   a. steadfast
   b. stubborn
   c. dishonest
   d. elusive

Choose the word or phrase closest in meaning to the underlined part of the word.

41. <u>uni</u>verse
   a. one
   b. three
   c. under
   d. opposite

42. <u>re</u>entry
   a. back
   b. push
   c. against
   d. forward

43. <u>bene</u>fit
   a. bad
   b. suitable
   c. beauty
   d. good

44. educa<u>tion</u>
   a. something like
   b. state of
   c. to increase
   d. unlike

45. urban<u>ite</u>
   a. resident of
   b. relating to
   c. that which is
   d. possessing

Circle the correct spelling of the word that fits in the blank.

46. The information was _____
   to the action.
   a. irelevent
   b. irrevelent
   c. irrelevant
   d. irrevelent

47. He made no _____ to take
   the job.
   a. comittment
   b. commitment
   c. comitment
   d. comittmint

48. He made an income _____
   to meet his needs.
   a. adaquate
   b. adequate
   c. adiquate
   d. adequet

49. We went to eat at a fancy new _____.
   a. restarant
   b. restaraunt
   c. restaurant
   d. resteraunt

50. The vote was _____ to elect
   the chairman.
   a. unannimous
   b. unanimous
   c. unanimus
   d. unaminous

ADDITIONAL RESOURCES

One of the best resources for any adult student is the public library. Many libraries have sections for adult learners or for those preparing to enter or change careers. Those sections contain skill books and review books on a number of subjects, including spelling and vocabulary. Here are some books you might consult:

- *Vocabulary and Spelling in 20 Minutes a Day* by Judith Meyers (LearningExpress, order information at the back of this book)
- *504 Absolutely Essential Words* by Murray Bromberg et al. (Barron's)
- *How to Build a Better Vocabulary* by M. and M. Rosenblum Nurnberg and Morris Rosenblum (Warner Books)

- *Merriam–Webster's Vocabulary Builder* by Mary Wood Cornog (Merriam–Webster)
- *500 SAT Words, and How to Remember Them Forever* by Charles Gulotta (Mostly Bright Ideas)
- *Spelling Made Simple* by Stephen V. Ross (Doubleday)
- *Spelling the Easy Way* by Joseph Mersand and Francis Griffith (Barron's)
- *Word Smart Revised* by Adam Robinson (The Princeton Review)
- *Instant Spelling Dictionary* by Margaret M. Dougherty (Warner Books)

ANSWERS TO PRACTICE QUESTIONS

26. a.
27. c.
28. c.
29. d.
30. b.
31. a.
32. c.
33. d.
34. a.
35. a.
36. b.
37. c.
38. a.
39. c.
40. d.
41. a.
42. a.
43. d.
44. b.
45. a.

C·H·A·P·T·E·R

MATH

12

CHAPTER SUMMARY

This chapter gives you some important tips for dealing with math questions on a civil service exam and reviews some of the most commonly tested concepts. If you've forgotten most of your high school math or have math anxiety, this chapter is for you.

ot all civil service exams test your math knowledge, but many do. Knowledge of basic arithmetic, as well as the more complex kinds of reasoning necessary for algebra and geometry problems, are important qualifications for almost any profession. You have to be able to add up dollar figures, evaluate budgets, compute percentages, and other such tasks, both in your job and in your personal life. Even if your exam doesn't include math, you'll find that the material in this chapter will be useful on the job.

The math portion of the test covers the subjects you probably studied in grade school and high school. While every test is different, most emphasize arithmetic skills and word problems.

MATH STRATEGIES

- **Don't work in your head!** Use your test book or scratch paper to take notes, draw pictures, and calculate. Although you might think that you can solve math questions more quickly in your head, that's a good way to make mistakes. Write out each step.
- **Read a math question in *chunks*** rather than straight through from beginning to end. As you read each *chunk*, stop to think about what it means and make notes or draw a picture to represent that *chunk*.
- **When you get to the actual question, circle it.** This will keep you more focused as you solve the problem.
- **Glance at the answer choices for clues.** If they're fractions, you probably should do your work in fractions; if they're decimals, you should probably work in decimals; etc.
- **Make a plan of attack** to help you solve the problem.
- **If a question stumps you, try one of the *backdoor* approaches** explained in the next section. These are particularly useful for solving word problems.
- **When you get your answer, reread the circled question to make sure you've answered it.** This helps avoid the careless mistake of answering the wrong question.
- **Check your work after you get an answer.** Test-takers get a false sense of security when they get an answer that matches one of the multiple-choice answers. Here are some good ways to check your work *if you have time*:
  - Ask yourself if your answer is reasonable, if it makes sense.
  - Plug your answer back into the problem to make sure the problem holds together.
  - Do the question a second time, but use a different method.
- **Approximate when appropriate.** For example:
  - $5.98 + $8.97 is a little less than $15. (Add: $6 + $9)
  - $.9876 \times 5.0342$ is close to 5. (Multiply: 1×5)
- **Skip hard questions and come back to them later.** Mark them in your test book so you can find them quickly.

BACKDOOR APPROACHES FOR ANSWERING QUESTIONS THAT PUZZLE YOU

Remember those word problems you dreaded in high school? Many of them are actually easier to solve by backdoor approaches. The two techniques that follow are terrific ways to solve multiple-choice word problems that you don't know how to solve with a straightforward approach. The first technique, *nice numbers*, is useful when there are unknowns (like *x*) in the text of the word problem, making the problem too abstract for you. The second technique, *working backwards*, presents a quick way to substitute numeric answer choices back into the problem to see which one works.

Nice Numbers

1. When a question contains unknowns, like *x*, plug nice numbers in for the unknowns. A nice number is easy to calculate with and makes sense in the problem.

2. Read the question with the nice numbers in place. Then solve it.

3. If the answer choices are all numbers, the choice that matches your answer is the right one.

4. If the answer choices contain unknowns, substitute the same nice numbers into **all** the answer choices. The choice that matches your answer is the right one. If more than one answer matches, do the problem again with different nice numbers. You'll only have to check the answer choices that have already matched.

Example: Judi went shopping with p dollars in her pocket. If the price of shirts was s shirts for d dollars, what is the maximum number of shirts Judi could buy with the money in her pocket?

a. psd b. $\frac{ps}{d}$ c. $\frac{pd}{s}$ d. $\frac{ds}{p}$

To solve this problem, let's try these nice numbers: $p = \$100$, $s = 2$; $d = \$25$. Now reread it with the numbers in place:

Judi went shopping with *$100* in her pocket. If the price of shirts was *2* shirts for *$25*, what is the maximum number of shirts Judi could buy with the money in her pocket?

Since 2 shirts cost $25, that means that 4 shirts cost $50, and 8 shirts cost $100. So our answer is *8*. Let's substitute the nice numbers into all 4 answers:

a. $100 \times 2 \times 25 = 5000$ b. $\frac{100 \times 2}{25} = 8$ c. $\frac{100 \times 25}{2} = 1250$ d. $\frac{25 \times 2}{100} = \frac{1}{2}$

The answer is b because it is the only one that matches our answer of 8.

Working Backwards

You can frequently solve a word problem by plugging the answer choices back into the text of the problem to see which one fits all the facts stated in the problem. The process is faster than you think because you'll probably only have to substitute one or two answers to find the right one.

This approach works only when:

- All of the answer choices are numbers.
- You're asked to find a simple number, not a sum, product, difference, or ratio.

Here's what to do:

1. Look at all the answer choices and begin with the one in the middle of the range. For example, if the answers are 14, 8, 2, 20, and 25, begin by plugging 14 into the problem.

2. If your choice doesn't work, eliminate it. Determine if you need a bigger or smaller answer.

3. Plug in one of the remaining choices.

4. If none of the answers work, you may have made a careless error. Begin again or look for your mistake.

Example: Juan ate $\frac{1}{3}$ of the jellybeans. Maria then ate $\frac{3}{4}$ of the remaining jellybeans, which left 10 jellybeans. How many jellybeans were there to begin with?

a. 60   b. 80   c. 90   d. 120   e. 140

Starting with the middle answer, let's assume there were **90** jellybeans to begin with:

Since Juan ate $\frac{1}{3}$ of them, that means he ate 30 ($\frac{1}{3} \times 90 = 30$), leaving 60 of them ($90 - 30 = 60$). Maria then ate $\frac{3}{4}$ of the 60 jellybeans, or 45 of them ($\frac{3}{4} \times 60 = 45$). That leaves 15 jellybeans ($60 - 45 = 15$).

The problem states that there were **10** jellybeans left, and we wound up with **15** of them. That indicates that we started with too big a number. Thus, 90, 120, and 140 are all wrong! With only two choices left, let's use common sense to decide which one to try. The next lower answer is only a little smaller than 90 and may not be small enough. So, let's try **60**:

Since Juan ate $\frac{1}{3}$ of them, that means he ate 20 ($\frac{1}{3} \times 60 = 20$), leaving 40 of them ($60 - 20 = 40$). Maria then ate $\frac{3}{4}$ of the 40 jellybeans, or 30 of them ($\frac{3}{4} \times 40 = 30$). That leaves 10 jellybeans ($40 - 30 = 10$).

Because this result of **10** jellybeans left agrees with the problem, the right answer is **a.**

WORD PROBLEMS

Many of the math problems on tests are word problems. A word problem can include any kind of math, including simple arithmetic, fractions, decimals, percentages, even algebra and geometry.

The hardest part of any word problem is translating English into math. When you read a problem, you can frequently translate it *word for word* from English statements into mathematical statements. At other times, however, a key word in the word problem hints at the mathematical operation to be performed. Here are the translation rules:

EQUALS   key words: is, are, has

English	Math
Bob **is** 18 years old.	B = 18
There **are** 7 hats.	H = 7
Judi **has** 5 books.	J = 5

ADDITION   key words: sum; more, greater, or older than; total; altogether

English	Math
The **sum** of two numbers is 10.	X + Y = 10
Karen has $5 **more than** Sam.	K = 5 + S
The base is 3″ **greater than** the height.	B = 3 + H
Judi is 2 years **older than** Tony.	J = 2 + T
The **total** of three numbers is 25.	A + B + C = 25
How much do Joan and Tom have **altogether**?	J + T = ?

SUBTRACTION   key words: difference, less or younger than, remain, left over

English	Math
The **difference** between two numbers is 17.	X − Y = 17
Mike has 5 **less** cats **than** twice the number Jan has.	M = 2J − 5
Jay is 2 years **younger than** Brett.	J = B − 2
After Carol ate 3 apples, R apples **remained**.	R = A − 3

MULTIPLICATION   key words: of, product, times

English	Math
20% **of** Matthew's baseball caps	$.20 \times M$
Half **of** the boys	$\frac{1}{2} \times B$
The **product** of two numbers is 12	$A \times B = 12$

DIVISION   key word: **per**

English	Math
15 drops **per** teaspoon	$\frac{15 \text{ drops}}{\text{teaspoon}}$
22 miles **per** gallon	$\frac{22 \text{ miles}}{\text{gallon}}$

DISTANCE FORMULA: DISTANCE = RATE × TIME

The key words are movement words like: plane, train, boat, car, walk, run, climb, swim

- How far did the **plane** travel in 4 hours if it averaged 300 miles per hour?

  $D = 300 \times 4$

  $D = 1200$ miles

- Ben **walked** 20 miles in 4 hours. What was his average speed?

  $20 = r \times 4$

  5 miles per hour $= r$

SOLVING A WORD PROBLEM USING THE TRANSLATION TABLE

Remember the problem at the beginning of this chapter about the jellybeans?

Juan ate $\frac{1}{3}$ of the jellybeans. Maria then ate $\frac{3}{4}$ of the remaining jellybeans, which left 10 jellybeans. How many jellybeans were there to begin with?

  a. 60 **b.** 80 **c.** 90 **d.** 120 **e.** 140

We solved it by *working backwards*. Now let's solve it using our translation rules.

Assume Juan started with *J* jellybeans. Eating $\frac{1}{3}$ of them means eating $\frac{1}{3} \times J$ jellybeans. Maria ate a fraction of the **remaining** jellybeans, which means we must **subtract** to find out how many are left: $J - \frac{1}{3} \times J = \frac{2}{3} \times J$. Maria then ate $\frac{3}{4}$, leaving $\frac{1}{4}$ of the $\frac{2}{3} \times J$ jellybeans, or $\frac{1}{4} \times \frac{2}{3} \times J$ *jellybeans. Multiplying out* $\frac{1}{4} \times \frac{2}{3} \times J$ gives $\frac{1}{6}J$ as the number of jellybeans left. The problem states that there were **10 jellybeans left**, meaning that we set $\frac{1}{6} \times J$ **equal to** 10:

$$\frac{1}{6} \times J = 10$$

Solving this equation for *J* gives *J* = **60**. Thus, the right answer is **a** (the same answer we got when we *worked backwards*). As you can see, both methods—working backwards and translating from English to math—work. You should use whichever method is more comfortable for you.

PRACTICE WORD PROBLEMS

You will find word problems using fractions, decimals, and percentages in those sections of this chapter. For now, practice using the translation table on problems that just require you to work with basic arithmetic. Answers are at the end of the chapter.

_____ **1.** Joan went shopping with $100 and returned home with only $18.42. How much money did she spend?

    a. $81.58   **b.** $72.68   **c.** $72.58   **d.** $71.68   **e.** $71.58

_____ **2.** Mark invited ten friends to a party. Each friend brought 3 guests. How many people came to the party, excluding Mark?

    a. 3   **b.** 10   **c.** 30   **d.** 40   **e.** 41

_____ **3.** The office secretary can type 80 words per minute on his word processor. How many minutes will it take him to type a report containing 760 words?

    a. 8   **b.** $8\frac{1}{2}$ **c.** 9   **d.** $9\frac{1}{2}$ **e.** 10

_____ **4.** Mr. Wallace is writing a budget request to upgrade his personal computer system. He wants to purchase 4 mb of RAM, which will cost $100, two new software programs at $350 each, a tape backup system for $249, and an additional tape for $25. What is the total amount Mr. Wallace should write on his budget request?

    a. $724   **b.** $974   **c.** $1049   **d.** $1064   **e.** $1074

FRACTION REVIEW

Problems involving fractions may be straightforward calculation questions, or they may be word problems. Typically, they ask you to add, subtract, multiply, divide, or compare fractions.

WORKING WITH FRACTIONS

A fraction is a part of something.

Example: Let's say that a pizza was cut into 8 equal slices and you ate 3 of them. The fraction $\frac{3}{8}$ tells you what part of the pizza you ate. The pizza below shows this: 3 of the 8 pieces (the ones you ate) are shaded.

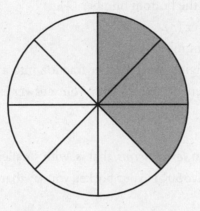

Three Kinds of Fractions

Proper fraction:	The top number is less than the bottom number:
	$\frac{1}{2}$; $\frac{2}{3}$; $\frac{4}{9}$; $\frac{8}{13}$
	The value of a proper fraction is less than 1.
Improper fraction:	The top number is greater than or equal to the bottom number:
	$\frac{3}{2}$; $\frac{5}{3}$; $\frac{14}{9}$; $\frac{12}{12}$
	The value of an improper fraction is 1 or more.
Mixed number:	A fraction written to the right of a whole number:
	$3\frac{1}{2}$; $4\frac{2}{3}$; $12\frac{3}{4}$; $24\frac{3}{4}$
	The value of a mixed number is more than 1: it is the sum of the whole number plus the fraction.

Changing Improper Fractions into Mixed or Whole Numbers

It's easier to add and subtract fractions that are mixed numbers rather than improper fractions. To change an improper fraction, say $\frac{13}{2}$, into a mixed number, follow these steps:

1. Divide the bottom number (2) into the top number (13) to get the whole number portion (6) of the mixed number:

$$2\overline{)13} \quad \begin{array}{r} 6 \\ \underline{12} \\ 1 \end{array}$$

2. Write the remainder of the division (1) over the old bottom number (2): $6\frac{1}{2}$
3. Check: Change the mixed number back into an improper fraction (see steps below).

Changing Mixed Numbers into Improper Fractions

It's easier multiply and divide fractions when you're working with improper fractions rather than mixed numbers. To change a mixed number, say $2\frac{3}{4}$, into an improper fraction, follow these steps:

1. Multiply the whole number (2) by the bottom number (4). $2 \times 4 = 8$

2. Add the result (8) to the top number (3). $8 + 3 = 11$

3. Put the total (11) over the bottom number (4). $\frac{11}{4}$

4. Check: Reverse the process by changing the improper fraction into a mixed number. If you get back the number you started with, your answer is right.

Reducing Fractions

Reducing a fraction means writing it in *lowest terms*, that is, with smaller numbers. For instance, 50¢ is $\frac{50}{100}$ of a dollar, or $\frac{1}{2}$ of a dollar. In fact, if you have 50¢ in your pocket, you say that you have half a dollar. Reducing a fraction does not change its value.

Follow these steps to reduce a fraction:

1. Find a whole number that divides *evenly* into both numbers that make up the fraction.

2. Divide that number into the top of the fraction, and replace the top of the fraction with the quotient (the answer you got when you divided).

3. Do the same thing to the bottom number.

4. Repeat the first 3 steps until you can't find a number that divides evenly into both numbers of the fraction.

For example, let's reduce $\frac{8}{24}$. We could do it in 2 steps: $\frac{8 \div 4}{24 \div 4} = \frac{2}{6}$; then $\frac{2 \div 2}{6 \div 2} = \frac{1}{3}$. Or we could do it in a single step: $\frac{8 \div 8}{24 \div 8} = \frac{1}{3}$.

Shortcut: When the top and bottom numbers both end in zeroes, cross out the same number of zeroes in both numbers to begin the reducing process. For example, $\frac{300}{4000}$ reduces to $\frac{3}{40}$ when you cross out 2 zeroes in both numbers.

Whenever you do arithmetic with fractions, reduce your answer. On a multiple-choice test, don't panic if your answer isn't listed. Try to reduce it and then compare it to the choices.

Reduce these fractions to lowest terms:

_____ **5.** $\frac{3}{12}$

_____ **6.** $\frac{14}{35}$

_____ **7.** $\frac{27}{72}$

Raising Fractions to Higher Terms

Before you can add and subtract fractions, you have to know how to raise a fraction to higher terms. This is actually the opposite of reducing a fraction.

Follow these steps to raise $\frac{2}{3}$ to 24ths:

1. Divide the old bottom number (3) into the new one (24): $\quad 3\overline{)24} = 8$

2. Multiply the answer (8) by the old top number (2): $\quad 2 \times 8 = 16$

3. Put the answer (16) over the new bottom number (24): $\quad \frac{16}{24}$

4. Check: Reduce the new fraction to see if you get back the original one: $\quad \frac{16 \div 8}{24 \div 8} = \frac{2}{3}$

Raise these fractions to higher terms:

_____ **8.** $\frac{5}{12} = \frac{}{24}$

_____ **9.** $\frac{2}{9} = \frac{}{27}$

_____**10.** $\frac{2}{5} = \frac{}{500}$

ADDING FRACTIONS

If the fractions have the same bottom numbers, just add the top numbers together and write the total over the bottom number.

Examples: $\quad \frac{2}{9} + \frac{4}{9} = \frac{2+4}{9} = \frac{6}{9} \qquad$ Reduce the sum: $\frac{2}{3}$

$\frac{5}{8} + \frac{7}{8} = \frac{12}{8} \qquad$ Change the sum to a mixed number: $1\frac{4}{8}$; then reduce: $1\frac{1}{2}$

There are a few extra steps to add mixed numbers with the same bottom numbers, say $2\frac{3}{5} + 1\frac{4}{5}$:

1. Add the fractions: $\qquad\qquad\qquad\qquad\qquad\qquad\qquad \frac{3}{5} + \frac{4}{5} = \frac{7}{5}$

2. Change the improper fraction into a mixed number: $\qquad \frac{7}{5} = 1\frac{2}{5}$

3. Add the whole numbers: $\qquad\qquad\qquad\qquad\qquad\quad 2 + 1 = 3$

4. Add the results of steps 2 and 3: $\qquad\qquad\qquad\quad 1\frac{2}{5} + 3 = 4\frac{2}{5}$

Finding the Least Common Denominator

If the fractions you want to add don't have the same bottom number, you'll have to raise some or all of the fractions to higher terms so that they all have the same bottom number, called the **common denominator.** All of the original bottom numbers divide evenly into the common denominator. If it is the smallest number that they all divide evenly into, it is called the **least common denominator (LCD).**

Here are a few tips for finding the LCD, the smallest number that all the bottom numbers evenly divide into:

- See if all the bottom numbers divide evenly into the biggest bottom number.
- Check out the multiplication table of the largest bottom number until you find a number that all the other bottom numbers evenly divide into.

- When all else fails, multiply all the bottom numbers together.

    Example: $\frac{2}{3} + \frac{4}{5}$

1. Find the LCD. Multiply the bottom numbers: $3 \times 5 = 15$

2. Raise each fraction to 15ths:

$$\frac{2}{3} = \frac{10}{15}$$
$$+ \frac{4}{5} = \frac{12}{15}$$
$$\frac{22}{15}$$

3. Add as usual:

Try these addition problems:

_____**11.** $\frac{3}{4} + \frac{1}{6}$

_____**12.** $\frac{7}{8} + \frac{2}{3} + \frac{3}{4}$

_____**13.** $4\frac{1}{3} + 2\frac{3}{4} + \frac{1}{6}$

SUBTRACTING FRACTIONS

If the fractions have the same bottom numbers, just subtract the top numbers and write the difference over the bottom number.

    Example: $\frac{4}{9} - \frac{3}{9} = \frac{4-3}{9} = \frac{1}{9}$

If the fractions you want to subtract don't have the same bottom number, you'll have to raise some or all of the fractions to higher terms so that they all have the same bottom number, or LCD. If you forgot how to find the LCD, just read the section on adding fractions with different bottom numbers.

    Example: $\frac{5}{6} - \frac{3}{4}$

1. Raise each fraction to 12ths because 12 is the LCD, the smallest number $\frac{5}{6} = \frac{10}{12}$
that 6 and 4 both divide into evenly: $- \frac{3}{4} = \frac{9}{12}$

2. Subtract as usual: $\frac{1}{12}$

Subtracting mixed numbers with the same bottom number is similar to adding mixed numbers.

    Example: $4\frac{3}{5} - 1\frac{2}{5}$

1. Subtract the fractions: $\frac{3}{5} - \frac{2}{5} = \frac{1}{5}$

2. Subtract the whole numbers: $4 - 1 = 3$

3. Add the results of steps 1 and 2: $\frac{1}{5} + 3 = 3\frac{1}{5}$

Sometimes there is an extra "borrowing" step when you subtract mixed numbers with the same bottom numbers, say $7\frac{3}{5} - 2\frac{4}{5}$:

1. You can't subtract the fractions the way they are because $\frac{4}{5}$ is bigger than $\frac{3}{5}$.

   So you borrow 1 from the 7, making it 6, and change that 1 to $\frac{5}{5}$ because

   5 is the bottom number: $\qquad$ $7\frac{3}{5} = 6\frac{5}{5} + \frac{3}{5}$

2. Add the numbers from step 1: $\qquad$ $6\frac{5}{5} + \frac{3}{5} = 6\frac{8}{5}$

3. Now you have a different version of the original problem: $\qquad$ $6\frac{8}{5} - 2\frac{4}{5}$

4. Subtract the fractional parts of the two mixed numbers: $\qquad$ $\frac{8}{5} - \frac{4}{5} = \frac{4}{5}$

5. Subtract the whole number parts of the two mixed numbers: $\qquad$ $6 - 2 = 4$

6. Add the results of the last 2 steps together: $\qquad$ $4 + \frac{4}{5} = 4\frac{4}{5}$

Try these subtraction problems:

_____ **14.** $\frac{4}{5} - \frac{2}{3}$

_____ **15.** $\frac{7}{8} - \frac{1}{4} - \frac{1}{2}$

_____ **16.** $4\frac{1}{3} - 2\frac{3}{4}$

   Now let's put what you've learned about adding and subtracting fractions to work in some real-life problems.

_____ **17.** Patrolman Peterson drove $3\frac{1}{2}$ miles to the police station. Then he drove $4\frac{3}{4}$ miles to his first assignment. When he left there, he drove 2 miles to his next assignment. Then he drove $3\frac{2}{3}$ miles back to the police station for a meeting. Finally, he drove $3\frac{1}{2}$ miles home. How many miles did he travel in total?

   a. $17\frac{5}{12}$ $\qquad$ **b.** $16\frac{5}{12}$ $\qquad$ **c.** $15\frac{7}{12}$ $\qquad$ **d.** $15\frac{5}{12}$ $\qquad$ **e.** $13\frac{11}{12}$

_____ **18.** Before leaving the fire station, Firefighter Sorensen noted that the mileage gauge on Engine 2 registered $4,357\frac{4}{10}$ miles. When he arrived at the scene of the fire, the mileage gauge then registered $4,400\frac{1}{10}$ miles. How many miles did he drive from the station to the fire scene?

   a. $42\frac{3}{10}$ $\qquad$ **b.** $42\frac{7}{10}$ $\qquad$ **c.** $43\frac{7}{10}$ $\qquad$ **d.** $47\frac{2}{10}$ $\qquad$ **e.** $57\frac{3}{10}$

MULTIPLYING FRACTIONS

Multiplying fractions is actually easier than adding them. All you do is multiply the top numbers and then multiply the bottom numbers.

   Examples: $\quad \frac{2}{3} \times \frac{5}{7} = \frac{2 \times 5}{3 \times 7} = \frac{10}{21} \qquad \frac{1}{2} \times \frac{3}{5} \times \frac{7}{4} = \frac{1 \times 3 \times 7}{2 \times 5 \times 4} = \frac{21}{40}$

   Sometimes you can *cancel* before multiplying. Cancelling is a shortcut that makes the multiplication go faster because you're multiplying with smaller numbers. It's very similar to reducing: if there is a number that divides evenly into a top number and bottom number, do that division before multiplying. If you forget to cancel, you'll still get the right answer, but you'll have to reduce it.

Example: $\frac{5}{6} \times \frac{9}{20}$

1. Cancel the 6 and the 9 by dividing 3 into both of them: $6 \div 3 = 2$ and $9 \div 3 = 3$. Cross out the 6 and the 9.

$\frac{5}{\cancel{6}_2} \times \frac{\cancel{9}^3}{20}$

2. Cancel the 5 and the 20 by dividing 5 into both of them: $5 \div 5 = 1$ and $20 \div 5 = 4$. Cross out the 5 and the 20.

$\frac{\cancel{5}^1}{\cancel{6}_2} \times \frac{\cancel{9}^3}{\cancel{20}_4}$

3. Multiply across the new top numbers and the new bottom numbers:

$\frac{1 \times 3}{2 \times 4} = \frac{3}{8}$

Try these multiplication problems:

_____**19.** $\frac{1}{5} \times \frac{2}{3}$

_____**20.** $\frac{2}{3} \times \frac{4}{7} \times \frac{3}{5}$

_____**21.** $\frac{3}{4} \times \frac{8}{9}$

To multiply a fraction by a whole number, first rewrite the whole number as a fraction with a bottom number of 1:

Example: $5 \times \frac{2}{3} = \frac{5}{1} \times \frac{2}{3} = \frac{10}{3}$ (Optional: convert $\frac{10}{3}$ to a mixed number: $3\frac{1}{3}$)

To multiply with mixed numbers, it's easier to change them to improper fractions before multiplying.

Example: $4\frac{2}{3} \times 5\frac{1}{2}$

1. Convert $4\frac{2}{3}$ to an improper fraction:

$4\frac{2}{3} = \frac{4 \times 3 + 2}{3} = \frac{14}{3}$

2. Convert $5\frac{1}{2}$ to an improper fraction:

$5\frac{1}{2} = \frac{5 \times 2 + 1}{2} = \frac{11}{2}$

3. Cancel and multiply the fractions:

$\frac{\cancel{14}^7}{3} \times \frac{11}{\cancel{2}_1} = \frac{77}{3}$

4. Optional: convert the improper fraction to a mixed number:

$\frac{77}{3} = 25\frac{2}{3}$

Now try these multiplication problems with mixed numbers and whole numbers:

_____**22.** $4\frac{1}{3} \times \frac{2}{5}$

_____**23.** $2\frac{1}{2} \times 6$

_____**24.** $3\frac{3}{4} \times 4\frac{2}{5}$

Here are a few more real-life problems to test your skills:

_____**25.** After driving $\frac{2}{3}$ of the 15 miles to work, Mr. Stone stopped to make a phone call. How many miles had he driven when he made his call?

    a. 5   **b.** $7\frac{1}{2}$ **c.** 10   **d.** 12   **e.** $15\frac{2}{3}$

_____**26.** If Henry worked $\frac{3}{4}$ of a 40-hour week, how many hours did he work?

    a. $7\frac{1}{2}$ **b.** 10   **c.** 20   **d.** 25   **e.** 30

_____**27.** Technician Chin makes \$14.00 an hour. When she works more than 8 hours a day, she gets over-time pay of $1\frac{1}{2}$ times her regular hourly wage for the extra hours. How much did she earn for working 11 hours in one day?

    a. \$77   **b.** \$154   **c.** \$175   **d.** \$210   **e.** \$231

DIVIDING FRACTIONS

To divide one fraction by a second fraction, invert the second fraction (that is, flip the top and bottom numbers) and then multiply. That's all there is to it!

    Example: $\frac{1}{2} \div \frac{3}{5}$

1. Invert the second fraction ($\frac{3}{5}$): $\frac{5}{3}$

2. Change the division sign ($\div$) to a multiplication sign ($\times$)

3. Multiply the first fraction by the new second fraction: $\frac{1}{2} \times \frac{5}{3} = \frac{1 \times 5}{2 \times 3} = \frac{5}{6}$

To divide a fraction by a whole number, first change the whole number to a fraction by putting it over 1. Then follow the division steps above.

    Example: $\frac{3}{5} \div 2 = \frac{3}{5} \div \frac{2}{1} = \frac{3}{5} \times \frac{1}{2} = \frac{3 \times 1}{5 \times 2} = \frac{3}{10}$

When the division problem has a mixed number, convert it to an improper fraction and then divide as usual.

    Example: $2\frac{3}{4} \div \frac{1}{6}$

1. Convert $2\frac{3}{4}$ to an improper fraction: $2\frac{3}{4} = \frac{2 \times 4 + 3}{4} = \frac{11}{4}$

2. Divide $\frac{11}{4}$ by $\frac{1}{6}$: $\frac{11}{4} \div \frac{1}{6} = \frac{11}{4} \times \frac{6}{1}$

3. Flip $\frac{1}{6}$ to $\frac{6}{1}$, change $\div$ to $\times$, cancel and multiply: $\frac{11}{\underset{2}{4}} \times \frac{\overset{3}{6}}{1} = \frac{11 \times 3}{2 \times 1} = \frac{33}{2}$

Here are a few division problems to try:

_____**28.** $\frac{1}{3} \div \frac{2}{3}$

_____**29.** $2\frac{3}{4} \div \frac{1}{2}$

_____**30.** $\frac{3}{5} \div 3$

_____**31.** $3\frac{3}{4} \div 2\frac{1}{3}$

Let's wrap this up with some real-life problems.

_____**32.** If four friends evenly split $6\frac{1}{2}$ pounds of candy, how many pounds of candy does each friend get?

     a. $\frac{8}{13}$ **b.** $1\frac{5}{8}$ **c.** $1\frac{1}{2}$ **d.** $1\frac{5}{13}$ **e.** 4

_____**33.** How many $2\frac{1}{2}$-pound chunks of cheese can be cut from a single 20-pound piece of cheese?

     a. 2   **b.** 4   **c.** 6   **d.** 8   **e.** 10

_____**34.** Ms. Goldbaum earned $36.75 for working $3\frac{1}{2}$ hours. What was her hourly wage?

     a. $10.00   **b.** $10.50   **c.** $10.75   **d.** $12.00   **e.** $12.25

DECIMALS

WHAT IS A DECIMAL?

A decimal is a special kind of fraction. You use decimals every day when you deal with money—$10.35 is a decimal that represents 10 dollars and 35 cents. The decimal point separates the dollars from the cents. Because there are 100 cents in one dollar, 1¢ is $\frac{1}{100}$ of a dollar, or $.01.

Each decimal digit to the right of the decimal point has a name:

Example: $.1 = 1$ tenth $= \frac{1}{10}$

                     $.02 = 2$ hundredths $= \frac{2}{100}$

                     $.003 = 3$ thousandths $= \frac{3}{1000}$

                     $.0004 = 4$ ten-thousandths $= \frac{4}{10,000}$

When you add zeroes after the rightmost decimal place, you don't change the value of the decimal. For example, 6.17 is the same as all of these:

6.170

6.1700

6.17000000000000000

If there are digits on both sides of the decimal point (like 10.35), the number is called a mixed decimal. If there are digits only to the right of the decimal point (like .53), the number is called a decimal. A whole number (like 15) is understood to have a decimal point at its right (15.). Thus, 15 is the same as 15.0, 15.00, 15.000, and so on.

CHANGING FRACTIONS TO DECIMALS

To change a fraction to a decimal, divide the bottom number into the top number after you put a decimal point and a few zeroes on the right of the top number. When you divide, bring the decimal point up into your answer.

Example: Change $\frac{3}{4}$ to a decimal.

1. Add a decimal point and 2 zeroes to the top number (3):   3.00

2. Divide the bottom number (4) into 3.00:

Bring the decimal point up into the answer:

$$4\overline{)3.00}$$

$$\begin{array}{r} .75 \\ 4\overline{)3.00} \\ 2\ 8 \\ \hline 20 \\ 20 \\ \hline 0 \end{array}$$

3. The quotient (result of the division) is the answer: .75

Some fractions may require you to add many decimal zeroes in order for the division to come out evenly. In fact, when you convert a fraction like $\frac{2}{3}$ to a decimal, you can keep adding decimal zeroes to the top number forever because the division will never come out evenly! As you divide 3 into 2, you'll keep getting 6's:

$$2 \div 3 = .6666666666 \text{ etc}$$

This is called a *repeating decimal* and it can be written as $.66\overline{6}$ or as $.66\frac{2}{3}$. You can approximate it as .67, .667, .6667, and so on.

CHANGING DECIMALS TO FRACTIONS

To change a decimal to a fraction, write the digits of the decimal as the top number of a fraction and write the decimal's name as the bottom number of the fraction. Then reduce the fraction, if possible.

Example: .018

1. Write 18 as the top of the fraction: $\frac{18}{}$

2. Three places to the right of the decimal means *thousandths,* so write
1000 as the bottom number: $\frac{18}{1000}$

3. Reduce by dividing 2 into the top and bottom numbers: $\frac{18 \div 2}{1000 \div 2} = \frac{9}{500}$

Change these decimals or mixed decimals to fractions:

_____**35.** .005

_____**36.** 3.48

_____**37.** 123.456

COMPARING DECIMALS

Because decimals are easier to compare when they have the same number of digits after the decimal point, tack zeroes onto the end of the shorter decimals. Then all you have to do is compare the numbers as if the decimal points weren't there:

Example: Compare .08 and .1

1. Tack one zero at the end of .1:   .10
2. To compare .10 to .08, just compare 10 to 8.
3. Since 10 is larger than 8, .1 is larger than .08.

ADDING AND SUBTRACTING DECIMALS

To add or subtract decimals, line them up so their decimal points are even. You may want to tack on zeroes at the end of shorter decimals so you can keep all your digits lined up evenly. Remember, if a number doesn't have a decimal point, then put one at the right end of the number.

Example: 1.23 + 57 + .038

1. Line up the numbers like this:

$$\begin{array}{r}1.230\\57.000\\+\ \ .038\\\hline\end{array}$$

2. Add:
$$58.268$$

Example: 1.23 − .038

1. Line up the numbers like this:
$$\begin{array}{r}1.230\\-\ \ .038\\\hline\end{array}$$

2. Subtract:
$$1.192$$

Try these addition and subtraction problems:

_____**38.** .905 + .02 + 3.075

_____**39.** .005 + 8 + .3

_____**40.** 3.48 − 2.573

_____**41.** 123.456 − 122

_____**42.** Officer Peterson drove 3.7 miles to the state park. He then walked 1.6 miles around the park to make sure everything was all right. He got back into the car, drove 2.75 miles to check on a broken traffic light and then drove 2 miles back to the police station. How many miles did he drive in total?

a. 8.05   b. 8.45   c. 8.8   d. 10   e. 10.05

_____**43.** The average number of emergency room visits at City Hospital fell from 486.4 per week to 402.5 per week. By how many emergency room visits per week did the average fall?

a. 73.9   b. 83   c. 83.1   d. 83.9   e. 84.9

MULTIPLYING DECIMALS

To multiply decimals, ignore the decimal points and just multiply the numbers. Then count the total number of decimal digits (the digits to the *right* of the decimal point) in the numbers you're multiplying. Count off that number of digits in your answer beginning at the right side and put the decimal point to the *left* of those digits.

Example: 215.7×2.4

1. Multiply 2157 times 24:

$$
\begin{array}{r}
2157 \\
\times\ \ 24 \\
\hline
8628 \\
4314\ \ \\
\hline
51768
\end{array}
$$

2. Because there are a total of 2 decimal digits in 215.7 and 2.4, count off 2 places from the right in 51768, placing the decimal point to the *left* of the last 2 digits: 517.68

If your answer doesn't have enough digits, tack zeroes on to the left of the answer.

Example: $.03 \times .006$

1. Multiply 3 times 6: $3 \times 6 = 18$

2. You need 5 decimal digits in your answer, so tack on 3 zeroes: 00018

3. Put the decimal point at the front of the number (which is 5 digits in from the right):   .00018

You can practice multiplying decimals with these:

_____**44.** $.05 \times .6$

_____**45.** $.053 \times 6.4$

_____**46.** $38.1 \times .0184$

_____ **47.** Joe earns $14.50 per hour. Last week he worked 37.5 hours. How much money did he earn that week?

  a. $518.00   **b.** $518.50   **c.** $525.00   **d.** $536.50   **e.** $543.75

_____ **48.** Nuts cost $3.50 per pound. Approximately how much will 4.25 pounds of nuts cost?

  a. $12.25   **b.** $12.50   **c.** $12.88   **d.** $14.50   **e.** $14.88

DIVIDING DECIMALS

To divide a decimal by a whole number, set up the division (8 ⟌.256) and immediately bring the decimal point straight up into the answer (8 ⟌.256). Then divide as you would normally divide whole numbers:

    Example:
$$\begin{array}{r} .032 \\ 8\overline{).256} \\ \underline{0} \\ 25 \\ \underline{24} \\ 16 \\ \underline{16} \\ 0 \end{array}$$

    To divide any number by a decimal, there is an extra step to perform before you can divide. Move the decimal point to the very right of the number you're dividing by, counting the number of places you're moving it. Then move the decimal point the same number of places to the right in the number you're dividing into. In other words, first change the problem to one in which you're dividing by a whole number.

    Example: .06 ⟌1.218

1. Because there are 2 decimal digits in .06, move the decimal point 2 places to the right in both numbers and move the decimal point straight up into the answer:
    .06. ⟌1.21.8

2. Divide using the new numbers:
$$\begin{array}{r} 20.3 \\ 6\overline{)121.8} \\ \underline{12} \\ 01 \\ \underline{00} \\ 18 \\ \underline{18} \\ 0 \end{array}$$

    Under certain conditions, you have to tack on zeroes to the right of the last decimal digit in number you're dividing into:

- If there aren't enough digits for you to move the decimal point to the right, or
- If the answer doesn't come out evenly when you do the division, or
- If you're dividing a whole number by a decimal. Then you'll have to tack on the decimal point as well as some zeroes.

Try your skills on these division problems:

_____**49.** $7\overline{)9.8}$

_____**50.** $.0004\overline{).0512}$

_____**51.** $.05\overline{)28.6}$

_____**52.** $.14\overline{)196}$

_____**53.** If James Worthington drove his truck 92.4 miles in 2.1 hours, what was his average speed in miles per hour?

        a. 41   **b.** 44   **c.** 90.3   **d.** 94.5   **e.** 194.04

_____**54.** Mary Sanders walked a total of 18.6 miles in 4 days. On average, how many miles did she walk each day?

        a. 4.15   **b.** 4.60   **c.** 4.65   **d.** 22.60   **e.** 74.40

PERCENTS

WHAT IS A PERCENT?

A percent is a special kind of fraction or part of something. The bottom number (the *denominator*) is always 100. For example, 17% is the same as $\frac{17}{100}$. Literally, the word *percent* means *per 100 parts*. The root *cent* means 100: a *cent*ury is 100 years, there are 100 *cent*s in a dollar, etc. Thus, 17% means 17 parts out of 100. Because fractions can also be expressed as decimals, 17% is also equivalent to .17, which is 17 hundredths.

    You come into contact with percents every day. Sales tax, interest, and discounts are just a few common examples.

    If you're shaky on fractions, you may want to review the fraction section before reading further.

CHANGING A DECIMAL TO A PERCENT AND VICE VERSA

To change a decimal to a percent, move the decimal point two places to the **right** and tack on a percent sign (%) at the end. If the decimal point moves to the very right of the number, you don't have to write the decimal point. If there aren't enough places to move the decimal point, add zeroes on the **right** before moving the decimal point.

    To change a percent to a decimal, drop off the percent sign and move the decimal point two places to the **left**. If there aren't enough places to move the decimal point, add zeroes on the **left** before moving the decimal point.

Try changing these decimals to percents:

_____**55.** .45

_____**56.** .008

_____**57.** .16$\frac{2}{3}$

Now change these percents to decimals:

_____**58.** 12%

_____**59.** 87$\frac{1}{2}$%

_____**60.** 250%

CHANGING A FRACTION TO A PERCENT AND VICE VERSA

To change a fraction to a percent, there are two techniques. Each is illustrated by changing the fraction $\frac{1}{4}$ to a percent:

Technique 1: Multiply the fraction by 100%.
Multiply $\frac{1}{4}$ by 100%:

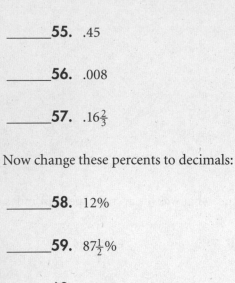

$$\frac{1}{\underset{1}{4}} \times \frac{\overset{25}{\cancel{100\%}}}{1} = 25\%$$

Technique 2: Divide the fraction's bottom number into the top number; then move the decimal point two places to the **right** and tack on a percent sign (%).
Divide 4 into 1 and move the decimal point 2 places to the right:

$$4\overline{|1.00}^{\,.25} \qquad .25 = 25\%$$

To change a percent to a fraction, remove the percent sign and write the number over 100. Then reduce if possible.

Example: Change 4% to a fraction

1. Remove the % and write the fraction 4 over 100: $\frac{4}{100}$
2. Reduce: $\frac{4 \div 4}{100 \div 4} = \frac{1}{25}$

Here's a more complicated example: Change 16$\frac{2}{3}$% to a fraction $\frac{16\frac{2}{3}}{100}$

1. Remove the % and write the fraction 16$\frac{2}{3}$ over 100:

2. Since a fraction means "top number divided by bottom number," rewrite the fraction as a division problem:

$$16\tfrac{2}{3} \div 100$$

3. Change the mixed number ($16\tfrac{2}{3}$) to an improper fraction ($\tfrac{50}{3}$):

$$\tfrac{50}{3} \div \tfrac{100}{1}$$

4. Flip the second fraction ($\tfrac{100}{1}$) and multiply:

$$\overset{1}{\tfrac{50}{3}} \times \tfrac{1}{\underset{2}{100}} = \tfrac{1}{6}$$

Try changing these fractions to percents:

_____ **61.** $\tfrac{1}{8}$

_____ **62.** $\tfrac{13}{25}$

_____ **63.** $\tfrac{7}{12}$

Now change these percents to fractions:

_____ **64.** 95%

_____ **65.** $37\tfrac{1}{2}\%$

_____ **66.** 125%

Sometimes it is more convenient to work with a percentage as a fraction or a decimal. Rather than have to *calculate* the equivalent fraction or decimal, consider memorizing the equivalence table below. Not only will this increase your efficiency on the math test, but it will also be practical for real life situations.

CONVERSION TABLE

Decimal	%	Fraction
.25	25%	$\tfrac{1}{4}$
.50	50%	$\tfrac{1}{2}$
.75	75%	$\tfrac{3}{4}$
.10	10%	$\tfrac{1}{10}$
.20	20%	$\tfrac{1}{5}$
.40	40%	$\tfrac{2}{5}$
.60	60%	$\tfrac{3}{5}$
.80	80%	$\tfrac{4}{5}$
$.33\overline{3}$	$33\tfrac{1}{3}\%$	$\tfrac{1}{3}$
$.66\overline{6}$	$66\tfrac{2}{3}\%$	$\tfrac{2}{3}$

PERCENT WORD PROBLEMS

Word problems involving percents come in three main varieties:

- Find a percent of a whole.

    Example: What is 30% of 40?

- Find what percent one number is of another number.

    Example: 12 is what percent of 40?

- Find the whole when the percent of it is given.

    Example: 12 is 30% of what number?

While each variety has its own approach, there is a single shortcut formula you can use to solve each of these:

$$\frac{is}{of} = \frac{\%}{100}$$

The *is* is the number that usually follows or is just before the word *is* in the question.

The *of* is the number that usually follows the word *of* in the question.

The *%* is the number that in front of the *%* or *percent* in the question.

Or you may think of the shortcut formula as:

$$\frac{part}{whole} = \frac{\%}{100}$$

To solve each of the three varieties, we're going to use the fact that the **cross-products** are equal. The cross-products are the products of the numbers diagonally across from each other. Remembering that *product* means *multiply*, here's how to create the cross-products for the percent shortcut:

$$\frac{part}{whole} = \frac{\%}{100}$$
$$part \times 100 = whole \times \%$$

Here's how to use the shortcut with cross-products:

- Find a percent of a whole.

    What is 30% of 40?

    30 is the % and 40 is the *of* number: $\frac{is}{40} = \frac{30}{100}$

    Cross-multiply and solve for *is*: $is \times 100 = 40 \times 30$

    $is \times 100 = 1200$

    $\mathbf{12} \times 100 = 1200$

    Thus, **12** *is* 30% of 40.

- Find what percent one number is of another number.

    12 is what percent of 40?

    12 is the *is* number and 40 is the *of* number: $\frac{12}{40} = \frac{\%}{100}$

    Cross-multiply and solve for %: $12 \times 100 = 40 \times \%$

    $1200 = 40 \times \%$

    $1200 = 40 \times \mathbf{30}$

    Thus, 12 is **30%** of 40.

- Find the whole when the percent of it is given.

  12 is 30% of what number?

  12 is the *is* number and 30 is the %:

  Cross-multiply and solve for the *of* number:

  $$\frac{12}{of} = \frac{30}{100}$$

  $$12 \times 100 = of \times 30$$

  $$1200 = of \times 30$$

  $$1200 = \mathbf{40} \times 30$$

  Thus 12 is 30% *of* **40**.

You can use the same technique to find the percent increase or decrease. The *is* number is the actual increase or decrease, and the *of* number is the original amount.

Example: If a merchant puts his $20 hats on sale for $15, by what percent does he decrease the selling price?

1. Calculate the decrease, the *is* number: $20 - $15 = $5

2. The *of* number is the original amount, $20

3. Set up the equation and solve for *of* by cross-multiplying:

$$\frac{5}{20} = \frac{\%}{100}$$

$$5 \times 100 = 20 \times \%$$

$$500 = 20 \times \%$$

$$500 = 20 \times \mathbf{25}$$

4. Thus, the selling price is decreased by **25%**.

If the merchant later raises the price of the hats from $15 back to $20, don't be fooled into thinking that the percent increase is also 25%! It's actually more, because the increase amount of $5 is now based on a lower original price of only $15:

$$\frac{5}{15} = \frac{\%}{100}$$

$$5 \times 100 = 15 \times \%$$

$$500 = 15 \times \%$$

$$500 = 15 \times \mathbf{33\tfrac{1}{3}}$$

Thus, the selling price is increased by **33%**.

Find a percent of a whole:

_____**67.** 1% of 25

_____**68.** 18.2% of 50

_____**69.** $37\tfrac{1}{2}$% of 100

_____**70.** 125% of 60

Find what percent one number is of another number.

_____**71.** 10 is what % of 20?

_____**72.** 4 is what % of 12?

_____**73.** 12 is what % of 4?

Find the whole when the percent of it is given.

_____**74.** 15% of what number is 15?

_____**75.** $37\frac{1}{2}$% of what number is 3?

_____**76.** 200% of what number is 20?

Now try your percent skills on some real life problems.

_____**77.** Last Monday, 20% of the 140-member nursing staff was absent. How many nurses were absent that day?
a. 14   b. 20   c. 28   d. 112   e. 126

_____**78.** 40% of Vero's postal service employees are women. If there are 80 women in Vero's postal service, how many men are employed there?
a. 32   b. 112   c. 120   d. 160   e. 200

_____**79.** Of the 840 crimes committed last month, 42 involved petty theft. What percent of the crimes involved petty theft?
a. .5%   b. 2%   c. 5%   d. 20%   e. 50%

_____**80.** Sam's Shoe Store put all of its merchandise on sale for 20% off. If Jason saved $10 by purchasing one pair of shoes during the sale, what was the original price of the shoes before the sale?
a. $12   b. $20   c. $40   d. $50   e. $70

ANSWERS TO MATH PROBLEMS

WORD PROBLEMS

1. a
2. d
3. d
4. e

FRACTIONS

5. $\frac{1}{4}$
6. $\frac{2}{5}$
7. $\frac{3}{8}$
8. 10
9. 6
10. 200
11. $\frac{11}{12}$
12. $\frac{55}{24}$ or $2\frac{7}{24}$
13. $7\frac{1}{4}$
14. $\frac{2}{15}$
15. $\frac{1}{8}$
16. $\frac{19}{12}$ or $1\frac{7}{12}$
17. a
18. b
19. $\frac{2}{15}$
20. $\frac{8}{35}$
21. $\frac{2}{3}$
22. $\frac{26}{15}$ or $1\frac{11}{15}$
23. 15
24. $\frac{33}{2}$ or $16\frac{1}{2}$
25. c
26. e
27. c
28. $\frac{1}{2}$
29. $5\frac{1}{2}$
30. $\frac{1}{5}$
31. $\frac{45}{28}$ or $1\frac{17}{28}$
32. b
33. d
34. b

DECIMALS

35. $\frac{5}{1000}$ or $\frac{1}{200}$
36. $3\frac{12}{25}$
37. $123\frac{456}{1000}$ or $123\frac{57}{125}$
38. 4
39. 8.305
40. .907
41. 1.456
42. b
43. d
44. .03
45. .3392
46. .70104
47. e
48. e
49. 1.4
50. 128
51. 572
52. 1400
53. b
54. c

PERCENTS

55. 45%
56. .8%
57. 16.67% or $16\frac{2}{3}$%
58. .12
59. .875
60. 2.5
61. 12.5% or $12\frac{1}{2}$%
62. 52%
63. 58.33% or $58\frac{1}{3}$%
64. $\frac{19}{20}$
65. $\frac{3}{8}$
66. $\frac{5}{4}$ or $1\frac{1}{4}$
67. $\frac{1}{4}$ or .25
68. 9.1
69. $37\frac{1}{2}$ or 37.5
70. 75
71. 50%
72. $33\frac{1}{3}$%
73. 300%
74. 100
75. 8
76. 10
77. c
78. c
79. c
80. d

CIVIL SERVICE EXAM 2

13

CHAPTER SUMMARY

This is the second practice exam covering the reading, writing, and math skills required on many civil service exams. This test will show you how much you've improved after working through the instructional chapters in this book.

Now that you've taken one practice civil service exam and studied how to answer reading comprehension, grammar, math, vocabulary, and spelling questions, you should be more confident as you go into this second exam.

For this second exam, simulate the actual test-taking experience as much as possible. Find a quiet place to work where you won't be interrupted. Tear out the answer sheet on the next page and find some number 2 pencils to fill in the circles with. Set a timer or stopwatch, and give yourself two hours for the entire exam. When that time is up, stop, even if you haven't finished the entire test.

After the exam, use the answer key that follows it to see how you did and to find out why the correct answers are correct. The answer key is followed by a section on how to score your exam.

1.	ⓐ	ⓑ	ⓒ	ⓓ
2.	ⓐ	ⓑ	ⓒ	ⓓ
3.	ⓐ	ⓑ	ⓒ	ⓓ
4.	ⓐ	ⓑ	ⓒ	ⓓ
5.	ⓐ	ⓑ	ⓒ	ⓓ
6.	ⓐ	ⓑ	ⓒ	ⓓ
7.	ⓐ	ⓑ	ⓒ	ⓓ
8.	ⓐ	ⓑ	ⓒ	ⓓ
9.	ⓐ	ⓑ	ⓒ	ⓓ
10.	ⓐ	ⓑ	ⓒ	ⓓ
11.	ⓐ	ⓑ	ⓒ	ⓓ
12.	ⓐ	ⓑ	ⓒ	ⓓ
13.	ⓐ	ⓑ	ⓒ	ⓓ
14.	ⓐ	ⓑ	ⓒ	ⓓ
15.	ⓐ	ⓑ	ⓒ	ⓓ
16.	ⓐ	ⓑ	ⓒ	ⓓ
17.	ⓐ	ⓑ	ⓒ	ⓓ
18.	ⓐ	ⓑ	ⓒ	ⓓ
19.	ⓐ	ⓑ	ⓒ	ⓓ
20.	ⓐ	ⓑ	ⓒ	ⓓ
21.	ⓐ	ⓑ	ⓒ	ⓓ
22.	ⓐ	ⓑ	ⓒ	ⓓ
23.	ⓐ	ⓑ	ⓒ	ⓓ
24.	ⓐ	ⓑ	ⓒ	ⓓ
25.	ⓐ	ⓑ	ⓒ	ⓓ
26.	ⓐ	ⓑ	ⓒ	ⓓ
27.	ⓐ	ⓑ	ⓒ	ⓓ
28.	ⓐ	ⓑ	ⓒ	ⓓ
29.	ⓐ	ⓑ	ⓒ	ⓓ
30.	ⓐ	ⓑ	ⓒ	ⓓ
31.	ⓐ	ⓑ	ⓒ	ⓓ
32.	ⓐ	ⓑ	ⓒ	ⓓ
33.	ⓐ	ⓑ	ⓒ	ⓓ
34.	ⓐ	ⓑ	ⓒ	ⓓ
35.	ⓐ	ⓑ	ⓒ	ⓓ
36.	ⓐ	ⓑ	ⓒ	ⓓ
37.	ⓐ	ⓑ	ⓒ	ⓓ
38.	ⓐ	ⓑ	ⓒ	ⓓ
39.	ⓐ	ⓑ	ⓒ	ⓓ
40.	ⓐ	ⓑ	ⓒ	ⓓ
41.	ⓐ	ⓑ	ⓒ	ⓓ
42.	ⓐ	ⓑ	ⓒ	ⓓ
43.	ⓐ	ⓑ	ⓒ	ⓓ
44.	ⓐ	ⓑ	ⓒ	ⓓ
45.	ⓐ	ⓑ	ⓒ	ⓓ
46.	ⓐ	ⓑ	ⓒ	ⓓ
47.	ⓐ	ⓑ	ⓒ	ⓓ
48.	ⓐ	ⓑ	ⓒ	ⓓ
49.	ⓐ	ⓑ	ⓒ	ⓓ
50.	ⓐ	ⓑ	ⓒ	ⓓ
51.	ⓐ	ⓑ	ⓒ	ⓓ
52.	ⓐ	ⓑ	ⓒ	ⓓ
53.	ⓐ	ⓑ	ⓒ	ⓓ
54.	ⓐ	ⓑ	ⓒ	ⓓ
55.	ⓐ	ⓑ	ⓒ	ⓓ
56.	ⓐ	ⓑ	ⓒ	ⓓ
57.	ⓐ	ⓑ	ⓒ	ⓓ
58.	ⓐ	ⓑ	ⓒ	ⓓ
59.	ⓐ	ⓑ	ⓒ	ⓓ
60.	ⓐ	ⓑ	ⓒ	ⓓ
61.	ⓐ	ⓑ	ⓒ	ⓓ
62.	ⓐ	ⓑ	ⓒ	ⓓ
63.	ⓐ	ⓑ	ⓒ	ⓓ
64.	ⓐ	ⓑ	ⓒ	ⓓ
65.	ⓐ	ⓑ	ⓒ	ⓓ
66.	ⓐ	ⓑ	ⓒ	ⓓ
67.	ⓐ	ⓑ	ⓒ	ⓓ
68.	ⓐ	ⓑ	ⓒ	ⓓ
69.	ⓐ	ⓑ	ⓒ	ⓓ
70.	ⓐ	ⓑ	ⓒ	ⓓ
71.	ⓐ	ⓑ	ⓒ	ⓓ
72.	ⓐ	ⓑ	ⓒ	ⓓ
73.	ⓐ	ⓑ	ⓒ	ⓓ
74.	ⓐ	ⓑ	ⓒ	ⓓ
75.	ⓐ	ⓑ	ⓒ	ⓓ
76.	ⓐ	ⓑ	ⓒ	ⓓ
77.	ⓐ	ⓑ	ⓒ	ⓓ
78.	ⓐ	ⓑ	ⓒ	ⓓ
79.	ⓐ	ⓑ	ⓒ	ⓓ
80.	ⓐ	ⓑ	ⓒ	ⓓ
81.	ⓐ	ⓑ	ⓒ	ⓓ
82.	ⓐ	ⓑ	ⓒ	ⓓ
83.	ⓐ	ⓑ	ⓒ	ⓓ
84.	ⓐ	ⓑ	ⓒ	ⓓ
85.	ⓐ	ⓑ	ⓒ	ⓓ
86.	ⓐ	ⓑ	ⓒ	ⓓ
87.	ⓐ	ⓑ	ⓒ	ⓓ
88.	ⓐ	ⓑ	ⓒ	ⓓ
89.	ⓐ	ⓑ	ⓒ	ⓓ
90.	ⓐ	ⓑ	ⓒ	ⓓ
91.	ⓐ	ⓑ	ⓒ	ⓓ
92.	ⓐ	ⓑ	ⓒ	ⓓ
93.	ⓐ	ⓑ	ⓒ	ⓓ
94.	ⓐ	ⓑ	ⓒ	ⓓ
95.	ⓐ	ⓑ	ⓒ	ⓓ
96.	ⓐ	ⓑ	ⓒ	ⓓ
97.	ⓐ	ⓑ	ⓒ	ⓓ
98.	ⓐ	ⓑ	ⓒ	ⓓ
99.	ⓐ	ⓑ	ⓒ	ⓓ
100.	ⓐ	ⓑ	ⓒ	ⓓ

CIVIL SERVICE EXAM 2

PART ONE: READING COMPREHENSION

Answer questions 1–5 on the basis of the following passages. The first is an excerpt from a Chamber of Commerce brochure about a restaurant; the second is a newspaper review of the same restaurant.

Excerpt from Chamber of Commerce brochure

Dilly's Deli provides a dining experience like no other! A rustic atmosphere, along with delicious food, provide an opportunity to soak up the local flavor. Recently relocated to the old market area, Dilly's is especially popular for lunch. At the counter, you can place your order for one of Dilly's three daily lunch specials or one of several sandwiches, all at reasonable prices. Once you get your food, choose a seat at one of the four charming communal tables. By the time you are ready to carry your paper plate to the trash bin, you have experienced some of the best food and most charming company our city has to offer.

Restaurant review

Yesterday I was exposed to what has been called "a dining experience like no other." At lunch-time, Dilly's Deli is so crowded that I wondered when the fire marshal had last visited the establishment. The line snaked out the door to the corner, and by the time I reached the counter, I was freezing. I decided on the hamburger steak special, the other specials being liver and onions and tuna casserole. Each special is offered with two side dishes, but there was no potato salad left and the green beans were cooked nearly beyond recognition. I chose the gelatin of the day and what turned out to be the blandest coleslaw I have ever eaten.

At Dilly's you sit at one of the four long tables. The couple sitting across from me was having an argument.

The truck driver sitting next to me told me more than I wanted to know about highway taxes. After I had tasted each of the dishes on my plate, I rose to leave, whereupon one of the people working behind the counter yelled at me to clean up after myself. Throwing away that plate of food was the most enjoyable part of dining at Dilly's.

1. If you go to lunch at Dilly's Deli, you could expect to see
   a. a long line of customers
   b. the fire marshal
   c. the restaurant critic from the newspaper
   d. homemade pie

2. Both passages suggest that if you eat lunch at Dilly's Deli, you should expect to
   a. sit next to a truck driver
   b. place your order with the waiter who comes to your table
   c. dress warmly
   d. carry your own food to your table

3. Which of the following illustrates the restaurant critic's opinion of the food at Dilly's Deli?
   a. "At Dilly's you sit at one of the four long tables."
   b. "At lunch-time, Dilly's is so crowded, I wondered when the fire marshal had last visited the establishment."
   c. "After I had tasted each of the dishes on my plate, I rose to leave, whereupon one of the people working behind the counter yelled at me to clean up after myself."
   d. "Throwing away that plate of food was the most enjoyable part of dining at Dilly's."

4. The main purpose of the restaurant review is to
   a. tell people they probably don't want to eat at Dilly's Deli
   b. make fun of couples who argue in public
   c. recommend the hamburger steak special
   d. warn people that Dilly's Deli tends to be crowded

5. The main purpose of the Chamber of Commerce brochure is to
   a. profile the owner of Dilly's Deli
   b. describe in detail the food served at Dilly's Deli
   c. encourage people to eat at Dilly's Deli
   d. explain the historical significance of the Dilly's Deli Building

Answer questions 6–11 on the basis of the following passage.

Although more and more people are exercising regularly, experts note that eating right is also a key to good health. Nutritionists recommend the "food pyramid" for a simple guide to eating the proper foods. At the base of the food pyramid are grains and fiber. You should eat six to eleven servings of bread, cereal, rice, and pasta everyday. Next up the pyramid are vegetables and fruit; five to nine daily servings from this group are recommended. The next pyramid level is the dairy group. Two or three servings a day of milk, yogurt, or cheese help maintain good nutrition. Moving up the pyramid, the next level is the meat, poultry, fish, beans, eggs, and nuts group, of which everyone should eat only two to three servings a day. At the very top of the pyramid are fats, oils, and sweets; these foods should be eaten only infrequently.

You don't have to shop in health food stores to follow the guidelines. One easy way to plan menus that follow the food pyramid is to shop only in the outer aisles of the grocery store. In most supermarkets, fresh fruit and vegetables, dairy, fresh meat, and frozen foods are in the outer aisles of the store. Grains, like pasta, rice, bread, and cereal, are located on the next aisles, the first inner rows. Finally, the farthest inside of the store is where you'll find chips and snacks, cookies and pastries, soda pop and drink mixes. These are the kinds of foods that nutritionists say everyone should eat rarely, if at all. If you stay in the outer aisles of the grocery store, you won't be tempted to buy foods you shouldn't eat, and you will find a wide variety of healthy foods to choose from. Another benefit of shopping this way is that grocery shopping takes less time.

6. A good title for this article would be
   a. Why You Should Shop in a Health Food Store
   b. How to Complete Your Grocery Shopping in Less Time
   c. How to Shop for Healthy Food
   d. How to Cook Healthy Food

7. According to the passage, the best way to shop in the grocery store is to
   a. make a list
   b. stay in the outside aisles
   c. find the best bargains
   d. check the newspaper ads each week

8. According to the food pyramid, people should
   a. eat more grains than meat
   b. never eat fats and sweets
   c. become vegetarians
   d. rarely eat bread

9. According to the passage, on the inside aisles of the grocery store you will find
   a. cleaning products
   b. dog and cat food
   c. wine and beer
   d. chips and snacks

10. According to the passage, to maintain good health, people should
   a. buy their food in health food stores
   b. worry more about nutrition than exercise
   c. exercise and eat right
   d. take up jogging

11. In order to follow the advice in the passage, it would be most helpful to know
   a. where to purchase a copy of "The Food Pyramid"
   b. whether rice has more calories than pasta
   c. which supermarket the author is referring to
   d. how much of each kind of food equals a serving

Answer questions 12–17 on the basis of the following passage.

As soon as she sat down on the airplane, Rachel almost began to regret telling the travel agent that she wanted an exotic and romantic vacation. As the plane hurled toward Rio de Janeiro, she read the information on Carnival that was in the pocket of the seat in front of hers. The very definition of Carnival made her shiver—"from the Latin *carnavale*, meaning a farewell to the flesh." She was searching for excitement, but had no intention of bidding her skin good-bye. Carnival, the brochure informed her, originated in Europe in the Middle Ages and served as a break from the requirements of daily life and society. Most of all, it allowed the hard-working and desperately poor serfs the opportunity to ridicule their wealthy and normally humorless masters. Rachel, a middle manager in a computer firm, wasn't entirely sure whether she was more serf or master. Should she be making fun, or would others be mocking her? She was strangely relieved when the plane landed, as though her fate were decided.

Rachel chewed on her lower lip as she stood before the mirror in her hotel room, choosing first one dress then another, trying to decide which outfit was the most serf-like. Nothing in her "dress for success" seminar had prepared her for this all-important decision. Finally, wearing her brightest blouse and skirt, she headed for the street, determined to find adventure.

12. Rachel was nervous on the airplane because she
   a. was afraid to fly
   b. thought Carnival sounded very exotic
   c. forgot her traveler's checks
   d. was worried she would lose her luggage

13. The passage implies that Rachel
   a. is traveling alone
   b. takes a vacation every year
   c. has never traveled abroad before
   d. speaks Portuguese

14. What is this passage mainly about?
   a. what life is like in Rio de Janeiro
   b. the history of Carnival
   c. a traveler on an exciting vacation
   d. how to dress for success

15. Rachel seems to be a person who
   a. does not usually travel
   b. is dissatisfied with her life
   c. works too hard
   d. is interested in trying new things

16. According to the passage Carnival
   a. lasts for several days
   b. originated in Europe
   c. occurs in February
   d. is famous for good food

17. Which of these sentences would most logically begin the next paragraph of this story?
   a. Settling herself comfortably at a table in the hotel coffee shop, Rachel began writing a post card to her mother.
   b. Later that night, as Rachel tossed in her bed, she wondered whether Bob ever thought about her.
   c. Rachel entered the huge office building and rode the elevator to the twelfth floor, the location of her 9:00 business meeting.
   d. As soon as she left the hotel, Rachel was surrounded by the sights and sounds of Carnival.

Answer questions 18–20 on the basis of the following passage.

Police officers must read suspects their Miranda rights upon taking them into custody. When a suspect who is merely being questioned incriminates himself, he might later claim to have been in custody, and seek to have the case dismissed on the grounds of not having been apprised of his Miranda rights. In such cases, a judge must make a determination as to whether or not a reasonable person would have believed himself to have been in custody, based on certain criteria. The judge must determine whether the suspect was questioned in a threatening manner (for example, if the suspect was seated while both officers remained standing) and whether the suspect was aware that he or she was free to leave at any time. Officers must be aware of these criteria and take care not to give suspects grounds for later claiming they believed themselves to be in custody.

18. What is the main idea of the passage?
   a. Officers must remember to read suspects their Miranda rights.
   b. Judges, not police officers, make the final determination as to whether or not a suspect was in custody.
   c. Officers who are merely questioning a suspect must not give the suspect the impression that he or she is in custody.
   d. Miranda rights needn't be read to all suspects before questioning.

19. According to the passage, a suspect is not in custody when he or she is
   a. free to refuse to answer questions
   b. free to leave the police station
   c. apprised of his or her Miranda rights
   d. not apprised of his or her Miranda rights

20. When must police officers read Miranda rights to a suspect?
   a. while questioning the suspect
   b. before taking the suspect to the police station
   c. while placing the suspect under arrest
   d. before releasing the suspect

To answer questions 21–26, read the following passage and choose the word or phrase that best fits in each numbered blank.

Some people say there is too little respect for the law, but I say there is too much respect for it. When people 21) _____ the law too much, they will follow it blindly. They will say, the majority of citizens have 22) _____ that this law is right; therefore I must heed it. They will not 23) _____ to consider whether or not the law is fair. If they do think the law is 24) _____, they think it is even more wrong to disobey it. They

25) _____ that people must not break the law but must live with it until the majority has been persuaded to change it. I am not saying that we should disobey laws because they are 26) _____ to us. I am saying that we must listen to our consciences first. Only then should we follow the law.

21. a. respect
b. underestimate
c. obey
d. hinder

22. a. affirmed
b. debated
c. repudiated
d. disregarded

23. a. request
b. imagine
c. stop
d. pretend

24. a. incomprehensible
b. reversible
c. unusual
d. wrong

25. a. reply
b. believe
c. disclaim
d. reminisce

26. a. inevitable
b. inconvenient
c. proper
d. agreeable

Answer questions 27–28 on the basis of the following passage.

After a snow or ice fall, city streets are treated with ordinary rock salt. In some areas, the salt is combined with calcium chloride, which is more effective in below-zero temperatures and better melts ice. This combination of salt and calcium chloride is also less damaging to foliage along the roadways.

27. In deciding whether to use ordinary rock salt or the salt and calcium chloride on a particular street, which of the following is NOT a consideration?
a. the temperature at the time of treatment
b. the plants and trees along the street
c. whether there is ice on the street
d. whether the street is a main or secondary road

28. According to the above snow treatment directions, which of the following is true?
a. If the temperature is below zero, salt and calcium chloride is effective in treating snow and ice covered streets.
b. Crews must wait until the snow or ice stops falling before salting streets.
c. The city always salts major roads first.
d. If the snowfall is light, the city will not salt the streets as this would be a waste of the salt supply.

Answer questions 29–30 on the basis of the following information.

Only supervisors of the Sanitation Department are qualified to handle hazardous waste. Hazardous waste is defined as any waste designated hazardous by the United States Environmental Protection Agency. If a sanitation worker is unclear whether a particular item is hazardous, he or she should not handle the item but instead should notify the supervisor for directions.

29. Sanitation Worker Wong comes upon a container of cleaning solvent that has been set out along with the regular garbage in front of a residence. The container does not list the contents of the cleaner. Wong should
   a. assume the solvent is safe and deposit it in the sanitation truck
   b. contact the supervisor for directions
   c. leave a note for the residents asking them to list the contents of the container
   d. leave the container on the curb

30. On the basis of the passage, which of the following is the best definition of hazardous waste?
   a. anything that would be life-threatening to sanitation workers
   b. anything picked up by special sanitation trucks
   c. anything so defined by the United States Environmental Protection Agency
   d. anything not allowed with regular residential garbage

PART TWO: GRAMMAR

Answer questions 31–37 by choosing the word or phrase that best completes the sentence.

31. If you don't stop playing _____ video games, your mind will become warped.
   a. that
   b. those
   c. them
   d. this

32. I am trying to become more skilled at weaving before winter _____.
   a. arrived
   b. will have arrived
   c. will arrive
   d. arrives

33. We have _____ more of these strange pods since those people moved in next door.
   a. saw
   b. been seeing
   c. been seen
   d. see

34. While trying to _____ his pet iguana from a tree, Travis Stevens fell and broke his ankle.
   a. be rescuing
   b. have rescued
   c. rescue
   d. rescuing

35. He _____ the gun down carefully.
   a. put
   b. putted
   c. been putting
   d. was putted

36. The main problem Jim had _____ too many parking tickets.
a. will have been
b. were
c. will have
d. was

37. If you steal _____ artichoke from Petra's garden, you'll be sorry.
a. them
b. those
c. that
d. these

Answer questions 38–39 by choosing the sentence that best combines the underlined sentences into one.

38. He did not return from his camping trip until 6:00 a.m.
We were all frantic with worry.
a. He did not return from his camping trip until 6:00 a.m.; however we were all frantic with worry.
b. While we were all frantic with worry, he did not return from his camping trip until 6:00 a.m.
c. He did not return from his camping trip until 6:00 a.m., whether we were all frantic with worry.
d. Because he did not return from his camping trip until 6:00 a.m., we were all frantic with worry.

39. Everyone likes Earl.
I think he is sneaky.
a. Everyone likes Earl, and I think he is sneaky.
b. Everyone likes Earl, whereas I think he is sneaky.
c. Everyone likes Earl, when I think he is sneaky.
d. Everyone likes Earl, or I think he is sneaky.

Answer questions 40–44 by choosing the sentences that are most clearly written.

40. a. We ate the popcorn and watch the movie.
b. While watching the movie, the popcorn was eaten.
c. Popcorn, while watching the movie, was eaten.
d. We ate the popcorn while we watched the movie.

41. a. I don't like fish as well as my sister does.
b. I don't like fish as well as my sister.
c. Fish isn't liked by me as well as my sister.
d. My sister likes it, but I don't like fish as well.

42. a. After renting him the room, a cat was discovered to belong to Mr. Morris.
b. A cat belonging to Mr. Morris was discovered by Alvin after renting him a room.
c. After renting him the room, Alvin discovered Mr. Morris owned a cat.
d. After renting him a room, Mr. Morris was discovered by Alvin to own a cat.

43. a. Though often romanticized in movies, the lives of criminals in reality are bleak and unrewarding.
b. In reality, the lives of criminals are bleak and unrewarding; however, it is often romanticized in movies.
c. Movies often romanticize the life of the criminal; however, in reality, they are bleak and unrewarding.
d. In reality bleak and unrewarding, movies often romanticize the lives of criminals.

44. a. Some people say jury duty is a nuisance that just takes up their precious time and that we don't get paid enough.
b. Some people say jury duty is a nuisance that just takes up your precious time and that one doesn't get paid enough.
c. Some people say jury duty is a nuisance that just takes up one's precious time and that one doesn't get paid enough.
d. Some people say jury duty is a nuisance that just takes up our precious time and that they don't get paid enough.

Answer questions 45–50 by choosing the sentences that are correctly written.

45. a. One of the first modern detectives in literature were created by Edgar Allen Poe.
b. One of the first modern detectives in literature was created by Edgar Allen Poe.
c. Edgar Allen Poe having created one of the first modern detectives in literature.
d. In literature, one of the first modern detectives, created by Edgar Allen Poe.

46. a. My brother and I going to see the ball game.
b. My brother and I seeing the ball game.
c. My brother and I are going to see the ball game.
d. My brother and I gone to the ball game.

47. a. As the old saying goes, a cat may look at a king.
b. A cat looking at a king, according to the old saying.
c. The old saying being, a cat may look at a king.
d. A cat looking at a king, in the old saying.

48. a. A longer happier life, caused by one's owning a pet.
b. Owning a pet, for one to live a longer, happier life.
c. To live a longer, happier life by one's owning a pet.
d. Owning a pet can help one live a longer, happier life.

49. a. Mr. Love felt it was time to find a new career, but he could not afford to go back to school.
b. Mr. Love felt it was time to find a new career, he could not afford to go back to school.
c. Mr. Love felt it was time to find a new career he could not afford to go back to school.
d. Mr. Love felt it was time. To find a new career, but he could not afford to go back to school.

50. a. Once the investigation begins, and there will be no turning back.
b. Once the investigation begins, there will be no turning back.
c. Once the investigation begins, so there will be no turning back.
d. Once the investigation begins, thus there will be no turning back.

PART THREE: MATHEMATICS

51. Which of the following is another way to write $\frac{4}{25}$?

    a. 4%

    b. 16%

    c. 40%

    d. 100%

Following is a list of ingredients needed to make 16 brownies. Use this list to answer questions 52–53.

Deluxe Brownies

$\frac{2}{3}$ cup butter

5 squares (1 ounce each) unsweetened chocolate

$1\frac{1}{2}$ cups sugar

2 teaspoons vanilla

2 eggs

1 cup flour

52. How much sugar is needed to make 8 brownies?

    a. 3 cups

    b. $\frac{2}{3}$ cup

    c. $\frac{5}{8}$ cup

    d. $\frac{3}{4}$ cup

53. What is the greatest number of brownies that can be made if the baker has only 1 cup of butter?

    a. 24

    b. 12

    c. 16

    d. 32

54. What is another way to write 3^4?

    a. 12

    b. 24

    c. 27

    d. 81

Use the information in the following passage to answer questions 55–56.

Basic cable television service, which includes 16 channels, costs $15 a month. The initial labor fee to install the service is $25. A $65 deposit is required but will be refunded within two years if the customer's bills are paid in full. Other cable services may be added to the basic service: the movie channel service is $9.40 a month; the news channels are $7.50 a month; the arts channels are $5.00 a month; the sports channels are $4.80 a month.

55. A customer's cable television bill totaled $20 a month. What portion of the bill was for basic cable service?

    a. 25%

    b. 33%

    c. 50%

    d. 75%

56. A customer's first bill after having cable television installed totaled $112.50. This customer chose basic cable and one additional cable service. Which additional service was chosen?

    a. the news channels

    b. the movie channels

    c. the arts channels

    d. the sports channels

57. Ms. Margaret Richbody wishes to insure items of jewelry valued as follows:

- 1 gold watch, valued at $240
- 2 rings, each valued at $150
- 1 ring, valued at $ 70
- 1 bracelet, valued at $ 95

Her insurance agent, Bill Ratchet, is preparing her policy on the jewelry. Which one of the following represents the total value of the jewelry?

a. $545
b. $555
c. $705
d. $785

58. A piece of ribbon 3 feet 4 inches long was divided in 5 equal parts. How long was each part?

a. 8 inches
b. 1 foot 2 inches
c. 10 inches
d. 6 inches

59. Bob tells his family that he wants the following birthday presents:

- 1 television, valued at $295
- 1 VCR, valued at $150
- 15 videotapes, each valued at $ 16
- Cash $225

How much will Bob's family have to pay so that Bob can have the presents he wants for his birthday?

a. $686
b. $700
c. $766
d. $910

60. What is 0.716 rounded to the nearest tenth?

a. 0.7
b. 0.8
c. 0.72
d. 1.0

61. Karen Green earns $26,000 a year. If she receives a 4.5% salary increase, how much will she earn?

a. $26,450
b. $27,170
c. $27,260
c. $29,200

62. Which of these has a 9 in the thousandths place?

a. 3.0095
b. 3.0905
c. 3.9005
d. 3.0059

63. Out of 100 shoppers polled, 80 said they buy fresh fruit every week. How many shoppers out of 30,000 could be expected to buy fresh fruit every week?

a. 2,400
b. 6,000
c. 22,000
d. 24,000

64. If it takes four workers 1 hour and 45 minutes to perform a particular job, how long would it take one worker working at the same rate to perform the same task alone?

a. 4.5 hours
b. 5 hours
c. 7 hours
d. 7.5 hours

65. On Monday morning, Officers Rosen and McNalty respond to a call of a burglary that apparently took place over the weekend at Datamation Computer Consultants. The owner of the business says that the following equipment is missing:

- 3 telephone sets, each valued at $ 125
- 2 computers, each valued at $1,300
- 2 computer monitors, each valued at $ 950
- 1 printer valued at $ 600
- 1 answering machine valued at $ 50

Officer McNalty is preparing a complaint report on the burglary. What should he write as the total value of the missing property?

a. $3,025
b. $5,400
c. $5,525
d. $6,525

66. Which of the following hose diameters is the smallest?

a. $\frac{17}{20}$ inches
b. $\frac{3}{4}$ inches
c. $\frac{5}{6}$ inches
d. $\frac{7}{10}$ inches

67. When a sprinkler system is installed in a home that is under construction, the system costs about 1.5% of the total building cost. The cost of the same system installed after the home is built is about 4% of the total building cost. How much would a homeowner save by installing a sprinkler system in a $150,000 home while the home is still under construction?

a. $600.00
b. $2,250.00
c. $3,750.00
d. $6,000.00

68. If one gallon of water weighs 8.35 pounds, a 25-gallon container of water would most nearly weigh

a. 173 pounds
b. 200 pounds
c. 209 pounds
d. 215 pounds

69. It takes a typist 0.75 seconds to type one word. At this rate, how many words can be typed in 60 seconds?

a. 4.5
b. 8
c. 45
d. 80

70. A safety box has three layers of metal, each with a different width. If one layer is $\frac{1}{8}$ inch thick, a second layer is $\frac{1}{6}$ inch thick, and the total thickness is $\frac{3}{4}$ inch thick, what is the width of the third layer?

a. $\frac{5}{12}$
b. $\frac{11}{24}$
c. $\frac{7}{18}$
d. $\frac{1}{2}$

PART FOUR: VOCABULARY AND SPELLING

To answer questions 71–76, choose the word or phrase that means the *same* or nearly the same as the underlined word.

71. articulate the philosophy

a. trust
b. refine
c. verify
d. express

72. expansive facility

a. obsolete
b. meager
c. spacious
d. costly

73. <u>detrimental</u> activity
   a. decisive
   b. harmful
   c. worthless
   d. advantageous

To answer questions 74–76, choose the word that most nearly means the *opposite* of the underlined word.

74. <u>abstract</u> thinking
   a. concentrated
   b. simple
   c. concrete
   d. understandable

75. remain <u>incognito</u>
   a. thoughtful
   b. hidden
   c. recognizable
   d. corrupt

76. <u>chronic</u> condition
   a. fatal
   b. quick
   c. bucolic
   d. infrequent

To answer questions 77–78, choose the word that means the same as *both* of the underlined phrases.

77. <u>to initiate by humiliating</u> and <u>fog</u>
   a. harass
   b. mist
   c. taunt
   d. haze

78. <u>a court proceeding</u> and <u>an article of clothing</u>
   a. suit
   b. collar
   c. case
   d. apparel

To answer questions 79–80, choose the word or phrase that means the same or nearly the same as the underlined prefix or suffix.

79. <u>im</u>mortal, <u>im</u>patient
   a. without
   b. not
   c. with
   d. until

80. father<u>hood</u>, adult<u>hood</u>
   a. a method of doing
   b. a state of being
   c. a way of behaving
   d. a mode of thinking

Answer questions 81–85 by choosing the word that best fills the blank in the following sentences.

81. I am especially interested in your views _____ political kickbacks.
   a. intending
   b. encumbering
   c. surmounting
   d. concerning

82. Because he felt he had been cheated, Mitchell _____ to see the president of the company.
   a. demanded
   b. commanded
   c. asserted
   d. persevered

83. Solar energy is as _____ as that which comes from fossil fuel.
a. preferable
b. effective
c. edifying
d. conciliatory

84. Maxine's stealing my computer disks was completely _____.
a. ephemeral
b. preemptive
c. intractable
d. reprehensible

85. We were jealous of Doug because he received _____ treatment from the teacher.
a. prefatory
b. irascible
c. preferential
d. susceptible

Answer questions 86–100 by choosing the word that is spelled correctly and best completes the sentence.

86. The Healthy Living Vitamins Corporation is soon to be _____ for fraud.
a. prosecuted
b. prossecuted
c. prosecutted
d. proseccuted

87. Martin's yellow-and-purple coat was quite _____ among all the gray suits.
a. conspiccuous
b. connspicuous
c. conspicuous
d. conspicious

88. The broccoli you bought will _____ up unless you put it in the refrigerator.
a. shrivel
b. shrivvel
c. shrivell
d. shrival

89. I just don't know what I'd do in her _____.
a. sittuation
b. situation
c. situachun
d. sitiation

90. Our basement apartment is so damp that my skin constantly feels _____.
a. clamby
b. clamy
c. clammy
d. clammby

91. The lovely blue sailboat sank in the _____ waters.
a. ruff
b. rouff
c. ruf
d. rough

92. The squirrel is actually a _____.
a. rodant
b. rodent
c. rodint
d. roddent

93. My math teacher has no sense of _____ at all.
a. humor
b. hummor
c. humorr
d. humer

94. It was a _____ day for the firefighter's annual picnic.
a. superb
b. supperb
c. supurb
d. sepurb

95. The first time he wore his Rolex watch, his friends were _____.
a. jellous
b. jealous
c. jealuse
d. jeolous

96. When we were halfway up the hill, we heard a _____ explosion.
a. teriffic
b. terrific
c. terriffic
d. terific

97. If elected, my brother Roy will make a fine _____.
a. sherrif
b. sherriff
c. sherif
d. sheriff

98. Working out every night at the local gym has become my _____.
a. obssession
b. obsessian
c. obsession
d. obsessiun

99. The bus driver would not drive during the blizzard because she did not want to place the children in _____.
a. jeoperdy
b. jepardy
c. jeapardy
d. jeopardy

100. Because of the danger they were in, the soldiers were unable to enjoy the _____ scenery.
a. magniffisent
b. magnifisent
c. magnificent
d. magnifficent

ANSWERS

PART ONE: READING COMPREHENSION

1. **a.** This is implied in the first passage, which says that Dilly's is "popular," and explicitly stated in the second passage.

2. **d.** This is the only one of the choices that is implied in both passages, which describe ordering at the counter.

3. **d.** This is the only quotation from the second passage that reveals the critic's opinion of the quality of the food.

4. **a.** The fact that the overall tone of the passage is quite negative points to the writer's purpose.

5. **c.** In contrast to the second passage, the first passage seems to be encouraging a visit to Dilly's. The other choices are not part of the passage.

6. **c.** This title most nearly captures the main idea of the passage. The other choices either are not mentioned or are secondary ideas in the passage.

7. **b.** This is the point of the second paragraph.

8. **a.** The first paragraph of the passage says that the food pyramid recommends six to eleven servings each day of grains and only two or three servings of meat.

9. **d.** See the second paragraph. The other choices are not mentioned in the passage.

10. **c.** This is implied in the first sentence of the passage.

11. **d.** This is the only choice that is important to the main point of the passage.

12. **b.** This is implied in the first paragraph.

13. **a.** We can infer that Rachel is traveling alone simply because no one else is mentioned. Any of the other choices could also be true, but there is nothing in the passage to support them.

14. **c.** This choice best captures the main theme. All the other choices are mentioned in the passage but are minor points.

15. **d.** This choice is the only one that is implied within the passage, which says that Rachel is "searching for excitement." The other choices could also be true, but we can't know for sure without further information.

16. **b.** See the first paragraph. The other choices also happen to be true of Carnival, but they are not mentioned in the passage.

17. **d.** The last line of the passage shows Rachel headed from her hotel room to the street where Carnival is taking place. Thus, a logical continuation is for Rachel to be experiencing the adventure she is "determined to find."

18. **c.** While **a** and **b** are also true, they are not the main idea, which is supported by the whole passage and spelled out in the last sentence.

19. **b.** This is implied in the next-to-last sentence.

20. **c.** See the first sentence of the passage.

21. **a.** *Respect* for the law is what the passage is about.

22. **a.** The passage does not mention any law that has been *debated* (choice **b**). Regarding choices **c** and **d**, in the context of the passage it would make more sense for a person to *heed* a law that had been affirmed by the majority than one that had been *repudiated* or *disregarded*.

23. **c.** The other choices are irrelevant and make no sense in the context of the sentence.

24. **d.** The phrase *even more wrong* would not seem reasonably to refer to any of the other choices.

25. b. There is no one mentioned in the passage to whom one might *reply* (choice **a**). The word *disclaim* (choice **c**) goes against the main thrust of the passage. The word *reminisce* (choice **d**) is irrelevant to the passage.

26. b. The word *inevitable* (choice **a**) makes no sense in the context of the passage. There would be no reason to even think of disobeying laws that are *proper* or *agreeable* to us (choices **c** and **d**), or to speak of respecting them too much.

27. d. The passage mentions nothing about main or secondary roads.

28. a. The other choices are not mentioned in the passage.

29. b. The passage indicates that Wong should call the supervisor.

30. c. According to the passage, hazardous waste is defined by the United States Environmental Protection Agency.

PART TWO: GRAMMAR

31. b. The pronoun *those* agrees in number with the noun *games* to which it refers.

32. d. The appropriate tense for the verb is the present tense, *arrives*.

33. b. The verbal form *been seeing* fits with the verb *have*.

34. c. The infinitive form of the verb *rescue* goes with *to* in the sentence.

35. a. The proper form for the verb is in the past tense, *put*; there is no such form as *putted*.

36. d. The verb *was* agrees with its subject, *problem*, and is in the past tense.

37. c. The pronoun *that* agrees in number with the noun to which it refers, *artichoke*.

38. d. The conjunction *because* establishes the correct causal relationship between the two sentences.

39. b. The transitional word *whereas* correctly establishes a contrast between the two sentences.

40. d. In choice **a**, the lack of agreement in tense makes the sentence unclear as to time; in choice **b** it is unclear who ate the popcorn; choice **c** contains a misplaced modifier, implying that the popcorn watched the movie.

41. a. This sentence is clearest. In choice **b**, the speaker likes his/her sister better than fish. Choice **c** is just plain confusing. Choice **d** has an unclear pronoun reference: *it* probably refers to *fish*, but who can tell?

42. c. In choice **a**, the cat seems to be renting the room. In choice **b**, it's unclear whether the pronoun *he* refers to the cat or to Mr. Morris. Choice **d** implies that Mr. Morris rented himself a room.

43. a. This is the only clear answer. In choices **b** and **c**, the pronouns *it* and *they* do not agree with the words they refer to. In choice **d**, the first phrase seems to refer to *movies* when it should refer to *the lives of criminals*.

44. c. The other choices are unclear because they contain unnecessary shifts in person, from *people* to *their* and *we* in choice **a**, to *your* and *one* in choice **b**, and to *our* and *they* in choice **d**.

45. b. In choice **a** the verb does not agree in number with its subject, *one*. Choices **c** and **d** are fragments.

46. c. This is a complete sentence; the others are fragments.

47. a. This is a complete sentence; the others are fragments.

48. d. This is a complete sentence; the others are fragments.

49. a. This is a complete sentence. Choice **b** is a comma splice; choice **c** is a run-on sentence; choice **d** contains a sentence fragment.

50. b. No connecting word is needed to relate the first half of the sentence to the second. Connecting words in the other choices turn them into sentence fragments.

PART THREE: MATHEMATICS

51. **b.** Four divided by 25 equals 0.16 or 16%.

52. **d.** The recipe is for 16 brownies. To make 8 brownies, you would reduce the ingredients by half. Half of $1\frac{1}{2}$ cups of sugar is $\frac{3}{4}$ cup.

53. **a.** The recipe for 16 brownies calls for $\frac{2}{3}$ cup butter. An additional $\frac{1}{3}$ cup would make 8 more brownies, for a total of 24 brownies.

54. **d.** The expression 3^4 means 3 times itself 4 times: $3 \times 3 \times 3 \times 3 = 81$.

55. **d.** The basic cable service fee of $15 is 75% of $20.

56. **a.** The labor fee ($25) plus the deposit ($65) plus the basic service ($15) equals $105. The difference between the total bill, $112.50, and $105 is $7.50, the cost of the news channels.

57. **c.** The two rings valued at $150 have a total value of $300, but remember that there is another ring valued at only $70.

58. **a.** Three feet 4 inches equals 40 inches; 40 divided by 5 is 8.

59. **d.** The total value of the 15 videotapes is $240; that number should be added with the other three numbers representing cash and property for a sum of $910.

60. **a.** Answer **b** is rounded up instead of down. Answer **c** is rounded to the thousandths place. Answer **d** is rounded to the nearest whole number.

61. **b.** There are three steps involved in solving this problem. First, convert 4.5% to a decimal: 0.045. Multiply that by $26,000 to find out how much the salary increases. Finally, add the result ($1,170) to the original salary of $26,000 to find out the new salary, $27,170.

62. **a.** In **b**, the 9 is in the hundredths place. In **c**, it is in the tenths place; in **d**, the ten thousandths place.

63. **d.** Eighty out of 100 is 80%. Eighty percent of 30,000 is 24,000.

64. **c.** To solve the problem you have to first convert the total time to minutes (105 minutes), then multiply by 4 (420 minutes), and then convert the answer back to hours by dividing by 60 minutes to arrive at the final answer (7 hours). Or you can multiply $1\frac{3}{4}$ hours by 4 to arrive at the same answer.

65. **c.** It is important to remember to include all three telephone sets ($375 total), both computers ($2,600 total), and both monitors ($1,900 total) in the total value.

66. **d.** To solve the problem, one must first find the common denominator, in this instance 60. Then the fractions must be converted: $\frac{17}{20} = \frac{51}{60}$ (for choice **a**); $\frac{3}{4} = \frac{45}{60}$ (for choice **b**); $\frac{5}{6} = \frac{50}{60}$ (for choice **c**); and $\frac{7}{10} = \frac{42}{60}$ (for the correct choice, **d**).

67. **c.** First you must subtract the percentage of the installation cost during construction (1.5%) from the percentage of the installation cost after construction (4%). To do this, begin by converting the percentages into decimals: 4% = 0.04; 1.5% = 0.015. Now subtract: $0.04 - 0.015 = 0.025$. This is the percentage of the total cost which the homeowner will save. Multiply this by the total cost of the home to find the dollar amount: $0.025 \times \$150,000 = \$3,750$

68. **c.** To solve the problem, take the weight of one gallon of water (8.35) and multiply it by the number of gallons (25): $8.35 \times 25 = 208.7$. Now round to the nearest unit, which is 209.

69. **d.** This problem is solved by dividing 60 by 0.75.

70. b. To solve the problem, you must first find the common denominator, in this instance, 24. Then the fractions must be converted: $\frac{1}{8} = \frac{3}{24}$; $\frac{1}{6} = \frac{4}{24}$; $\frac{3}{4} = \frac{18}{24}$. Add the values for first and second layers together: $\frac{3}{24} + \frac{4}{24} = \frac{7}{24}$, then subtract the sum from the total thickness ($\frac{18}{24}$): $\frac{18}{24} - \frac{7}{24} = \frac{11}{24}$.

PART FOUR: VOCABULARY AND SPELLING

If you don't understand why the correct answers in this section are correct, refer to any standard dictionary.

71. d.
72. c.
73. b.
74. c.
75. c.
76. d.
77. d.
78. a.

79. b.
80. b.
81. d.
82. a.
83. b.
84. d.
85. c.
86. a.
87. c.
88. a.
89. b.
90. c.
91. d.
92. b.
93. a.
94. a.
95. b.
96. b.
97. d.
98. c.
99. d.
100. c.

SCORING

As with the first exam, the first step in determining your score is to count up the questions you got right. Write the number of questions you answered correctly in each part of the exam below, and then add up the part scores for your total score.

Part One: _____ out of 30
Part Two: _____ out of 20
Part Three: _____ out of 20
Part Four: _____ out of 30
Total: _____ out of 100

Now practice your math skills by finding the percentage you got right in each part of the exam. Divide the number you got right by the total number of questions in that section. Move the decimal point two places to the right and you have your percentage. For example, if you got 17 questions right on Part Two, you would divide 17 by 20, which gives you 0.85. Move the decimal two places right and you have 85 percent.

Your percentage on the exam on the whole is simply the total number right you recorded above. If you got 75 questions right, your percentage is 75 percent. Most civil service exams require a score of 70 percent or more to pass, but in many cases just passing isn't enough. If the agency you apply to ranks candidates on an eligibility list based on their test scores, and if there are lots of people applying for this kind of job, you'll probably need a score well into the 90s to have a chance of actually getting the job.

Here's what you should do next, depending on how well you did on this exam:

- **If your total score is less than 60 percent,** you are probably not yet ready to face a real civil service exam. Instead, you should take some courses in basic reading, writing, and math skills. Many community colleges and high schools offer low-cost courses for adults who need to brush up these skills.

- **If your total score is between 60 and 70 percent,** you want to start by getting up to that magic 70 percent line on these basic skills before you start thinking about studying the other kinds of questions that might appear on a given civil service exam. You could also take courses in your weakest areas.

- **If your total score is between 70 and 80 percent,** you can probably pass the basic skills portion of your civil service exam. Continue to work on your weakest areas by using some of the additional resources listed in the relevant chapters of this book. If you've decided on a particular civil service job, you can also start finding out what will be on your exam and working on any additional kinds of questions that will be on that test.

- **If your total score is between 80 and 90 percent,** you can feel pretty confident about your basic skills. For the few extra points that could make the difference in whether you're offered a job, use some of the additional resources listed in the chapters that cover your weakest areas. Meanwhile, if you've decided on a particular civil service job, find out what's on that exam and start studying any additional kinds of questions it contains.

- **If your total score is above 90 percent,** congratulations! You can achieve a high score on any portions of your civil service exam that cover basic skills. It's time to focus on a particular exam for a particular career.

The biggest key to success on any civil service exam is self-confidence. Having put in time and effort to build up your basic skills is the first step; now you know you can handle questions on reading, grammar, vocabulary, spelling, and math. Next, you can take the same steps in preparing for other, more specific kinds of questions that appear on exams for the civil service job you want.

INDEX

INDEX